Fundamentals of Risk Management for Accountants and Managers

T0332615

Fundamentals of Risk Management for Accountants and Managers

Tools & Techniques

Paul M Collier
Monash University

ELSEVIER

AMSTERDAM • BOSTON • HEIDELBERG • LONDON • NEW YORK • OXFORD
PARIS • SAN DIEGO • SAN FRANCISCO • SINGAPORE • SYDNEY • TOKYO
Butterworth-Heinemann is an imprint of Elsevier

Butterworth-Heinemann is an imprint of Elsevier
Linacre House, Jordan Hill, Oxford OX2 8DP, UK
30 Corporate Drive, Suite 400, Burlington, MA 01803, USA

First edition 2009

Notice
No responsibility is assumed by the publisher for any injury and/or damage to persons or
property as a matter of products liability, negligence or otherwise, or from any use or operation of any methods, products, instructions or ideas contained in the material herein. Because
of rapid advances in the medical sciences, in particular, independent verification of diagnoses
and drug dosages should be made.

British Library Cataloguing in Publication Data
A catalogue record for this book is available from the British Library

Library of Congress Cataloguing in Publication Data
A catalog record for this book is available from the Library of Congress

ISBN–13: 978-0-7506-8650-1

For information on all Butterworth-Heinemann publications
visit our website at http://books.elsevier.com

Printed and bound in Great Britain

07 08 09 10 10 9 8 7 6 5 4 3 2 1

Working together to grow
libraries in developing countries

www.elsevier.com | www.bookaid.org | www.sabre.org

ELSEVIER   BOOK AID
            International   Sabre Foundation

For Loredana and Alexis
for their encouragement, support and advice in our family's own
risk management.

Contents

Introduction

At the time of writing, at least three major global risks can be identified which impact on organisations throughout the world. The first is the fallout from the United States sub-prime mortgage crisis which has reduced credit availability, increased interest rates and put significant pressure on many financial institutions around the world, some of whom have already failed or face failure. The second is climate change and the effect that proposed emissions trading schemes may have on costs. Third is the rapidly increasing price of oil and concerns over limited supply from the Middle East, exacerbated by long drawn out fighting in Iraq, Afghanistan and tensions in Iran and Pakistan. Both climate change and oil prices are likely to have significant impacts on economies, industries and consumers over the long term.

Had this book been written in 2001, the most high profile risk would have been the threat of terrorism following the September 11 attacks on the World Trade Centre and Pentagon. Two years before that, industry and government faced the threat of widespread computer failure as a result of the Millennium Bug (the 'Y2K' rollover).

Whilst these and other high profile events may seem distant from any particular organisation, the knock-on effect to economies, industries, individual organisations (public, private and not-for-profit) as well as on consumers can be significant. These events bring to the forefront the importance of risk management.

At the level of the individual organisation, the effect of these global risks cannot be ignored (the failure of Northern Rock in the UK is an example) but individual organisations also face more day-to-day risks, for example the entry of new competitors, changing customer demand, new technologies, loss of key staff, computer failure, loss of reputation, loss of investor confidence, etc.

Risk management has come to the forefront in many organisations. By risk management we mean the process by which risks are identified, assessed, estimated, evaluated, treated and reported. The risk management process has existed for many years but often in specialist areas, for example occupational health and safety, project risk management, credit risk, insurance, hedging of foreign currency and interest rates, etc. However, enterprise risk management has emerged more recently.

By enterprise risk management (ERM) we mean a focus on risk management at the corporate level, a more holistic approach than that usually associated with specialist areas. Whilst many of the principles are common, the often quantitative tools and techniques used in specific areas need to give way to more subjective judgments about the likelihood and consequences of risk at the level of the whole organisation – the enterprise and the strategic (as well as operational) risks it faces. Although ERM will encapsulate all these specialist areas, it is much broader in its focus. For example, at the enterprise level we need to consider the effect of the sub-prime mortgage crisis, emissions trading schemes, oil prices, the impact of the growth of the Chinese and

Indian economies etc. in both the short and long terms. These risks may not be recognised or evaluated by a narrowly specialist attention to risk.

The meaning of risk at the enterprise level has also shifted, from a concern with 'downside' risk: what can go wrong; to a recognition that taking risks is necessary to earning rewards, the 'upside' of risk in terms of the risk/return trade-off, and a focus on the risk of not achieving organisational objectives. ERM is as much about performance as conformance. This broader meaning of risk also encapsulates the recognition that different organisations define their appetite for risk differently and that any discussion of the risk/return trade-off is meaningless without an explicit recognition by an organisation's Board of Directors of the organisation's risk appetite. In ERM, risk is not something that is eliminated but which is managed in line with organisational objectives and risk appetite, and for which a risk culture is developed that is consistent with the organisation's strategy for managing risk.

The increasing importance of governance has contributed to the development of enterprise risk management. In the UK, the Cadbury Code and its followers, culminating in the Combined Code on Corporate Governance, and similar codes in other countries have emphasised the importance of Boards of Directors devoting considerable attention to risk management and the internal controls necessary to mitigate risk. This then follows through to internal audit processes which like controls should be risk-based. In the US, Sarbanes-Oxley has had a significant effect, albeit limited largely to risks in relation to financial reporting. Increasingly therefore, enterprise risk management cannot be separated from corporate governance, risk-based control and risk-based auditing.

This book is written for a number of audiences. First, financial and non-financial managers will each find the book essential to their understanding of ERM – managing risk at the whole enterprise level as well as risk at the level of their business unit – their own 'enterprise'. Managers who are responsible for performance – financial or non-financial – are automatically responsible for managing risk – the risk of not achieving their targets. The book is also written for business management and accounting students at undergraduate and postgraduate levels who need a solid understanding of enterprise risk management.

There are many books that purport to be about ERM but which take a very narrow approach to the topic. Many books emphasise banking and financial services and the requirements of Basel2, or are primarily concerned with hedging and derivatives. This book covers those topics (see chapters 12 and 22) but it is not a specialist book for those in banking and finance. Readers who need specialist knowledge of particular techniques e.g. financial hedging, insurance, etc. can then use this book as a springboard from which to delve into the detail of specific tools, techniques and methods of measurement.

The primary focus of this book is to encompass all organisations at the broader level of risk management for the whole enterprise, where a consistent approach to risk management can be taken. Readers will be introduced to enterprise risk management from each of three perspectives: financial, non-financial quantitative and qualitative (social/cultural), emphasising the strengths and limitations of each approach. The aim of the book is to help practitioners and students to become more effective managers by increasing their awareness and understanding of enterprise risk management;

being able to play a more important role in an organisation's risk management process; and producing information and implementing controls that contribute to the effective management of risk in their organisations and business units.

The book is international in its appeal, because part of the nature of ERM is the
globalisation of its concepts. It draws equally from US sources such as COSO and
Sarbanes-Oxley, from the UK and Europe through the Combined Code and Institute
of Risk Management, and from Australia and New Zealand in their AS4360 risk
management standard. The work of professional bodies such as the Institute of Internal Auditors and the Chartered Institute of Management Accountants is also used.
Equally global is the application of governance, risk and control to the public sector
and third (or not-for-profit) sectors. The use of international case studies illustrates
the ideas in the book, including Enron and WorldCom, Parmalat and Société Générale, Equitable Life, Royal Dutch/Shell, Barings Bank and Northern Rock.

The book is organised as follows. Part A provides an introduction to the development of ERM and the corporate governance agenda. Part B describes the structure
and the various models and approaches that are the foundations of enterprise risk
management. Part C looks at risk through a variety of organisational applications.
Part D looks at how the risk management process is itself managed. The book also has
an extensive further reading list and a comprehensive index.

About the Author

Paul Collier is Professor of Management Accounting at Monash University in Melbourne, Australia. He was previously at Aston Business School in the UK where he was an ESRC AIM Public Sector fellow. Paul's research interests are in performance management, governance, enterprise risk management and knowledge management. He has published widely in books and journals on these subjects.

Prior to joining academia, Paul held financial and general management positions in a number of organisations in Australia and the UK. His experience encompasses public, private and non-profit distributing sectors. He has held roles as diverse as chief financial officer for a listed manufacturing company, and head of training and development for a police force. He was a board member and chair of the audit committee of a charitable housing association with assets of £200 million. He was also an examiner for the Chartered Institute of Management Accountants in their strategic level subject *Risk and Control Strategy*.

Part A. Introducing Risk Management

In this first part, we consider the history of risk as a subject of interest (chapter 1), show the importance of the corporate governance agenda to risk management (chapter 2) and explore the similarities and differences between risk as seen in the private, public and non-profit distributing sectors (chapter 3). This part provides a useful background and introduction to the more detailed coverage of the structure of enterprise risk management that follows in Part B.

Chapter 1

The Emergence of Risk

A search through Amazon under 'risk management' reveals hundreds of books on the subject. Many cover generic risk management processes although most of these books are oriented to the US market and many are produced by professional service firms with the aim of promoting their own services. Other books specialize in a particular type of risk, for example financial, credit, information systems, etc. These books tend to be too detailed unless the reader is a specialist in these areas but the topics are nevertheless important to gain an understanding of risk management.

This book is concerned with what is called 'enterprise risk management' or ERM. ERM is a whole-organization approach to risk, so it is less concerned with the intricate detail of specific techniques and narrow functional specialties and more with how boards of directors and senior managers, both financial and non-financial, address risk and the management of risk at the corporate, whole-of-organization level.

What is risk?

We are all faced with a multitude of risks on a day-to-day basis, even if it is just crossing the road, driving our car, concern about school or university grades for ourselves or a member of our family, whether we will get the job we want or the salary increase or promotion we expect.

We are more aware of risks when we take out insurance policies on our lives, our homes or cars. We also face risk in our workplaces as occupational health and safety regulations are properly concerned with what we do and how we do it, so that we can return home safely at the end of each day.

But most of the risks that we might more readily recognize are those that come via television, radio, and newspapers. It seems that there is always some real or imagined risk that the world faces. I grew up during the cold war and my first exposure to risk was the Cuban missile crisis in the 1960s and the threat of mutually assured destruction (MAD) in the event of nuclear war between the United States and the then Soviet Union. This is no longer a risk we face but instead September 11, 2001 and the bombings in Madrid, London and other places have increased the risk of terrorism.

There are also risks that result from natural disasters over which we have no control: earthquakes, fires, floods, hurricanes. Over the last few years these events seem to have increased in frequency and severity as events such as the 2004 Indian Ocean earthquake and tsunami, Hurricane Katrina in New Orleans in 2005, and the flooding in China in 2008. Whether these are merely cyclic events or the results of global warming may not be known for decades.

Like global warming, environmental risks are often attributed to accident or negligence at the organizational level. These man-made disasters include Bhopal, Chernobyl, Three Mile Island, Challenger, Piper Alpha, and Exxon Valdez. Other man-made events are purely financial in nature, like Nick Leeson and Barings Bank, Enron and WorldCom.

Other crises emerge and decline. From the less likely such as asteroid collisions to the risk of widespread computer failures at the turn of the millennium (the Y2K bug failed to materialize) and our undiminished reliance on oil despite the steadily increasing price.

These are all risks, natural and man-made, affecting us all in different ways, some large and some small, some with high impacts, others with little effect, and some are risks that never eventuate but which we still guard against.

Risk in plain usage is something going wrong. The *Risk Management Standard* (Institute of Risk Management, 2002) defined risk as the combination of the probability of an event and its consequences, with risk management being concerned with both positive and negative aspects of risk. Risk is gradually losing the stigma of only being concerned with the negative or downside. We now recognize the risk of us not meeting our goals, a risk of missing an opportunity, a risk of not recognising that something good is happening. This is the positive, upside of risk, evident in the widely used 'risk/return' tradeoff. If there is no risk, there is often little return, and there is often a higher return when the risk is higher.

Financial examples are the easiest to recognize. We invest our savings and our pension funds in bank deposits, property and the stock market. We know that bank deposits are basically risk-free but we also know that they have relatively low interest rates. Shares achieve much higher returns but they are subject to substantial fluctuations in the stock market. Property rises in value over the long term even though the rental return may not be as good as shares, but as those caught by negative gearing (when the value of a home falls below the mortgage value) know, even property can be a risky investment in the short term. The international fallout from the crisis in the US subprime market attests to that.

A family example is more subtle but no less important. As children grow, we give them more freedom, to stop over at a friend's home, to go to the movies or shopping in town without parents. These are risky endeavours because, although children are taught safe practices, they are out of their parent's control. Things can go wrong. Things do go wrong. There is a real risk in giving children freedom, but the return is that children grow into confident and independent adults. To totally protect a child and not allow them any freedom may avoid many external risks. But it will also likely result in a child growing without confidence or independence, a different kind of risk altogether.

Each of us has an appetite for risk. Some have a huge appetite, climbing mountains, deep sea diving, or motorcycle racing. Others may be much happier in the garden or walking along the beach. Whether and how we perceive risk, our appetite for risk, and how we cope with risk is an individual matter. At the level of the organization where many people work together, there will be many different perceptions of risk, different appetites for risk (some risk taking, others risk avoiding) and many views as to the most appropriate response to risk (should it be ignored? avoided? insured?)

Can risk be managed?

While we may have no control over natural disasters, we can manage our response to those disasters, whether that is building in safer locations or using different construction methods, preparing flood defences, having rescue plans and resources available, etc. Risks can be reduced if we understand the risk. The risk of fire can be reduced by taking care not to have flammable materials on our premises, and reduced further still by having smoke detectors, fire alarms, water sprinklers, and fire extinguishers. Despite all precautions, a fire may still eventuate, so we need insurance to cover any loss, and a plan to resume our life (or our business) should the worse happen. This might include moving to other premises, having secure fireproof storage of our most valuable possessions and copies of all our computer-based information.

Some risks are more likely than others. It is more likely that someone has a workplace accident or that there is an environmental spillage than there is a terrorist incident. But some events have more consequences than others. One may cause injury or death, some may be written off as bad luck, and others may destroy our whole business. The way we manage those risks depends on how likely they are to eventuate, and the impact they will have if they do eventuate.

Some risks, like workplace accidents and environmental spillages can be avoided, although perhaps never eliminated altogether, because the cost of doing so may be prohibitive. But avoidance is preferred to remedial work so organizations put in place controls to avoid the identified risks from occurring, and if they do occur, to provide early warning so that corrective action can be taken.

In simple terms, a control is the exercise of some power of restraint or providing direction. Management controls have always existed, in order to control the behaviour of employees with the purpose of ensuring that organizational objectives are achieved. Many of these controls are accounting controls, such as budgets, standard costs, and variance analysis, etc. As organizations become more sophisticated, non-financial controls are added. These controls may include targets for quality, waste, delivery lead time, customer satisfaction, etc., often linked in what is frequently referred to as the *Balanced Scorecard* (Kaplan & Norton, 1992, 2001). When other controls, such as those in respect of personnel (recruitment, training, supervision), information systems (security of access, authorization, backups), corporate policies, procedures and working practices, etc. are added, the result is a 'system' of management control, although often the components of the 'system' can lead to different and inconsistent behaviours.The emergence of risk management is covered in the next section. However, it is worthwhile summarising, in simple terms, the common-sense approach to how risk is managed, which underlies more sophisticated models of risk management and control that feature in this and later chapters. The steps involved in managing risk are:

1. Identify the risk, because if it cannot be identified, it cannot be managed.
2. Assess the impact the risk is likely to have if it does eventuate.
3. Prioritise the importance of each risk in terms of its likelihood and impact, because we do not have the time or money to manage every risk.
4. Evaluate the risk in terms of the organization's risk appetite.
5. Decide on action to lessen either the likelihood or impact of the risk.
6. Record each risk and the decisions made about them.
7. Report the risks, decisions about their treatment and who is responsible.

Risk management is the process of understanding and managing risks that the organization faces in attempting to achieve its objectives. Perhaps the best definition of risk management is that in relation to ERM. ERM aligns risk management with business strategy and embeds a risk management culture into the business. It encompasses the whole organization and sees risks as opportunities as much as hazards.

All managers, whether financial or non-financial, are accountable for performance at either a corporate level or for their particular business unit. Accountability for performance cannot be separated from risk management, not just in terms of something going wrong which affects the organization or business unit, but also in terms of failing to achieve the organization's objectives. We are all, whether as individuals or managers, intimately involved in risk management.

The emergence of risk in business

Risk management has evolved from various but distinct functional areas: occupational health and safety; insurance; the hedging of financial risks (foreign exchange and interest rates); credit risk; and project management. The first two were largely the historical focus of risk managers in organizations, while hedging was the province of finance and treasury managers. Credit controllers had accounting or administrative backgrounds and were concerned with the risk of default by customers. Project managers tended to come from construction or engineering backgrounds, where risk was seen in terms of failing to complete to specification, on time and on budget. ERM ties these, and many other functional approaches to risk together.

In 1921, Frank Knight published *Risk, Uncertainty and Profit* (Knight, 1921), a book that is regularly referred to in risk management. According to Knight, risk was a state of not knowing what future events will happen, but having the ability to estimate the odds, while uncertainty was a state of not knowing the odds. While the first was calculable, the second was not and any estimates were subjective. Accounting texts, so far as they discuss risk, typically do so in terms of decision trees, probability distributions, cost–volume–profit analysis, discounted cash flow etc. Finance texts are typically concerned with portfolios, capital assets pricing models and hedging techniques to reduce the risks of currency and interest rate exposure. Engineering and other technically based texts use a variety of mathematically based techniques, often applying probability analysis.

These approaches to risk, valuable as they are in relation to their functional specializations, can be very restrictive at the wider organizational level, as much risk is the result of subjective judgement, experience, intuition, and insight. It is often difficult or impossible to measure risk using wholly quantitative techniques. This has been partially recognized in the banking industry where quantitative techniques (such as Value at Risk or VaR) have to be balanced with more subjective judgements of operational risk (see Chapter 22).

Risk came to be seen on a much wider basis through the publication of books such as *Risk Society* (Beck, 1986, 1992 in translation); *Risk* (Adams, 1995); *Against the Gods* (Bernstein, 1998) and more recently *Organized Uncertainty* (Power, 2007).

We can identify several motivators behind the emergence and continuing importance of risk management and each of these is discussed in turn.

Risk: from hazard to opportunity

The (International Federation of Accountants, 1999) published a study on *Enhancing Shareholder Wealth by Better Managing Business Risk*. The IFAC report defined risks as uncertain future events that could influence the achievement of the organization's strategic, operational and financial objectives. The IFAC report shifted the focus of risk from a negative concept of hazard to a positive interpretation that managing risk is an integral part of generating sustainable shareholder value. The report argued that business risk management establishes, calibrates and realigns the relationship between risk, growth and return. Similarly, the Turnbull Report (Institute of Chartered Accountants in England & Wales, 1999) now part of the *Combined Code on Corporate Governance* (Financial Reporting Council, 2003), defined risk as any event that might affect a listed company's performance, including environmental, ethical and social risks.

The standardization of risk

Standards for risk management are now international, and remarkably consistent in their focus (Committee of Sponsoring Organizations of the Treadway Commission (COSO), 2004); (Institute of Risk Management, 2002); (Standards Australia, 2004). As Michael Power explains in his recent book *Organized Uncertainty* (Power, 2007), risk has become very important in the language of managers and a major element of organizational accountability.

Perhaps the most widely recognized international standard is that produced by the Committee of Sponsoring Organizations of the Treadway Commission (COSO) in the US, which produced *Internal Control – Integrated Framework* (Committee of Sponsoring Organizations of the Treadway Commission (COSO), 1992) and followed this with *Enterprise Risk Management – Integrated Framework* (Committee of Sponsoring Organizations of the Treadway Commission (COSO), 2004). COSO's *Enterprise Risk Management – Integrated Framework* states that internal control is an integral part of ERM.

Building on work by the International Organization for Standardization (ISO/IEC Guide 73), the *Risk Management Standard* (Institute of Risk Management, 2002) was published in the UK and in Australia, the first risk management standard was produced in 1999 as Australian and New Zealand Standard AS4360 (Standards Australia, 2004).

Risk and corporate governance

Corporate governance is the system by which companies are directed and controlled. Boards of directors are responsible to their shareholders and have a stewardship function for the governance of their company. The responsibilities of Boards include setting the company's strategic goals, providing the leadership to put those goals into effect, supervising the management of the business and reporting to shareholders. This role involves the management of risk and the review of the effectiveness of internal control.

The trend towards improved corporate governance has emphasized risk management as a core function of the Board. In the UK, high profile corporate failures led to a series of reports, beginning with that by Sir Adrian Cadbury on corporate governance (Cadbury Code, 1992) and culminating in the *Combined Code on Corporate Governance* (Financial Reporting Council, 2003). The *Combined Code* requires that boards of directors review the effectiveness of internal controls in response to the risks facing the organization. This risk-based approach to control, as for audit, should lead to the development of controls that are a response to risks, rather than being developed incrementally over time (International Federation of Accountants, 2006) often for political purposes unrelated to risk.

Even before the spate of corporate governance reports culminating in the *Combined Code*, a growing number of institutional investors were starting to encourage greater disclosure of governance processes and emphasizing the quality and sustainability of earnings, rather than short-term profits alone. For example, a survey published by KPMG in 2002 reported that 80% of fund managers would pay more for the shares of a demonstrably well-governed company, with the average premium being 11%. Research by management consultants McKinsey also showed that an overwhelming majority of institutional investors were prepared to pay a significant premium for companies exhibiting high standards of corporate governance.

Risk and financial statements

The introduction of the US Sarbanes-Oxley (SOX) Act in 2002 was the legislative response in the US to the financial and accounting scandals of Enron and WorldCom and the misconduct at the accounting firm Arthur Andersen. Its main aim was to deal with issues of transparency, integrity and oversight of financial markets. SOX as it is called requires the certification of annual and quarterly financial reports by the chief executive and chief financial officer of all companies with US securities registrations, with criminal penalties for knowingly making false certifications. SOX is criticized for having increased corporate costs as a result of the greater emphasis on internal controls and the audit of financial reporting.

Risk and Basel

The notion of risk in relation to financial derivatives in the banking industry was first formulated by the Basel Committee on Banking Supervision (1994). For banks and regulated financial institutions, the Basel Committee has had an important impact, particularly as it affects risk and internal control. Part of the Bank for International Settlements, the objectives of the Basel Committee include enhancing the understanding of key supervisory issues and improving the quality of banking supervision worldwide.

Basel II is the second group of Accords from the Basel Committee. It contains international standards for banking laws and regulations aimed at helping to protect the international financial system from the results of the collapse of a major bank or a series of banks. Basel II establishes rigorous risk and capital management requirements to ensure each bank holds reserves sufficient to guard against its risk exposure given its lending and investment practices.

The rise of ERM on Board and management agendas has been a result of the changing understanding of risk, its standardization and globalization, and the role of corporate governance, Sarbanes-Oxley and Basel on its development. Each of these motivators of risk management is considered in greater detail in subsequent chapters.

Is risk management just another management fad?

There have been many management fads, often pushed by consultants, to help managers improve the performance of their organizations. These have ranged from Management by Objectives (MBO) in the 1960s; to total quality management, the quality standard ISO 9000 and Six Sigma; the balanced scorecard for non-financial performance measurement; Investors in People (IiP); and the Business Excellence model of the European Foundation for Quality Management (EFQM).

This is not to detract from what are doubtless helpful tools, but they are in the main either piecemeal approaches or layered over the top of existing business practices. By contrast, risk management, particularly in its ERM form, takes a holistic view of the organization incorporating the risks (and their treatment) of achieving strategy, maintaining quality, achieving financial and non-financial performance targets, and continual improvement to build and maintain competitive advantage.

Given that risk management has become embedded in corporate governance frameworks, and in various international standards, as well as in financial reporting and banking, it is unlikely that risk management will disappear from the corporate agenda. It has been dismissed to some extent by Power (2007) as merely a 'box-ticking' compliance exercise, although his view does reinforce the importance of Boards and managers not being solely dominated by a concern with conformance alone.

In 2003, the publication by Chartered Institute of Management Accountants (2003) of *Enterprise Governance: Getting the Balance Right*, emphasized the importance of a dual concern with conformance and performance. While conformance is related to issues of accountability and assurance, driven by corporate governance requirements, performance is concerned with resource utilization and value creation. CIMA's enterprise governance framework argued the need to balance conformance requirements with the need to deliver long-term performance to achieve strategic success.

▌ Case study: the subprime crisis

A global financial crisis commenced in 2007 and continued into 2008 as a result of falling US house prices and defaults on 'subprime' mortgages. The subprime market relates to poor quality loans where the interest rate is higher because of the higher risk involved. Borrowers typically have poor credit histories. Some commentators believe that subprime lending leads to predatory lending practices while others argue that it provides credit to those who otherwise have no access to credit.

Access to subprime loans enabled US homeowners to borrow up to the full value of their homes, with low initial repayments. Homeowners were unable to refinance when interest rates increased and the fall in housing prices led to many unwilling or unable to repay their mortgages, leading to foreclosure by mortgage lenders and the sale of houses at a loss, leading to a further decline in the housing market and increased unemployment in the sector.

The US Secretary to the Treasury called it the most significant risk to the US economy. The Wall Street Journal compared the crisis to the biggest financial disasters of the last half-century including the savings and loan crisis of the 1980s and the hi-tech stock crash of 2000. The effects were subsequently felt throughout the world in terms of reduced credit availability and interest rates.

In September 2007, Northern Rock plc was a top five UK mortgage lender, on the FTSE 100 index with over £100 billion in assets. Northern Rock raised over 70% of the money it used in its growing mortgage lending business from banks and other financial institutions. A bank run (the first on a UK bank for 150 years) on Northern Rock by its customers led to the government providing 'lender of last resort' funding and guarantees for the bank's depositors totalling about £20 billion. The result was a 90% fall in the bank's share price, a deteriorating credit rating and a loss of reputation. The CEO resigned and several directors also left the board. In 2008 Northern Rock was nationalized by the UK government after two unsuccessful bids to buy the bank.

The initial round of finger pointing at institutions that lost billions on subprime mortgage-linked investments focused on their chief executives and those at Citi, UBS and Merrill Lynch were forced to leave their companies. Bear Stearns, one of the largest US brokers and investment banks collapsed in 2008 despite emergency loans from the Federal Reserve. Bear Stearns was subsequently sold to JP Morgan Chase.

In 2008, the US Government intervened to protect mortgage giants Fannie Mae (the Federal National Mortgage Association) and Freddie Mac (the Federal Home Loan Mortgage Corporation) from insolvency after their share price plunged. Together, these listed companies hold or guarantee more than 50% of US housing mortgages. Fannie Mae and Freddie Mac are listed on the stock exchange and with an implicit government guarantee had been seen as safe and secure, so able to borrow money more cheaply than other mortgage providers which they then lend on to mortgage brokers and banks. These mortgages are then packaged and sold to investors, a process of securitization.

The subprime crisis, and its results in housing prices, construction, and employment in the US and a global tightening of credit and increased interest rates raises the question of whether ERM was being used effectively by organizations that have been involved. Did banks and financial institutions that invested in subprime mortgages really understand the risk involved and the dependence on economic factors? Did organizations understand how global credit tightening and increased interest rates would affect them? Did Northern Rock adequately assess its dependence for liquidity on funds and the effect of a credit tightening? One commentator argued that Northern Rock could not have foreseen such an event. Yet history shows us (e.g. the US savings and loan crisis and the bust in the stock market for 'dot com' stocks) that these lessons repeat themselves and are not necessarily learned by organizations. ERM emphasizes the need to stand back from the day-to-day business, question the assumptions behind the business model, consider 'what if' scenarios and identify responses that can avoid or mitigate the effects of these events if they do arise.

References

Adams J. 1995. *Risk*. London: UCL Press.

Basel Committee on Banking Supervision. 1994. *Risk Management Guidelines for Derivatives*. Basel: Bank for International Settlements.

Beck U. 1986. *Risk Society*. London: Sage, (1992 in translation).

Bernstein PL. 1998. *Against the Gods: The Remarkable Story of Risk*. New York: John Wiley.

Cadbury Code. 1992. *Report of the Committee on the Financial Aspects of Corporate Governance: The Code of Best Practice*. London: Professional Publishing.

Chartered Institute of Management Accountants. 2003. *Enterprise Governance: Getting the Balance Right*: CIMA & IFAC.

Committee of Sponsoring Organizations of the Treadway Commission (COSO). 1992. *Internal Control – Integrated Framework*.

Committee of Sponsoring Organizations of the Treadway Commission (COSO). 2004. *Enterprise Risk Management – Integrated Framework*.

Financial Reporting Council. 2003. *The Combined Code on Corporate Governance*. London: Financial Reporting Council.

Institute of Chartered Accountants in England & Wales. 1999. *Internal Control: Guidance for Directors on the Combined Code* (Turnbull Report).

Institute of Risk Management. 2002. *A Risk Management Standard*. London: IRM.

International Federation of Accountants. 1999. Enhancing Shareholder Wealth by Better Managing Business Risk. *Report on International Management Accounting Study No. 9*.

International Federation of Accountants. 2006. *Internal Controls – A Review of Current Developments*. New York Professional Accountants in Business Committee.

Kaplan RS, Norton DP. 1992. The Balanced Scorecard – Measures That Drive Performance. *Harvard Business Review*, (Jan.–Feb. 1992).

Kaplan RS, Norton DP. 2001. *The Strategy-Focused Organization: How Balanced Scorecard Companies Thrive in the New Business Environment*. Boston, MA: Harvard Business School Press.

Knight FH. 1921. *Risk, Uncertainty, and Profit*. Boston, MA: Houghton Mifflin Co.

Power M. 2007. *Organized Uncertainty: Designing a World of Risk Management*. Oxford: Oxford University Press.

Standards Australia. 2004. *Australian and New Zealand Risk Management Standard AS/NZS 4360*, 3rd edition. Sydney: Standards Australia.

Chapter 2

Risk in the Corporate Governance Agenda

Corporate governance is the system by which companies are directed and controlled. Boards of directors are responsible to their shareholders and have a stewardship function for the governance of the company. The responsibilities of Boards include setting the company's strategic goals, providing the leadership to put those goals into effect, supervising the management of the business and reporting to shareholders.

Models of corporate governance

There are two models of corporate governance:

- Shareholder value/agency model
- Stakeholder model.

Each model represents a different means by which the functioning of boards of directors and top management can be understood. In UK company law, there is no doubt that shareholders are in a privileged position compared with other stakeholders. Hence, corporate governance in the UK is founded on the shareholder value/agency model. However, other models of governance take a broader view, for example that found in South Africa.

Boards of directors are responsible for the governance of their companies. The shareholders' role in governance is to appoint the directors and the auditors and to satisfy themselves that an appropriate governance structure is in place. The responsibilities of the board include setting the company's strategic aims, providing the leadership to put them into effect, supervising the management of the business and reporting to shareholders on their stewardship.

The Board is held accountable by shareholders for achieving satisfactory returns from their investment. Traditionally, business performance has been measured through accounting ratios such as return on capital employed (ROCE), return on investment (ROI), earnings per share, etc. However, it has been argued that these are historical rather than current measures, and they vary between companies as a result of different accounting treatments.

One of the most important developments over the last 10 years has been the notion of shareholder value. During the 1990s institutional investors (pension funds, insurance companies, investment trusts, etc.), through their dominance of share ownership, increased their pressure on management to improve the financial performance of companies. Shareholder value analysis, or value-based management emphasizes the processes by which shareholder value is achieved. In practice, the pursuit of shareholder value (also called economic value added, or EVA) can be achieved through the introduction of new or redesigned products and services; the management of costs; the development of performance measurement systems; and through improved decision-making. Value-based management (VBM) emphasizes shareholder value, on the assumption that this is the primary goal of every business. VBM approaches include total shareholder return, market value added, shareholder value added and economic value added.

- *Total shareholder return (TSR)* compares the dividends received by shareholders and the increase in the share price with the original shareholder investment, expressing the TSR as a percentage of the initial investment.
- *Market value added (MVA)* is the difference between total market capitalization (number of shares issued times share price plus the market value of debt) and the total capital invested in the business by debt and equity providers. This is a measure of the value generated by managers for shareholders.
- *Shareholder value added (SVA)* refers to the increase in shareholder value over time, defined as the economic value of an investment, which can be calculated by using the cost of capital to discount forecast future cash flows (free cash flows) into present values using discounted cash flow techniques. The business must generate profits that exceed the cost of capital in the capital market for value to be created (if not, shareholder value is eroded).
- *Economic Value Added*^{TM} *(EVA)* is a financial performance measure developed by consultants Stern Stewart & Co. which claims to capture the economic profit of a business that leads to shareholder value creation. In simple terms, EVA is net operating profit after deducting a charge to cover the opportunity cost of the capital invested in the business (and which is similar, albeit more complicated than the Residual Income approach used by accountants). EVA's 'economic profit' is the amount by which earnings exceed (or fall short of) the minimum rate of return that shareholders and financiers could get by investing in other securities with a comparable risk (see Stern Stewart's website at www.sternstewart.com).

The King Report on Corporate Governance in South Africa (King Committee on Corporate Governance, 2002) provides an integrated approach to corporate governance in the interest of all stakeholders, embracing social, environmental and economic aspects of organizational activities. It therefore takes, to some extent at least, a broader stakeholder model of governance. The King Report (King II) acknowledges that there is a move away from the single bottom line (that is, profit for shareholders) to a triple bottom line, which embraces the economic, environmental and social aspects of a company's activities.

Risk management may be embedded in legislation, as has been done for the US through the Sarbanes-Oxley Act, or in 'soft law' like the South African King II or the UK Combined Code on Corporate Governance which operates on a 'comply or explain' basis.

Corporate reform in the UK

In the UK, a series of reports has had a marked influence on the development of corporate governance. The first report, by Sir Adrian Cadbury, followed a number of high-profile corporate failures including Polly Peck (1990), BCCI (1991), and pension funds in the Maxwell Group (1991).

The Cadbury Report (Cadbury Code, 1992) was in relation to *Financial Aspects of Corporate Governance*. The Greenbury report (Greenbury, 1995) was published in 1995 on Directors' Remuneration. The Hampel report (Committee on Corporate Governance, 1998) was set up to review the implementation of the Cadbury Code. It was responsible for the *Corporate Governance Combined Code* which was published in 1998 and incorporated the recommendations of the Cadbury, Greenbury and Hampel Committees (Financial Reporting Council, 2003).

The Turnbull Guidance on internal control (Institute of Chartered Accountants in England & Wales, 1999) was subsequently incorporated into the *Combined Code*, as was the Higgs report (Higgs, 2003)[1] on the role of non-executive directors and the Smith report (Financial Reporting Council, 2005a)[2] on the role of audit committees, both published in 2003. The Higgs and Smith Reports were followed by the Tyson Report (Tyson, 2003)[3] on the recruitment and development of non-executive directors. *Internal Control: Revised Guidance for Directors on the Combined Code* was published by the Financial Reporting Council (Financial Reporting Council, 2005b).

A report produced in 2007 by King's College, London for the Department of Trade and Industry (Filatotchev et al., 2007) considered the key drivers of good corporate governance and how appropriate the policy environment was in the UK to promote

---

[1] http://www.berr.gov.uk/files/file23012.pdf.
[2] http://www.frc.org.uk/documents/pagemanager/frc/Smith%20Report%202005.pdf.
[3] http://facultyresearch.london.edu/docs/TysonReport.pdf.

good governance practices. The report[4] identified 18 key mechanisms for corporate governance, ranging from board independence to shareholder activism, information disclosure, audit and internal control effectiveness, executive remuneration, takeovers and stakeholder involvement. The researchers identified gaps in government policy that supported these mechanisms, mainly relating to executive remuneration, employees and stakeholders generally. The report also found that it was important to balance and recognise trade-offs between mandatory regulations and 'soft law' such as codes based on comply or explain principles (such as the Combined Code on Corporate Governance) and the self-regulation of professional groups. The cost of regulation should also be considered.

Corporate reform in the US

Corporate governance emerged in the United States with the Treadway Commission's Report on *Fraudulent Financial Reporting* in 1987 (Treadway Commission, 1987). The report affirmed the important role played by audit committees in governance. The report was later reinforced by the Securities and Exchange Commission in its listing requirements.

A subgroup of the Treadway Commission, the Committee of Sponsoring Organisations (COSO) developed *Internal Control – Integrated Framework* in 1992 (Committee of Sponsoring Organizations of the Treadway Commission (COSO), 1992) and in 2003 a report was published on *Enterprise Risk Management* (Committee of Sponsoring Organizations of the Treadway Commission (COSO), 2003).

As a result of accounting scandals at Enron and WorldCom, the US introduced the Sarbanes-Oxley Act of 2002. Sarbanes-Oxley (SOX) introduced the requirement to disclose all material off-balance sheet transactions and for the chief executive officer and chief financial officer to give assurances regarding the effectiveness of internal controls. Section 404 of Sarbanes-Oxley requires companies to state the responsibility of management for establishing and maintaining an adequate internal control structure and procedures for financial reporting; and to make an assessment of the effectiveness of the internal control structure and procedures for financial reporting.

An important role of a Board of Directors is to understand the significant risks an organization faces and to ensure that controls are in place in relation to those risks. The publication by the International Federation of Accountants (IFAC) in August 2006 of *Internal Controls – A Review of Current Developments* (International Federation

---

[4]The full report including a detailed description of the eighteen drivers can be downloaded from www.berr.gov.uk/files/file36671.pdf.

of Accountants, 2006) emphasized the risk-based approach to internal control as encompassing all an organization's activities, an approach that is much wider than the Sarbanes-Oxley regulations for financial reporting.

This approach is evident in the US by the Committee of Sponsoring Organizations of the Treadway Commission (COSO) in their reports on *Internal Control Integrated Framework* (1992) and *Enterprise Risk Management Integrated Framework* (2004), and in the UK by the Turnbull report, now part of the Financial Reporting Council's (FRC) *Combined Code on Corporate Governance*. COSO has also influenced the approach taken in relation to IT governance in the *Control Objectives for Information and Related Techno*logy (COBIT)[5], the latest version of which was published in 2005. The COSO/Turnbull approach has been adopted in Canada (the *Criteria of Control Board Guidance on Control*, or CoCo), in Hong Kong by the Hong Kong Stock Exchange, and in Europe by the Fédération des Experts Comptables Européens (FEE). In each of these countries, the narrow approach taken in the US has been rejected. Similarly, Australia largely follows the UK model in its Company Law Economic Reform Program (CLERP9).

The principles-based approach adopted by COSO and the Financial Reporting Council, where risk management and internal control is embedded in organizational processes, is in sharp contrast with the narrow and more rules-based approach taken by the Sarbanes-Oxley (SOX) Act which applies to all companies registered with the US Securities and Exchange Commission (SEC). However, the International Federation of Accountants (2006) report recognises that the emphasis in SOX on internal control over financial reporting may be detrimental to broader aspects of internal control and risk management as it may lead organizations to see internal control as a compliance issue rather than as a part of managing a successful organization.

Responsibility for risk and control

Code C.2 of the *Combined Code on Corporate Governance* (Financial Reporting Council, 2003) relates to internal control. The *Combined Code* encompasses the Turnbull Guidance (Institute of Chartered Accountants in England & Wales, 1999), specifying that

> *The board should maintain a sound system of internal control to safeguard shareholders' investment and the company's assets.*

---

[5]Available to download from http://www.isaca.org/Content/NavigationMenu/Members_and_Leaders/ COBIT6/Obtain_COBIT/Obtain_COBIT.htm.

The Turnbull Guidance is based on the adoption by a company's board of a risk-based approach to establishing a sound system of internal control and reviewing its effectiveness (para. 9).

The Board is responsible for the company's system of internal control and should set policies on internal control and seek assurance that the system is working effectively and is effective in managing risks. However, it is management's role to identify and evaluate the risks faced by the company for consideration by the Board. Management must also implement the Board's policies on risk and control by designing, operating and monitoring a suitable system of internal control.

The Smith Guidance (Financial Reporting Council, 2005a) notes:

The company's management is responsible for the identification, assessment, management and monitoring of risk, for developing, operating and monitoring the system of internal control and for providing assurance to the board that it has done so (para. 4.6).

Reports from management to the board should provide a balanced assessment of the significant risks facing the organization and the effectiveness of the system of internal control in managing those risks. Any significant control failings or weaknesses identified should be discussed in the reports, including the impact that they have had, could have had, or may have, on the company and the actions being taken to rectify them (Turnbull Guidance, para. 30: Institute of Chartered Accountants in England & Wales, 1999).

Enterprise governance: conformance and performance

In a report published by Chartered Institute of Management Accountants (2004) *Enterprise Governance: Getting the Balance Right*, enterprise governance was described as constituting the entire accountability framework of the organization, with two dimensions: conformance, and performance. These dimensions need to be in balance.

- Conformance is what is generally referred to as corporate governance and covers board structures, roles and remuneration. Conformance takes place through assurance, ensuring that the organization understands and is managing its risks effectively. Codes such as Turnbull and the Combined Code address the conformance dimension through compliance, audit assurance and oversight such as through the audit committee.

■ Performance is the need to take risks to achieve objectives, and in order to do this, risk management needs to be integrated with decision-making at each organizational level. Performance focuses on strategy, resource utilization and value creation, helping the board to make strategic decisions, understand its appetite for risk and the key performance drivers. Performance does not fit easily with codes, audit and oversight but relies on a strategic focus, taking advantage of opportunities as they arise.

The CIMA/IFAC report found four key corporate governance issues that underpinned success and failure: culture and tone at the top; the chief executive; the board of directors; and internal controls. The report also identified four key strategic issues that underpinned success and failure: choice and clarity of strategy; strategy execution; the ability to respond to sudden changes and/or fast moving market conditions; and the ability to undertake successful mergers and acquisitions (M&A). Unsuccessful M&As were the most significant issue in strategy-related failure. The report recommended the establishment of a strategy committee to undertake regular reviews of strategy and to better inform the full board's discussions about strategic decisions. This would balance the audit committee's conformance role. The relationship between conformance and performance in CIMA's enterprise governance model is shown in Figure 2.1.

The responsibility of the Board of Directors

The Board must acknowledge that it is responsible for the company's system of internal control and for reviewing its effectiveness. It should also explain that the system is designed to manage rather than eliminate the risk of failure to achieve business objectives, and can only provide reasonable but not absolute assurance against material mis-statement or loss. The Board should also disclose the process it has applied to deal with material internal control aspects of any significant problems disclosed in the annual report and accounts.

When reviewing management reports on internal control, the board should:

■ Consider the significant risks and assess how they have been identified, evaluated and managed.
■ Assess the effectiveness of internal controls in managing the significant risks, having regard to any significant weaknesses in internal control.
■ Consider whether necessary actions are being taken promptly to remedy any weaknesses.

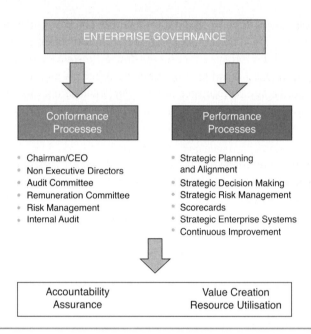

Figure 2.1   CIMA Enterprise Governance model.
Source: http://www.ifac.org/Store/Details.tmpl?SID=11559337241982775&
Cart=1157581557690125.

■ Consider whether the findings indicate a need for more exhaustive monitoring of the system of internal control.

In determining its policies for a system of internal control, the Board needs to consider:

■ The nature and extent of the risks facing the company.
■ The extent and types of risk which are acceptable for the company to bear.
■ The likelihood of the risks materializing.
■ The ability of the company to reduce the incidence and severity of risks that do materialize.
■ The costs of operating controls compared with the benefit obtained in managing the risk.

Combined Code provision C.2.1 states:

> *The board should, at least annually, conduct a review of the effectiveness of the group's system of internal controls and should report to shareholders that*

they have done so. The review should cover all material controls, including financial, operational and compliance controls and risk management systems.

Reviewing the effectiveness of internal control is one of the Board's responsibilities and this function needs to be carried out on a continuous basis. Directors are expected to apply the same standard of care when reviewing the effectiveness of internal control as when they exercise their general duties. It is important that a review of internal controls is not limited to financial controls. The Board should regularly review reports on internal control in order to carry out an annual assessment for the purpose of making its public statement on internal control to ensure that it has considered all significant aspects of internal control.

The Board's annual assessment should consider:

- Any changes since the last annual assessment in the nature and extent of significant risks, and the company's ability to respond to changes in its business and the external environment.
- The scope and quality of management's ongoing monitoring of risks and of the system of internal control and the work of the internal audit function and other providers of assurance.
- The extent and frequency of the communication of the results of the monitoring to the Board which enables it to build up a cumulative assessment of the state of control in the company and the effectiveness with which risk is being managed.
- The incidence of significant control weaknesses that have been identified during the period and the extent to which they have resulted in unforeseen outcomes that have had, or could have, a material impact on the company's financial performance.
- The effectiveness of the company's public reporting processes.

(Turnbull Guidance, para. 33).

The board's statement on internal control should disclose that there is an ongoing process for identifying, evaluating and managing the significant risks faced by the company, that it has been in place for the year and up to the date of approval of the annual report and accounts, and that it has been regularly reviewed by the Board and conforms to the Turnbull Guidance.

Boards are required to confirm in their annual report that necessary action has been or is being taken to remedy any significant failings or weaknesses identified from their review of the effectiveness of the internal control system, and to include in the annual report such information as considered necessary to assist shareholders' understanding of the main features of the company's risk management processes and system of internal control.

The Audit Committee

Code C3 of the *Combined Code* (Financial Reporting Council, 2003) states:

> *The Board should establish an audit committee of at least three, or in the case of smaller companies[6] two, members, who should all be independent non-executive directors. The board should satisfy itself that at least one member of the audit committee has recent and relevant financial experience.*

The Smith Guidance (Financial Reporting Council, 2005a) states that there should be no less than three audit committee meetings each year, held to coincide with key dates in the financial reporting and audit cycle as well as board meetings. Between meetings, the chairman of the audit committee will maintain contact with the board chairman, chief executive, finance director, external audit lead partner and the head of internal audit.

An audit committee is

> *a formally constituted sub-committee of the main board which should normally meet at least twice a year. Membership of the committee should comprise at least three directors, all non-executive. A majority of the committee members should be independent of the company. The primary function of the audit committee is to assist the board to fulfil its stewardship responsibilities by reviewing the systems of internal control, the external audit process, the work of internal audit and the financial information which is provided to shareholders (Chartered Institute of Management Accountants, 2005).*

The audit committee should have terms of reference tailored to the needs of the company, which must be approved by the board. The audit committee should review its terms of reference and its own effectiveness annually. The main role and responsibilities of the audit committee should be established in the terms of reference but should include:

- Monitoring the integrity of the company's financial statements; significant judgments made in relation to the financial statements; and formal announcements made by the company to the stock exchange.
- Reviewing the company's internal control and risk management systems (although in some cases financial controls may be the responsibility of the audit

---

[6]Below FTSE 350.

committee while non-financial controls and risk management may be the responsibility of a separate risk committee of the board, in which case the principles
should also apply to the risk committee).

■   Monitoring and reviewing the effectiveness of the internal audit function.
■   Making recommendations to the Board for the Board to place a resolution before
    shareholders in an annual general meeting for the appointment, re-appointment
    and removal of the external auditor and to approve the terms of engagement and
    remuneration of the external auditor.
■   Reviewing and monitoring the external auditor's independence and objectivity
    and the effectiveness of the audit process.
■   Developing and implementing policy on the engagement of the external audi-
    tor to supply non-audit services in order to maintain auditor objectivity and
    independence.

The board should also review the effectiveness of the audit committee annually.

It is not the duty of the audit committee to carry out functions that belong to others,
such as management in the preparation of financial statements, or auditors in the
planning and conduct of audits. Audit committees need to satisfy themselves that there
is a proper system and allocation of responsibilities for the day-to-day monitoring of
financial controls but they should not seek to do the monitoring themselves. However,
this oversight function may lead to more detailed work if there are signs that something
is wrong.

The audit committee should report to the Board, identifying any matters where
it considers action or improvement is needed and making appropriate recommendations. The audit committee should also review arrangements by which staff may
confidentially raise their concerns about possible improprieties in matters of financial
reporting and, more generally, how those investigations take place and are followed
up with appropriate action.

The audit committee and audit

The audit committee should review and approve the scope of work of the internal
audit function, with regard to the complementary roles of internal and external audit.
The audit committee should ensure that the internal audit function has access to the
information it needs and the resources necessary to carry out its function. The audit
committee should approve the appointment or termination of the Head of Internal
Audit. The audit committee should, at least annually, meet the external and internal
auditors, without management being present, to discuss the scope of work of the
auditors and any issues arising from the audit.

In its review of the work of internal audit, the audit committee should:

■ Ensure that the internal auditor is accountable to the audit committee and has direct access to the Board chairman and audit committee.

■ Review and assess the internal audit work plan.

■ Receive regular reports on the results of the work of the internal auditor.

■ Review and monitor management's responsiveness to the internal auditor's findings and recommendations.

■ Monitor and assess the role and effectiveness of the internal audit function in the overall context of the company's risk management system.

The audit committee is also responsible for making a recommendation on the appointment, re-appointment and removal of the external auditors and oversight of relations between the company and the external auditor. Each year the audit committee should assess the qualification, expertise, resources and independence of the external auditors and the effectiveness of the audit process. This should include obtaining a report on the audit firm's own internal quality control procedures. If the external auditor resigns, the audit committee should investigate the reasons and consider whether any further action is required.

The audit committee should approve the terms of engagement and remuneration of the external auditor and should review and agree with the engagement letter issued by the external auditor at the start of each audit, ensuring that it has been updated to reflect any changed circumstances. The scope of the audit work should be reviewed by the audit committee and if unsatisfied with its adequacy, it should arrange for additional work to be done.

The audit committee should have procedures to ensure the objectivity and independence of the external auditor, taking into account professional requirements. This assessment should consider all relationships between the external auditor and the company, including any non-audit services carried out by the external auditor for the company. The audit committee should monitor the audit firm's compliance with ethical guidance in relation to the rotation of audit partners, the level of fees the company pays to the external auditor in proportion to the total fee income of the firm, office and partner.

The audit committee should review with the external auditors their findings and should in particular:

■ Discuss major issues that arose during the audit and have subsequently been resolved and those issues that remain unresolved.

■ Review key accounting and audit judgments.

■ Review levels of error identified during the audit, obtaining explanations from management and the external auditors, as to any errors that remain unadjusted.

At the end of the audit cycle, the audit committee should review the effectiveness of the audit by:

- Reviewing whether the auditor has met the agreed audit plan, and understood why any changes have been made to that plan.
- Considering the robustness and perceptiveness of the auditors in their handling of the key accounting and audit judgments; in responding to questions from the audit committee and in their commentary on the systems of internal control.
- Obtaining feedback about the conduct of the audit from key people involved, notably the finance director and head of internal audit.
- Reviewing and monitoring the content of the external auditor's management letter, in order to assess whether it is based on a good understanding of the company's business and establish whether recommendations have been acted upon.

The chairman of the audit committee should be present at the annual general meeting to answer questions on the report of the audit committee's activities and matters within the scope of the audit committee's responsibilities.

Benefits of corporate governance

It is difficult to directly relate organizational benefits to good governance but it can be assumed that the benefits are likely to include:

- Reductions in risk as Boards of Directors play a more active role in risk management.
- Stimulation of performance by focusing on performance as well as conformance, and the need to be aware of risks that prevent organizational goals from being achieved.
- Improved access to capital markets as investors value good governance and risk management compared with companies that have weak processes.
- Enhancing the marketability of product/services by creating confidence among stakeholders.
- Improved leadership.
- Demonstrated transparency and accountability.

A model of governance, risk and control

An understanding of enterprise risk management needs to take place in the context of governance. It is important to understand the links between governance, risk

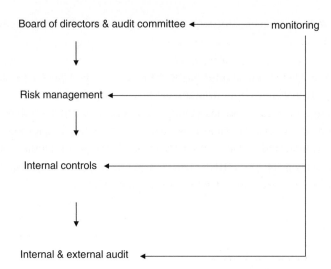

Figure 2.2   A model of governance, risk and control.

management and internal control and the interaction between the board of directors, the audit committee, external and internal auditors. This relationship is shown in Figure 2.2.

Figure 2.2 shows that the Board is responsible for establishing the risk management, internal control and audit framework and strategy for the organization, with risk guiding both internal controls and internal audit (we return to the issue of risk-based control and risk-based audit in subsequent chapters). The Board is also responsible for continual monitoring of the effectiveness of risk management, control and audit. The following case study highlights the failure of governance in relation to risk management and control.

Case study: Equitable Life

During the 1960s–1980s the 242-year-old Equitable Life sold thousands of policies with guaranteed returns, some as high as 12%. The company ran into problems in 2000 when it closed to new business after years of excessive returns to special policy holders had left the company with no money to absorb deterioration in the value of its stock market investments. It had a 'black hole' in its finances estimated at £4.4 billion because it had been paying out more to policy holders than it held in reserves. Equitable lost a case in the House of Lords in 2000 that led to a further deterioration in its financial position of £1.5 billion.

A report by Lord Penrose published in 2004[7] said that the former management was primarily culpable for Equitable's near collapse, aided by the failure of regulators to identify the mutual insurer's financial position. The autocratic former Chief Executive and chief actuary Roy Ranson was blamed for keeping regulators and the Board of Equitable in the dark about the precarious state of Equitable's financial position throughout the 1990s. The Penrose report also said that there had been weaknesses in the way that insurance companies were supervised throughout that period. The 'light touch' approach to regulation had not been changed to meet the requirements of an increasingly sophisticated and risky investment industry.

The Penrose report said that management had been dominated by 'unaccountable' actuaries, a board of non-executive directors who had no idea what was going on at the company they were charged with overseeing, and a regulator that failed to act as any kind of protector for policy holders. Lord Penrose said that at no stage had the Board been fully to grips with the company's financial situation, information was too fragmented, and the collective skills of the Board were inadequate for the task.

References

Cadbury Code. 1992. *Report of the Committee on the Financial Aspects of Corporate Governance: The Code of Best Practice*. London: Professional Publishing.

Chartered Institute of Management Accountants. 2005. *CIMA Official terminology: 2005 Edition*. Oxford: Elsevier.

Chartered Institute of Management Accountants, International Federation of Accountants. 2004. *Enterprise Governance: Getting the Balance Right*.

Committee of Sponsoring Organizations of the Treadway Commission (COSO). 1992. *Internal Control – Integrated Framework*.

Committee of Sponsoring Organizations of the Treadway Commission (COSO). 2003. *Enterprise Risk Management Framework*.

Committee on Corporate Governance. 1998. *Final Report* (Hampel Committee).

Filatotchev I, Jackson G, Gospel H, Allcock D. 2007. *Key Drivers of 'Good' Corporate Governance and the Appropriateness of UK Policy Responses: Final Report*. London: King's College.

Financial Reporting Council. 2003. *The Combined Code on Corporate Governance*.

Financial Reporting Council. 2005a. *Guidance on Audit Committees (The Smith Guidance)*. London: Financial Reporting Council.

Financial Reporting Council. 2005b. *Internal Control: Revised Guidance for Directors on the Combined Code*. London: Financial Reporting Council.

Greenbury R. 1995. *Directors' Remuneration: Report of a Study Group Chaired by Sir Reichard Greenbury*.

---

[7]The full report by Lord Penrose can be downloaded from http://www.hm-treasury.gov.uk/independent_ reviews/penrose_report/indrev_pen_index.cfm.

Higgs D. 2003. Review of the role and effectiveness of non-executive directors. *Department of Trade and Industry*. London: Department of Trade and Industry.

Institute of Chartered Accountants in England & Wales. 1999. *Internal Control: Guidance for Directors on the Combined Code* (Turnbull Report).

International Federation of Accountants. 2006. *Internal Controls – A Review of Current Developments*. New York Professional Accountants in Business Committee.

King Committee on Corporate Governance. 2002. *King Report on Corporate Governance for South Africa – 2002 (King II Report)*. South Africa: Institute of Directors.

Treadway Commission. 1987. *Report of the National Commission on Fraudulent Financial Reporting*.

Tyson L. 2003. *The Tyson Report on the Recrutment and Development of Non-Executive Directors*. London: London Business School.

Chapter 3

Risk and Governance in the Public and Third Sectors

The public sector is undergoing wide-ranging change and new governance arrangements are emerging, including partnerships with the private sector to deliver programs and services. The traditional mode of delivery of government services has increasingly shifted to outside organizations, including the third sector that is non-profit distributing organizations. This reinforces the need for extra care to ensure that sound systems of governance are in place and effective in line with increasing public expectations of behaviour from the public sector.

The International Federation of Accountants has argued that the 'corporate' in corporate governance has a broad application to all public sector organizations. The issues raised in the Cadbury report and laid down in the Combined Code on Corporate Governance (see Chapter 2) are just as relevant to public sector organizations.

Private sector risk management is chiefly concerned with profitability whereas public sector risk management is more focused upon service delivery, for which responsibility is often distributed between various public sector agencies. In the public sector and non-profit distributing bodies, governance may be through an elected and/or appointed governing body with 'governors', 'trustees' or 'members' rather than a Board of 'directors'.

Governance in the public sector

The principles of governance in public services have been laid down in *The Good Governance Standard for Public Services* (Independent Commission on Good Governance in Public Services, 2004).[1]

The public sector plays a significant role in society, and effective governance in the public sector can encourage the efficient use of resources, strengthen accountability for the stewardship of resources, improve service delivery, and contribute to improving peoples' lives.

---

[1] Available from http://www.cipfa.org.uk/pt/download/governance_standard.pdf.

"In virtually all jurisdictions, the public sector plays a major role in society, and effective governance in the public sector can encourage the efficient use of resources, strengthen accountability for the stewardship of those resources, improve management and service delivery, and thereby contribute to improving peoples' lives. Effective governance is also essential for building confidence in public sector entities – which is in itself necessary if public sector entities are to be effective in meeting their objectives." – (International Federation of Accountants, 2001).[2]

Public sector governance encompasses the policies and procedures used to direct an organization's activities to provide reasonable assurance that objectives are met and that operations are carried out in an ethical and accountable manner. In the public sector, governance relates to the means by which goals are established and accomplished. It also includes activities that ensure a government's credibility, establish equitable provision of services, and assure the appropriate behaviour of government officials thereby reducing the risk of public corruption.

Governance in the public sector is considered a serious issue because of concerns about excessive confidentiality in decision-making, the need to avoid undue influence caused by the lobbying of special interest groups, and to ensure efficiency in public expenditure. The public is now demanding increased openness by and accountability of government, has a greater willingness to challenge decisions, and has high expectations for an independent public service administration.

Public sector governance principles arise from the unique nature of government. For example, political forces are an essential part of the public sector, as is the not-for-profit nature of service delivery. Governments also hold coercive (police, taxation, and regulatory) powers over citizens and economic enterprises, and protection must exist to ensure accountability in the use of those powers and in service delivery. The absence of good governance structures and the lack of adherence to basic governance principles increases the risk of public corruption, which is defined as the misuse of entrusted power for private gain (Institute of Internal Auditors, 2006).[3]

In the public sector context, Boards of Directors can be difficult to identify and define, as they operate under different statutory and regulatory frameworks. Public sector organizations have to satisfy a complex range of political, economic and social objectives, which subject them to a different set of constraints than private sector, for-profit organizations face from shareholders.

Public sector organizations are accountable to various stakeholders including Cabinet Ministers, Parliament, other government officials, the electorate, client groups,

---

[2] Available from http://www.ifac.org/Members/DownLoads/Study_13_Governance.pdf.
[3] Available from http://www.theiia.org/download.cfm?file=3512.

etc. as well as the tax-paying public, each with a legitimate interest in public sector service delivery, but without the 'ownership rights' of the private sector.

In United Kingdom, the *Combined Code on Corporate Governance* (Financial Reporting Council, 2003) applies only to companies listed on the Stock Exchange. However, the Code is seen as an example of best practice and there are many examples of the principles being adopted by the public sector and by non-profit organizations as well as by privately owned unlisted organisations.

In 2001, a CIPFA/SOLACE Joint Working Group published *'Corporate Governance in Local Government – A Keystone for Community Governance'*.[4] The report recommended that a corporate governance assurance statement should be included in local authorities' financial statements. The Joint Working Group proposed that local authorities should make a statement on how they have complied with their local code of corporate governance and how they have monitored the effectiveness of their corporate governance arrangements in their financial statements. A revised *Delivering Good Governance in Local Government: Framework* document was published by CIPFA in 2007[5] provides a structure to help individual authorities with their own approach to governance. In United Kingdom, the preparation and publication of an annual governance statement in accordance with the *Framework* will be necessary to meet statutory requirements for authorities to prepare a statement of internal control in accordance with 'proper practices'.

Six principles have been developed by *The Good Governance Standard for Public Services* (Independent Commission on Good Governance in Public Services, 2004). Good governance means:

1. Being clear about the organization's purpose and its intended outcomes for citizens and service users – making sure that users receive a high quality service and that taxpayers receive value for money.

2. Performing effectively in clearly defined functions and roles – being clear about the functions of the governing body, the responsibilities of non-executives and the executive, and making sure that those responsibilities are carried out, and being clear about relationships between governors and the public.

3. Promoting values for the whole organization and demonstrating the values of good governance through behaviour that is putting organizational values into practice, and individual governors behaving in ways that uphold and exemplify effective governance.

4. Taking informed, transparent decisions and managing risk by being rigorous and transparent about how decisions are taken, having and using good quality

---

[4]The report is no longer available online.

[5]The framework document can be purchased from http://secure.cipfa.org.uk/cgi-bin/CIPFA.storefront/EN/ product/BU012.

information, advice and support, and making sure that an effective risk management system is in operation.

5. Developing the capacity and capability of the governing body to be effective by making sure that appointed and elected governors have the skills, knowledge and experience they need to perform well, by developing the capability of people with governance responsibilities and evaluating their performance, as individuals and as a group, and by striking a balance, in the membership of the governing body, between continuity and renewal.

6. Engaging stakeholders and making accountability real, through understanding formal and informal accountability relationships, taking an active and planned approach to dialogue with and accountability to the public, taking an active and planned approach to responsibility to staff, and engaging effectively with institutional stakeholders.

Risk management in the public sector

Then-UK Prime Minister Tony Blair's Strategy Unit conducted a study of modern risk, and how governments might better manage it.[6] One of the Unit's early conclusions was that it was not only the accelerating pace of change in science and technology and the greater connectedness of the world that was heightening the risk environment for government. Escalating risk, especially political risk, was also due to 'rising public expectations ... [and] declining trust in institutions, declining deference, and increased activism around specific risk issues, with messages amplified by the news media'. On the changing nature and severity of risk it referred to 'unforeseen events, programmes going wrong, projects going awry' including:

- Manufactured risks – from genetically modified food and drugs, to industrial processes or cloning methods.
- Direct threats such as the events of September 11 and the threat of chemical and biological attack.
- Risks resulting from the increasing vulnerability of citizens to distant events including economic crises in other countries, attacks on IT networks, diseases carried by air travellers, or the indirect impact of civil wars and famines.
- Safety risk issues such as BSE ('Mad Cow' disease), the Measles, Mumps and Rubella (MMR) vaccine, rail safety, adventure holidays, and flooding.
- Risks imposed on the public by individuals or businesses that necessitate government intervention.

[6]http://www.r2a.com.au/publications/5th_Edition/03_goverance.html.

- Risks of infrastructure disruption from industrial action, protest or the failure of transport or IT networks.
- Risks to government from the transfer of risk, for example, in capital projects and service delivery to the private sector.
- Risks of damage to government's reputation in the eyes of stakeholders and the public that impact government's ability to carry out its programs.

In United Kingdom, the Civil Contingencies Act of 2004 defines 'emergency' broadly to include not only war or attack by a foreign power but also terrorism which poses a threat of serious damage to the security of the UK and events which threaten serious damage to human welfare. Events such as the disruption of fuel supplies, contamination of land with a chemical matter or an epidemic could also satisfy the definition, should they reach the required level of seriousness. The Act imposes duties on local government bodies including the duty to assess the risk of an emergency occurring and to maintain plans for the purposes of responding to an emergency. The Act's implications for risk management are significant. Government bodies must produce risk assessments and adapt continuity planning accordingly. However, if organization-wide risk management practices are in place, compliance with the Act is less daunting.

The UK's Comprehensive Performance Assessment (CPA) system has also pushed risk management to the front of the local authority agenda. While most organizations have a risk management strategy in place, the focus of CPA is changing from a silo approach to risk management to it becoming an integral part of a sound corporate governance framework. CPA requires that councils demonstrate a proactive, practical approach to risk management. Good planning alone is no longer enough as local authorities are now judged on the performance of their risk management strategies such that risk management has to be part of all local government processes.

Both the Civil Contingencies Act and the Comprehensive Performance Assessment highlight the importance of the integration of risk management strategies with performance, business continuity and emergency planning into their enterprise risk management.

In the United Kingdom, CIPFA (the Chartered Institute of Public Finance and Accountancy) and SOLACE (the Society of Local Authority Chief Executives) have issued guidance for the public services which recognizes effective risk management as a component of good corporate governance. Just as the Turnbull Report recognized that internal control requires a system of risk management, for which boards of directors should be held responsible, public services are also encouraged to follow the private sector governance model by similarly regarding risk management as an essential ingredient of internal control. In the public sector, governing bodies have to accept a similar responsibility.

ALARM (the National Forum for Risk Management in the Public Sector) has published *Corporate Governance in the Public Sector – The Role of Risk Management*.[7] The report explains that a common feature of disasters such as the '*Herald of Free Enterprise*' Zeebrugge ferry disaster, the Kings Cross, London Underground fire and the Piper Alpha North Sea oil rig fire was that they highlighted gross deficiencies in general management practices. This was particularly evident in the '*Herald of Free Enterprise*' disaster where Mr Justice Sheen described Townsend Thorensen, operator of the ferry, and their governing body as being '... *infected with the disease of sloppiness*'.

The number of well-publicised governance failures in the health sector, particularly in the area of clinical risk management, may indicate that focussing on financial controls as a means of achieving an effective standard of overall corporate governance may not be sufficient. The reward for successful risk-taking is an increase in stakeholder value.

ALARM has produced a 10-point plan for risk management in public bodies:

1. The organization has a formal framework for managing risk and has implemented an effective strategy which is supported by the Chief Executive and Chief Officers or governing body.

2. There is a documented and approved framework for risk management implementation.

3. The risk management framework and its effectiveness are subject to at least annual review.

4. The board makes an objective analysis of external opportunities and threats to business operations.

5. Internal analysis identifies key strengths, weaknesses and competencies of the organization.

6. The goals and objectives of risk management programmes are communicated and embraced throughout the organization.

7. The objectives are measurable, have associated plans, are deadline driven, command specific resource allocations and address qualitative as well as quantitative outcomes.

8. Responsibility for implementing action plans is clearly assigned and reconciles resource allocation and availability.

9. There is an organized procedure for monitoring and reporting activity to the Board on a periodic and progressive basis.

10. Business Continuity planning is regularly reviewed and tested at executive level.

---

[7]http://www.alarm-uk.org/PDF/corpgovsum.pdf.

As whole-of-government approaches become more common, state-sector risks – risks that affect the State as a whole – are becoming more significant. Agencies need to understand state-sector risks, and to pay greater attention to identifying and managing them. The links between risks are important so whilst a risk may not look significant in isolation, it may become significant when its flow-on effect is considered. There are three types of state-sector risk, each of which calls for a different response:

▪ Agency-level risks. Agencies often face risks that significantly influence other risks (such as inadequate staff skills or low morale that influence the risk of losing key customers). These can become risks to the State because of their size and significance, because of the wider impact of measures to manage them, or because of poor management by agencies.

▪ Interagency risks, which if unmitigated by one agency, become risks for other agencies (such as if young people do not complete school, they may require employment support and adult and community education).

▪ Statewide risks, which are beyond the boundaries of any one agency and call for a response across agencies coordinated by a central agencies (such as floods and other emergencies).

IFACs *Governance in the Public Sector: A Governing Body Perspective* (International Federation of Accountants, 2001)[8] highlights the role of public sector governing bodies in risk management and control:

▪ Ensure that effective systems of risk management are established as part of the framework of control.

▪ Ensure that a framework of internal control is established, operates in practice, and that a statement on its effectiveness is included in the entity's annual report.

▪ Ensure that an effective internal audit function is established as part of the framework of control.

▪ Establish an audit committee, comprising non-executive members, with the responsibility for independent review of the framework of control and of the external audit process.

Risk management in public and private sectors are little different. In the UK, "*The Orange Book – Management of Risk: Principles and Concepts*" (HM Treasury, 2004a)[9] establishes the principles of risk management, and a 'Risk Management

---

[8] http://www.ifac.org/Members/DownLoads/Study_13_Governance.pdf.
[9] http://www.hm-treasury.gov.uk/media/3/5/FE66035B-BCDC-D4B3-11057A7707D2521F.pdf.

Assessment Framework' provides a means of assessing the maturity of risk management.

The Orange Book contrasts the private sector pursuit of shareholder value with the purpose of government being the delivery of service or the delivery of a beneficial outcome in the public interest. The task of public sector management is to respond to risks so as to maximize the likelihood of achieving the purpose, recognizing that the resources available for doing so are finite, so the aim is to achieve an optimum response to risk, prioritized in accordance with an evaluation of the risks. A hierarchy of risks is established, encompassing strategic, programme and project levels.

Under the UK's *Modernising Government* programme, departments have to set out their approach to risk management in their areas of responsibility. HM Treasury works with departments to improve risk management and internal control as part of the corporate governance agenda. This includes the requirement that Accounting Officers sign a Statement of Internal Control as part of the annual accounts for their departments.

The Treasury's aim is to raise the rate of economic growth, and achieve rising prosperity, through creating economic and employment opportunities for all. This aim and the objectives in the Treasury's Public Service Agreements (PSA) are underpinned by targets which cover the key areas of each government department's activity. Those targets are set out in the PSA and in the Treasury's Service Delivery Agreement. Performance against the targets is monitored quarterly, and reported to Parliament annually. Supporting targets are set for units within the organization, and are regularly monitored by management. The anticipation and assessment of risks to delivery of these objectives and targets is a central part of the Treasury's activities.

HM Treasury (2004b) has produced a *Risk Management Assessment Framework: A tool for Departments*.[10] This framework is adapted from the EFQM Business Excellence Model but is simplified and targeted to provide a flexible tool to assist in monitoring and evaluating performance systematically and identifying opportunities for improvement. The framework contains seven questions to address:

Capabilities

1. Leadership: do senior management and Ministers support and promote risk management?
2. Are people equipped and supported to manage risk well?
3. Is there a clear risk strategy and risk policies?
4. Are there effective arrangements for managing risks with partners?

---

[10] Available from http://www.hm-treasury.gov.uk/media/6/6/17A8166B-BCDC-D4B3-16668DC702198931.pdf.

5. Do the organization's processes incorporate effective risk management?
   Risk handling
6. Are risks handled well?
   Outcomes
7. Does risk management contribute to achieving outcomes?

These seven key questions are each underpinned by a lower level, non-exhaustive set of questions which are intended to be indicative of the range of issues and extent of evidence needed to come to a decision in respect of the key questions and to help guide evidence gathering.

A scale provides a means of quantifying performance and can assist in monitoring existing performance, in identifying and setting targets for improvement and in judging progress towards those targets. It can also be used to establish a basis for planning and priority setting for future work plans and for peer review and/or benchmarking, both within and between organizations.

Governance and risk in the third sector

The 'Nolan Principles', set out by Lord Nolan, the Chair of the Committee on Standards in Public Life[11] were originally established for individuals involved in public and government positions, but are also seen as having wider relevance, including for the trustees of voluntary and community organizations. Many organizations in the third sector (not-for-profit, voluntary organizations) have found the Nolan principles of public life a useful basis for understanding the role of a trustee, and the principles often appear in trustee job descriptions or codes of conduct. The principles are: selflessness, integrity, objectivity, accountability, openness, honesty and leadership.

Principles of good governance for third sector boards have been published by the National Hub of Expertise in Governance (2005) as *Good Governance: A Code for the Voluntary and Community Sector*.[12] The principles are:

- Board leadership: every organization should be led and controlled by an effective Board of trustees which collectively ensures delivery of its objects, sets its strategic direction and upholds its values.
- The Board in control: the trustees as a Board should collectively be responsible and accountable for ensuring and monitoring that the organization is performing well, is solvent, and complies with all its obligations.

---

[11] See http://www.public-standards.gov.uk/.
[12] http://www.changeup.org.uk/documents/governance/GoodGovernanceCodeVCS.pdf.

- The high performance Board: the Board should have clear responsibilities and functions, and should compose and organize itself to discharge them effectively.
- Board review and renewal: the Board should periodically review its own and the organization's effectiveness, and take any necessary steps to ensure that both continue to work well.
- Board delegation: the Board should set out the functions of sub-committees, officers, the chief executive, other staff and agents in clear delegated authorities, and should monitor their performance.
- Board and trustee integrity: the Board and individual trustees should act according to high ethical standards, and ensure that conflicts of interest are properly dealt with.
- The open Board: the Board should be open, responsive and accountable to its users, beneficiaries, members, partners and others with an interest in its work.

Risk management is explicit within the principle of 'the Board in control':

The Board must act prudently to protect the assets and property of the organization, and ensure that they are used to deliver the organization's objectives. The Board must regularly review the risks to which the organization is subject, and take action to mitigate risks identified.

Charities face some level of risk in most of the things that they do. The UK's Charity Commission[13] states that the responsibility for the management and control of a charity rests with the trustee body and as such their involvement in the key aspects of the risk management process is essential, particularly in setting the parameters of the process and in the review and consideration of the results. This should not be interpreted, as meaning the trustees must undertake each aspect of the process themselves. In all but the smallest charities trustees are likely to delegate elements of the risk management process to managers ensuring that they, as trustees, review and consider the key aspects of the process and results. The level of involvement should be such that the trustees can make the required statement on risk management with reasonable confidence. Trustees, staff and charity volunteers handle risk as an everyday part of any charity's work. Risk is often seen as going hand in hand with the rewards and opportunities of advancing a charity's work. 'Risk" here describes the uncertainty surrounding events and their outcomes that may have a significant effect, either enhancing or inhibiting operational performance, the achievement of aims and objectives, or meeting the expectations of stakeholders.

---

[13] See http://www.charitycommission.gov.uk.

Under Accounting and Reporting by Charities – Statement of Recommended Practice (SORP)[14] trustees are required to make a statement confirming that 'the major risks to which the charity is exposed, as identified by the trustees, have been reviewed and systems have been established to manage those risks'. The SORP firmly places the reporting of risk management on the agenda of all auditable charities. A charity that has identified the major risks it faces, and established systems to manage such risks, will be able to make a positive statement on risk in its trustees' Annual Report. This will help to demonstrate the charity's accountability to its stakeholders (beneficiaries, donors and other funders, employees, and the general public).

References

Financial Reporting Council. 2003. *The Combined Code on Corporate Governance*.

HM Treasury. 2004a. *The Orange Book – Management of Risk: Principles and Concepts*. London: HM Treasury.

HM Treasury. 2004b. *Risk Management Assessment Framework: A Tool for Departments, The Risk Programme*. London: HM Treasury.

Independent Commission on Good Governance in Public Services. 2004. *The Good Governance Standard for Public Services*. London: OPM & CIPFA.

Institute of Internal Auditors. 2006. *The Role of Auditing in Public Sector Governance*. Altamonte Springs, FL: IIA.

International Federation of Accountants. 2001. Governance in the public sector: A governing body perspective. *Report Study 13*. New York IFAC.

National Hub of Expertise in Governance. 2005. *Good Governance: A Code for the Voluntary and Community Sector*. London: National Hub of Expertise in Governance.

---

[14]http://www.charity-commission.gov.uk/Library/publications/pdfs/sorp05text.pdf.

Part B. The Structure of Enterprise Risk Management

In Part B, we look at the structure of enterprise risk management (ERM). By structure, we mean the underlying principles behind all the particular applications of risk that are described in the various chapters in Part C.

In this Part, we introduce the various models of risk management (chapter 4) and explain the importance of categorising risks (chapter 5). We look at the relationship between organisational strategy and its risk appetite and how this is translated into a risk culture (chapter 6). The particular techniques of ERM are covered in chapter 7 (identifying, assessing and estimating risk) and chapter 8 (evaluating, treating and reporting risk). We then look at general approaches to internal control and the manager's role in risk management in chapter 9.

Part B: The Structure of Enterprise
Risk Management

Chapter 4

Towards Enterprise Risk Management

Risk management

The traditional view of risk management has been one of protecting the organization from loss through avoiding the downside. A more sophisticated approach to risk management is about 'seeking the upside while managing the downside'. Building on work by the International Organization for Standardization (ISO/IEC Guide 73), the *Risk Management Standard* (Institute of Risk Management, 2002) defines risk as the combination of the probability of an event and its consequences, with risk management being concerned with both positive and negative aspects of risk.

International Federation of Accountants (1999) (IFAC) published a study on *Enhancing Shareholder Wealth by Better Managing Business Risk*. The IFAC report defined risks as uncertain future events which could influence the achievement of the organization's strategic, operational and financial objectives. However, the report shifted the focus of risk from a negative concept of hazard to a positive interpretation that managing risk is an integral part of generating sustainable shareholder value. The report argued that business risk management 'establishes, calibrates and realigns the relationship between risk, growth and return'.

Similarly, the Turnbull report (Institute of Chartered Accountants in England & Wales, 1999) defined risk as any event that might affect a listed company's performance, including environmental, ethical and social risks.

The Institute of Risk Management provides a more detailed definition of risk management as

The process by which organizations methodically address the risks attaching to their activities with the goal of achieving sustained benefit within each activity and across the portfolio of all activities. The focus of good risk management is the identification and treatment of these risks. Its objective is to add maximum sustainable value to all the activities of the organization. It marshals the understanding of the potential upside and downside of all those factors which can affect the organization. It increases the probability of success, and reduces both the probability of failure and the uncertainty of achieving the organization's overall objectives.

Common features of risk management

Through these definitions, risk management can be seen as

- Linked closely with achieving business objectives;
- Addressing both 'upside' and 'downside' risks;
- Involving the identification and treatment of risks;
- Reducing both uncertainties and the probability of failure.

A natural progression in managing risk can therefore be seen:

- from managing the risk associated with compliance and prevention (the downside);
- through managing to minimize the risks of uncertainty in respect of operating performance; and
- moving to the higher level of managing opportunity risks (the upside) which need to be taken in order to increase and sustain shareholder value.

This natural progression requires answers to two questions:

(a) What are the drivers of business value?
(b) What are the key risks associated with these drivers of value?

The International Federation of Accountants (1999) report argued that these questions could be answered by mapping the business processes that drive value; and then identifying and analysing the business risks and establishing the appropriate responses that will have the most impact on the value drivers. This is the process of risk management.

Threat, uncertainty and opportunity

Risk can be understood in a number of different ways:

- Risk as hazard or threat.
- Risk as uncertainty.
- Risk as opportunity.

Risk as hazard or threat is what managers most often mean when they talk about risk, referring mainly to negative events. Managing risk in this context means using management techniques to reduce the probability of the negative event (the downside) without undue cost. Risk, as hazard is typically a concern of those responsible for conformance: financial controllers; internal auditors and insurance specialists.

Risk as uncertainty is the notion of the distribution of all possible outcomes, both positive and negative. Managing risk in this context means reducing the variance between anticipated and actual outcomes. Risk as uncertainty concerns chief financial officers and line managers responsible for operations.

Risk as opportunity accepts that there is a relationship between risk and return and usually, the greater the risk, the greater the potential return, but equally, the greater the potential loss. Managing risk in this context means using techniques to maximize the upside while minimising the downside. Risk as opportunity is the outlook of senior managers and corporate planners.

Shareholders understand the risk/return trade-off as they invest in companies and expect boards to achieve a higher return than is possible from risk-free investments such as government securities. This implies that they expect boards and managers to be entrepreneurial, but that risks taken will be considered and managed within the accepted risk profile of the organization.

Conformance and performance

We saw in Chapter 2 that a report published by Chartered Institute of Management Accountants (2003), *Enterprise Governance: Getting the Balance Right*, emphasized the importance of enterprise governance with its two dimensions: conformance, and performance, both of which needed to be in balance.

Conformance is what is generally addressed by corporate governance, including board structures, roles and remuneration. Codes such as the Combined Code on Corporate Governance address the conformance dimension through compliance, audit assurance and oversight through an audit committee. This has been the traditional domain of risk management. Performance focuses on strategy, resource utilization and value creation, helping the board to make strategic decisions, understand its appetite for risk and the key drivers of business performance. Performance does not fit easily with codes and audit and oversight but is the focus of taking calculated risks to achieve shareholder value.

Figure 4.1 shows how risk management can reconcile the two perspectives of conformance and performance.

Figure 4.1   Risk management reconciles conformance and performance.
Source: International Federation of Accountants, Enhancing Shareholder Wealth by Better Managing Business Risk (1999, p. 6).

Enterprise risk management (ERM)

A weakness of traditional approaches to risk management is that it has tended to be implemented within functional or divisional (business unit) silos such that it may have been done very well in one part of an organization, but not well in others. These silo approaches may not have considered how the actions of each function or division affected the risks faced by other functions or divisions. Silo-based or functional approaches may also overlook the most significant risks that the organization as a whole faces. An effective ERM process must be applied within the context of strategy setting and achieving corporate objectives. This is a fundamental difference from most traditional risk models that tend to view only the downside of risk – what could go wrong.

Viewing risk in terms of both downside and upside, recognizing the important link between risk and achieving organizational objectives, the risk/return relationship, and the need for balance between conformance and performance leads to a broader, enterprise-wide approach to risk management that takes a more holistic and integrated approach than other, often piecemeal approaches to managing risk.

ERM includes the methods and processes used by organizations to manage risks (or seize opportunities) related to the achievement of their objectives. ERM provides a framework for risk management, which typically involves identifying particular events or circumstances relevant to the organization's objectives (risks and opportunities), assessing them in terms of likelihood and magnitude of impact, determining a response strategy, and monitoring progress. By identifying and proactively addressing risks and opportunities, organizations protect and create value for their stakeholders, including owners, employees, customers, regulators, and society overall.

ERM is a risk-based approach to managing an enterprise, integrating concepts of strategic planning, operations management, performance management and internal control. ERM is continually evolving to address the needs of various stakeholders, who want to understand the broad spectrum of risks facing complex organizations to ensure they are appropriately managed and monitored. ERM is an approach that is equally important to the Board of Directors and to operational managers.

ERM aligns risk management with business strategy and embeds a risk management culture into business operations. It encompasses the whole organization and seeks to foster a change in the culture of the organization towards one where risks are considered as a normal part of the management process.

World-class ERM encompasses a framework of:

- Risk management structure: to facilitate the identification and communication of risk;
- Resources: to support effective risk management;
- Risk culture: to strengthen decision-making processes by management;
- Tools and techniques: to enable the efficient and consistent management of risks across the organization.

Alternative approaches to managing risk

Various approaches exist to manage risk. There are also other models available from professional consultancies, as well as those developed by various organizations for their internal use. However, the principles underlying all these approaches (or models) are virtually the same. The main models include:

- COSO's ERM framework.
- The Institute of Risk Management standard.
- Australia/New Zealand Standard AS/NZS 4360:2004.
- CIMA's risk management cycle.

Each will be considered in this chapter.

The COSO model

In 2003, the Committee of Sponsoring Organizations of the Treadway Commission (COSO: 2003) published *Enterprise Risk Management Framework*. The framework describes the critical principles and components of an effective ERM process, showing how all-important risks should be identified, assessed, responded to and controlled. It also provides a common language for risk management.

The original framework was updated in COSO's *Enterprise Risk Management – Integrated Framework* (Committee of Sponsoring Organizations of the Treadway Commission (COSO), 2004). ERM is defined as

> *a process, effected by an entity's board of directors, management and other personnel, applied in strategy setting and across the enterprise, designed to identify potential events that may affect the entity, and manage risk to be within its risk appetite, to provide reasonable assurance regarding the achievement of entity objectives.*

In the COSO model, ERM encompasses:

- Aligning risk appetite with strategy;
- Enhancing risk response decisions (whether avoidance, reduction, sharing or acceptance);
- Reducing operational surprises and losses;
- Identifying the inter-related impact of multiple and cross-enterprise risks and the integrated response to those risks;
- Proactively seizing opportunities as they arise; and
- Improving the deployment of capital.

The ERM framework seeks to achieve four categories of organizational objectives:

- Strategic: high-level goals which are aligned with the organization's mission;
- Operations: the efficient and effective use of resources;
- Reliability of financial reporting; and
- Compliance with laws and regulations.

These categories may be the responsibility of different managers and address different needs of the organization.

COSO's ERM model consists of eight inter-related components:

- Internal environment: the tone of the organization, which sets the basis of how risk is viewed, including the risk management philosophy and risk appetite.
- Objective setting: a process to set objectives that are aligned with the organization's mission and are consistent with its risk appetite. Risk appetite is explained in Chapter 6.

- Event identification: internal and external events affecting achievement of objectives must be identified, distinguishing between risks and opportunities.

- Risk assessment: risks are analyzed, considering likelihood and impact, as a basis for determining how they should be managed, both on an inherent (gross) and residual (net) basis. Gross and net risks are described in Chapter 8.

- Risk response: management decides whether to avoid, accept, reduce or share risk, developing a set of actions to align risks with its risk appetite. Risk response is covered in Chapter 8.

- Control activities: policies and procedures help ensure the risk responses are effectively carried out. Internal control is explained in Chapter 9.

- Information and communication: relevant information is identified, captured and communicated that enables people to carry out their responsibilities.

- Monitoring: the entire ERM is monitored through ongoing management activities and separate evaluations and modified where necessary.

The Framework is supported by an Application Techniques document that contains detailed implementation guidance.

The COSO ERM model comprises a three dimensional matrix in the form of a cube, which reflects the relationships between the objectives, components, and different organizational levels. The COSO ERM 'cube' is shown in Figure 4.2.

COSO's ERM 'cube' provides the ability to focus on the whole organization's risk management, or the risk management of each objective (whether strategic, operational, reporting or compliance), by any of the eight components of risk management (see above), or from an individual business unit perspective. It shows the importance of the relationship between each of these dimensions in understanding ERM.

The Institute of Risk Management process

The Institute of Risk Management (IRM) standard (Institute of Risk Management, 2002) was developed in the UK jointly by the IRM, the Association of Insurance and Risk Managers (AIRMIC) and ALARM, the National Forum for Risk Management in the Public Sector (it is hereinafter referred to as the IRM Standard). The standard has been adopted by the Federation of European Risk Management Associations (FERMA). Figure 4.3 shows the risk management process developed by the Institute of Risk Management (2002).

In the IRM risk management process, risk assessment comprises risk analysis and risk evaluation. Risk analysis takes place through processes of identification, description and estimation of risk. The purpose of risk assessment is to undertake

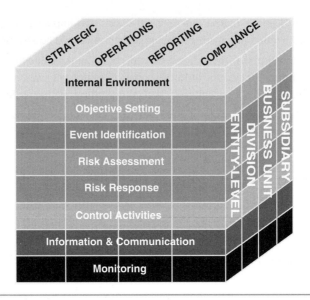

Figure 4.2   COSO ERM framework.
Source: COSO (2004) Enterprise risk management – integrated framework.

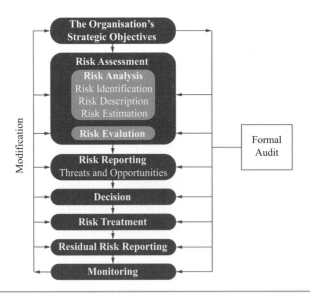

Figure 4.3   Risk management process.
Source: Institute of Risk Management (2002, p. 4).

risk evaluation. Risk evaluation is used to make decisions about the significance of risks to the organization and whether each specific risk should be accepted or treated. Risk evaluation takes place against various criteria including costs and benefits, legal requirements, and wider social and environmental factors.

Risk treatment (also called risk response) is the process of selecting and implementing measures to modify the risk. This may include risk control/mitigation, risk avoidance, risk transfer, risk financing (e.g. hedging, insurance), etc. Risk reporting is concerned with regular reports to the Board and to stakeholders setting out the organization's policies in relation to risk and enabling the monitoring of the effectiveness of those policies. These processes are explained in more detail in Chapters 7 and 8.

Australia/New Zealand Standard AS/NZS 4360:2004

AS/NZS 4360 (Standards Australia, 2004) was first published in 1995 and revised in 1999 and again in 2004. The Standard provides a generic guide for managing risk which can be applied to a wide range of activities in public, private or community enterprises. The Standard specifies the elements of the risk management process, but it is generic and independent of any specific industry or economic sector. It recognizes that the design and implementation of an organization's risk management system will be influenced by its varying needs, objectives, and its products and services.

The Standard has a companion Handbook, HB 436 *Risk Management Guidelines – Companion to AS/NZS 4360*. The two documents are intended to be used together, with the Handbook providing important commentary, guidance and examples on the implementation of the Standard.

Figure 4.4 shows the risk management process for AS/NZS 4360.

It comprises five steps:

1. Establish the goals and context for risk management;
2. Identify risks;
3. Analyze risks in terms of likelihood and consequences and estimate the level of risk faced;
4. Evaluate and rank those risks;
5. Treat the risks through the most appropriate options.

Communication and monitoring and review are ongoing processes in AS/NZS 4360 that inter-relate with all of the five steps.

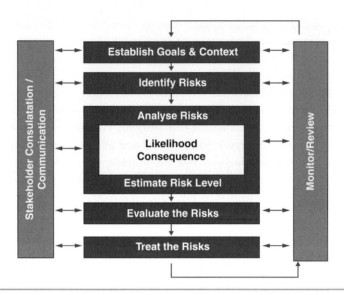

Figure 4.4   The AS/NZS risk management process.
Source: AS/NZS 4360:2004

CIMA's risk management cycle

The Chartered Institute of Management Accountants (CIMA) has taken a particular interest in the role that financial managers can play in risk management. CIMA's risk management cycle is shown in Figure 4.5.

The cycle begins with identifying risks, assessing the scale of risks, developing a risk response strategy, implementing the strategy (which involves allocating responsibilities), implementing and monitoring controls and reviewing the effectiveness of the process. At the centre of the cycle is the provision of information for decision-making.

Comparison of approaches

While all four approaches are similar, the IRM standard and the CIMA cycle provide only brief guidance rather than the detailed supporting information that is available from COSO (in an Application Techniques document) and AS/NZS 4360 (in the Guidelines document).

AIRMIC (the Association of Insurance and Risk Managers) has carried out a comparison of the COSO, IRM, and AS/NZS 4360 standards. There are minor differences in terminology and the sequence in which the approach to risk management is presented. AIRMIC acknowledges that the setting of objectives is a core part of COSO

The risk management cycle

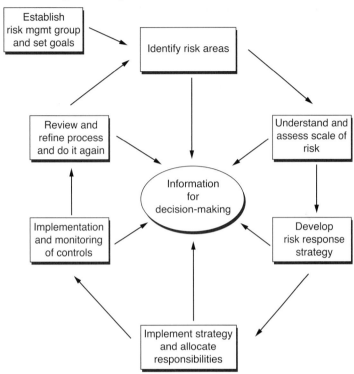

Figure 4.5   CIMA Risk management cycle.
Source: Chartered Institute of Management Accountants, Risk Management: A guide to good practice (2002) CIMA.

and AS/NZS 4360, although there is only passing mention of it in the IRM standard. Both the IRM and COSO standards are more explicit than AS/NZS 4360 about the role of the Board of Directors, the risk management function and internal auditors. COSO's more detailed Application Techniques is more financially oriented than the other approaches, while AS/NZS 4360 emphasizes qualitative, semi-quantitative and quantitative techniques to estimate likelihood and consequences. Only COSO identifies the limitations of ERM (see below).

Benefits of risk management

There are a number of 'payoffs' for effective risk management. Epstein and Rejc (2005) list these as enhanced reporting; compliance with laws and regulations;

improved resource allocations; assured business continuity; enhanced working environment; increased productivity; reduced earnings volatility; decreased cost of capital; improved reputation; increased sales; and reduced costs. All of these can lead to increased organizational success and shareholder value

Discussions with risk managers and senior executives have identified the following benefits:

- Being seen by stakeholders as profitable and successful;
- Being seen by stakeholders as predictable, with analysts comfortable with what the organization is saying;
- Not issuing profit warnings, or having major exceptional items to report to shareholders;
- Proactively managing mergers and acquisitions;
- Reducing the impact of any impairment of goodwill;
- Maintaining brand reputation;
- Being seen by stakeholders to be adopting corporate social responsibility and being a good corporate citizen;
- Having a well-managed supply chain;
- Having a good credit rating.

Limitations of risk management

No matter how well designed and implemented it may be, ERM is only able to provide reasonable assurance to management and the Board of Directors about the achievement of organizational objectives. This is because future events are inherently uncertain and therefore unpredictable. While ERM can alert managers and directors to the degree to which the organization is meeting its objectives, ERM cannot provide assurance that objectives will be achieved.

ERM can fail because of poor judgment, mistake, negligence, collusion or fraud, or by deliberately ignoring or circumventing risk management processes and controls. ERM can also be costly to implement and maintain.

References

Chartered Institute of Management Accountants. 2003. *Enterprise Governance: Getting the Balance Right*: CIMA & IFAC.

Committee of Sponsoring Organizations of the Treadway Commission (COSO). 2003. *Enterprise Risk Management Framework.*

Committee of Sponsoring Organizations of the Treadway Commission (COSO). 2004. *Enterprise Risk Management – Integrated Framework.*

Epstein MJ, Rejc A. 2005. *Identifying, Measuring, and Managing Organizational Risks for Improved Performance.* Society of Management Accountants of Canada & American Institute of Certified Public Accountants.

Institute of Chartered Accountants in England & Wales. 1999. *Internal Control: Guidance for Directors on the Combined Code* (Turnbull Report).

Institute of Risk Management. 2002. *A Risk Management Standard.* London: IRM.

International Federation of Accountants. 1999. Enhancing Shareholder Wealth by Better Managing Business Risk. *Report on International Management Accounting Study No. 9.*

Standards Australia. 2004. *Australian and New Zealand Risk Management Standard AS/NZS 4360:2004,* 3rd edition.

Chapter 5

Risk Categorization

One of the first stages of risk management is that internal and external events affecting achievement of objectives must be identified. It is common for the risk management process to identify many hundreds of risks, even for a smaller organization. Larger companies may easily identify thousands of risks, some of importance only to an individual business unit or function, while others have a more strategic significance. Risk categorization provides a way of grouping individual risks into meaningful groups so that they can be managed as a group.

The advantages of categories

The advantages of risk categorization are that:

- The list of individual risks facing an organization is potentially endless. By grouping risks into categories, they can be managed in common through the use of similar controls.
- Categorization forces managers to think holistically as well as at operational levels. Categories of risks are more easily communicated upwards in the organization where senior managers and Boards of Directors need to consider 'big picture' risks rather than the details of individual risks.
- Once a risk has been identified, it becomes possible to think of tools that may be used to measure and control those risks. Categorization helps managers to identify how they can use their past experience to treat risks as a class, rather than to identify an appropriate treatment for each individual risk.
- Risk categorization provides a framework that can be used to define who is responsible, design appropriate internal controls and assist in simplified risk reporting for management and Board review.
- The development of a sound risk management system would be difficult without grouping risks into categories. Such a systematic approach may help organizations to identify inter-related risks in the same category.

It is important to recognize that there is no one widely accepted listing of categories for risk, as they will vary according to the nature of the business, its size, competitive intensity, etc. What is important is that risks are classified in some way that is relevant to the needs of the business.

Risk drivers

We know from the value chain (Porter, 1985) that various business activities add value that is reflected in prices charged to customers. Value drivers may be purchasing power, production economies, distribution efficiency, after-sales service, etc. We also know that each of these value drivers also has cost drivers and it is important to recognize that the price able to be charged for the added value must exceed the cost of the activity that adds that value. However, we can take this one step further by recognizing that each driver has associated with it particular risks. For example, if after-sales service is a value driver, this requires trained and experienced staff with good attitudes towards customer service. There is a cost of providing the staff; training them and monitoring the service they deliver. However, there are also risks associated with this. Employees may leave, standards of service may slip relative to competitors, information systems may fail, or customer expectations may change. Risk is therefore intimately concerned with value adding activities.

One way of considering risk is to use the drivers of risk as categories, which may be internal or external. The Institute of Risk Management model shown in Figure 5.1 categorizes risk in terms of financial, strategic, operational, and hazard. Some of these risks are driven by external factors (competition, customer demand, interest rates, regulation, contracts, natural events) and some are driven by internal factors (research and development, cash flow, information systems, etc.). Some risks have both external and internal drivers (e.g. employees, supply chains, products and services, and the integration of merger and acquisitions).

Simple classification of risk

Risks can be classified in any number of ways. A simple categorization of risks, for example, is:

- *Business* or operational: relating to the activities carried out within an organization;
- *Financial*: relating to the financial operation of a business;
- *Environmental*: relating to changes in the political, economic, social and financial environment;
- *Reputation risk*: caused by failing to address some other risk.

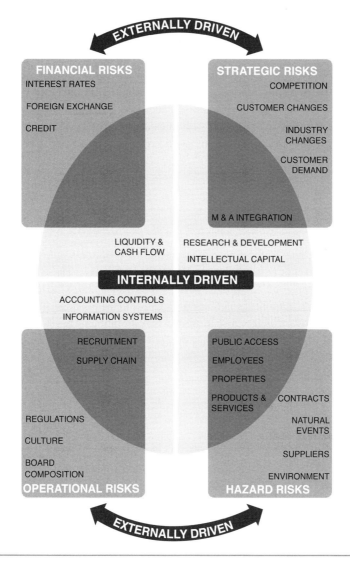

Figure 5.1   Risk drivers.
Source: Institute of Risk Management (2002) *A Risk Management Standard*, p. 3. Available from: http://www.theirm.org/publications/documents/Risk_Management_Standard_030820.pdf.

We explore each of these in turn. However, these categories may vary substantially between industries. For example, credit risk may be particularly appropriate for a bank, technology risk for a call centre, or compliance risk for a regulated utility. The risk categories that are specific to banking are described in Chapter 22.

Business or operational risk

Business or operational risk relates to the activities carried out within an organization, arising from structure, systems, people, products or processes. Business or operational risks include business interruption, errors or omissions by employees, product failure, health and safety, failure of IT systems, fraud, loss of key people, litigation, loss of suppliers, etc. These factors are to a considerable extent within the control of the organization through risk assessment and risk management practices, including internal control and insurance.

Financial risk

Financial risk relates to the financial operation of a business, such as credit risk, liquidity risk, currency risk, interest rate risk and cash flow risk. These are described in more detail in Chapter 12. Some of these risks arise from cultural and legal differences between countries, such that obtaining money from customers in other countries or recovering the cost of goods lost in transit may be difficult due to different legal or banking regulations. While these are typically outside the organization's control, action can be taken to mitigate those risks, for example, by credit control procedures, hedging, export insurance, etc.

Environmental risk

Environmental risk relates to changes in the political, economic, social and financial environment over which an organization has no influence. Environmental risks include legislative or regulatory change, climate change, natural disasters, changing customer demand, competition, economic slowdown and stock market fluctuations. These are outside the organization's control but can be mitigated to some extent through environmental scanning and contingency planning.

Political risk refers to the detrimental consequence of political activities in other countries that have an effect on the organization. Examples include discrimination against foreign businesses; nationalization by government of private property; regulations requiring a specified use of local materials or labour; exchange controls that limit transfers of funds or exchange into foreign currencies; changes in taxation regulations or rates of tax; or restrictions on access to local loans. A good although extreme example of political change is the erratic policies of President Robert Mugabe in Zimbabwe which has effectively destroyed much of that country's economy.

Table 5.1   Classification of risks

Type of risk	Description and explanation
Strategic risks	
Economic	Macroeconomic policies and economic cycles, e.g. government monetary & fiscal policy
Industry	Industry competition and concentration, profit margins, market structure, competition law
Strategic transactions	Significant changes in strategic direction, e.g. mergers and acquisitions, joint ventures, etc.
Social	Changing demographics and social attitudes affecting consumer behaviour
Technology	Obsolescence, new technologies that change industries and markets
Political	Changes in government policy, regulatory environment, political instability, terrorism
Organizational	Business policies, culture, control systems, performance measurement and reward systems
Operational risks	
Environmental	Earthquake, fire, flood, pollution that could impact the business
Financial	Changes in credit, interest rates, currency rates and in the stock market
Business continuity	Conditions that could affect production, distribution, customers, suppliers, employees, outsourcing or compliance issues
Innovation	Poor performance in research and development or new product or market development
Commercial	Poor quality in marketing, engineering, production, etc. leading to warranty claims or product failure and liability
Project	Technical difficulties or commercial obstacles to completing projects on time, to budget and to quality
Human resources	Loss of skilled personnel, industrial relations problems, lack of training, unethical conduct
Health and safety	Workplace accidents or work-caused sickness
Property	Security of assets including spoilage, theft, loss of intellectual property

Table 5.1　*(Continued)*

Type of risk	Description and explanation
Reputation	Perception of the organization by the public, media, government about business model, controls, ethical practices
Reporting risks	
Information	Poor quality and accessibility of information including problems with data accuracy or security
Reporting	Reliability and completeness of financial reports for internal and external decision-making
Compliance risks	
Legal and regulatory	Corporate governance, industrial relations, environmental standards
Control	Internal control systems and security that could result in fraud, computer failure and errors
Professional	Organizational and personal liability of directors and managers

Adapted from Epstein and Rejc (2005).

Reputation risk

Reputation risk is caused by failing to address some other risk. This is within the organization's control but requires the organization to take a wider view of its role in society and to consider how it is seen by its customers, suppliers, competitors and regulators. For example, the failure of accountants Arthur Andersen was to a large extent a direct result of its loss of reputation following its audit and other work on behalf of WorldCom and Enron.

Sophisticated classification of risk

A more sophisticated classification of risks is shown in Table 5.1, adapted from Epstein and Rejc (2005).

The Epsetein and Rejc categorization has four main categories: strategic, operational, reporting and compliance. Within each of these main categories are a number of subcategories, and individual risks are assigned to these subcategories. For example, in this approach reputation risk is a subcategory of operational risk rather than a category in its own right.

Most importantly, each organization needs to group its risks into manageable categories that enable the application of risk management processes described in detail in Chapters 7 and 8. The categories that an organization uses need to be enterprise-wide and specific to its needs.

References

Epstein MJ, Rejc A. 2005. *Identifying, Measuring, and Managing Organizational Risks for Improved Performance.* Society of Management Accountants of Canada & American Institute of Certified Public Accountants.

Porter ME. 1985. *Competitive Advantage: Creating and Sustaining Superior Performance..* New York: Free Press.

Chapter 6

Strategy, Culture and Risk Appetite

The identification, assessment, evaluation, treatment and reporting of risk, individually or in their categories takes place in relation to various criteria including organizational objectives and strategy, and the organization's risk appetite. This enterprise-wide approach to risk management then becomes part of the organization's culture.

Objectives, strategy and control

Ansoff (1988) provided a typical description of strategy formulation: objectives and goals were established; followed by an internal appraisal of strengths and weaknesses and an external appraisal of opportunities and threats. These led to strategic decisions such as diversification or the formulation of competitive strategy. A contrasting approach was developed by Quinn (1980), which he called *logical incrementalism*. Quinn argued against formal planning systems, which he believed had become 'costly paper-shuffling exercises', observing that 'most major strategic decisions seemed to be made outside the formal planning structure' (p. 2). Similarly, Mintzberg and Waters (1985) separated the *intended* from the *realized* strategy, arguing that *deliberate* strategies provided only a partial explanation, as some intended strategies were unable to be realized while other strategies *emerged* over time.

Strategy can be crucial in enabling a business to be proactive in increasingly competitive and turbulent business conditions. The absence of strategy can lead to reactivity and a steady erosion of market share. In the public and third sectors it can lead to stagnation and increasing marginalization.

Porter (1980) developed his 'five forces' model for analyzing an industry. This focused on the effects of rivalry among existing firms, the threat of new entrants, the bargaining power of suppliers and customers, and the threat of substitute products and services. Porter also identified three 'generic strategies' for competitive advantage: cost leadership, differentiation and focus. Cost leadership required efficiency, tight cost control and the avoidance of unprofitable work, with low cost a defence against competition. Differentiation was achieved through, for example, brand image, technology or a unique distribution channel. These factors insulate against price competition because of brand loyalty and lower customer sensitivity to pricing differences. Focus emphasizes servicing a particular market segment (whether customer, territory or product/service) better than competitors who may be competing more broadly.

Kaplan and Norton (2001) built on the success of their *Balanced Scorecard* approach to non-financial performance measurement to emphasize the 'strategy-focused organization' that links financial performance with non-financial measures. Non-financial measures in the Balanced Scorecard measure how well the organization is meeting the targets established in its strategy. Kaplan and Norton use 'strategy maps' to identify cause–effect relationships, which they argue should be modified over time as a result of experience gained within organizations. They also argued that budgetary allocations and incentives need to be consistent with strategy, while reflecting the importance of continual learning and improvement.

Management control theory has its roots in systems theory, in which organizations are goal-oriented with control exercised in pursuit of those goals by influencing behaviour amidst environmental change (Anthony, 1965; Berry et al., 2005). Management control systems have been identified with strategic and long-range plans; annual budgets; non-financial performance measures; employee performance appraisal; and policies and procedures (Daft & Macintosh, 1984). A further category of control includes objectives; strategies and plans; target-setting; incentive and reward structures; and information feedback loops (Otley, 1999). However, the definition of management control systems has evolved over the years from a focus on formal, financially quantifiable information to assist managerial decision-making to include external information relating to markets, customers, competitors, non-financial information about production processes, predictive information and a broad array of decision support mechanisms and informal personal and social controls (Chenhall, 2003).

Inherent in the identification and selection of goals and strategy is risk, in particular, as we have seen in previous chapters, the risk of not achieving stated goals. Even in the case of emergent, rather than deliberate strategy, the risk is that opportunities are missed. The selection of a particular competitive strategy is also fraught with risk, as the strategy may be wrong, particularly if competitors are better at satisfying customer demand. An organization focused on strategy may set financial and non-financial goals, but there is a risk in setting goals as the goals themselves may be wrong, and the targets may be unachievable or simply demotivating. Management control systems may not be consistent or sufficiently focused on strategy.

Although Simons (1990) was not writing specifically about risk, he did make reference to it in defining two of his four types of management control system: belief systems, boundary systems, diagnostic control systems and interactive control systems:

- Belief systems define, communicate and reinforce the organization's core values.
- Boundary systems establish explicit limits through codes of conduct, strategic planning systems and directives, influenced by the *risks to be avoided*.
- Diagnostic control systems are formal feedback systems to monitor outcomes and correct deviations from preset standards of performance, both financial and non-financial.
- Interactive control systems are used by top managers to regularly and personally involve themselves in the decision activities of subordinates. Controls become interactive through top management attention and interest, influenced by *strategic uncertainties* and the resultant need to focus on those strategic uncertainties.

Risk is therefore explicitly recognized in Simons (1990) categorization of boundary and interactive controls. Simons argued that control systems were the methods by which information could be used to maintain or alter patterns in organizational activity. His research suggested that control systems could be used to learn and that learning could be used to influence strategy. Simons (1990) developed a model of the relationship between strategy, control systems and organizational learning in order to reduce strategic uncertainty. Simons' model can be summarized as follows:

- The intended business strategy creates strategic uncertainties that top managers monitor;
- Top managers make selected control systems interactive to personally monitor the strategic uncertainties;
- The choice to make certain control systems interactive provides signals to organizational participants about what should be monitored and where new ideas should be proposed and tested;
- This signal activates organizational learning and through interactive management control, new strategies emerge.

The selection of goals, strategy and management controls explicitly or implicitly is (or at least should be) concerned with risk (although we return to this problem in Chapter 10). We therefore need to consider how risk is a fundamental element of organizational strategy, because the organization's appetite for taking or avoiding risk is fundamental to how it shapes its strategy, sets its targets and its approach to control.

Risk appetite

Both risk appetite and risk tolerance set boundaries of how much risk an organization is prepared to accept. Risk appetite is a high level statement that considers broadly the levels of risk that management deems acceptable. Risk tolerances are narrower and set the acceptable level of variation around objectives. For example, a company that says that it does not accept risks that could result in a significant loss of its revenue base is expressing appetite. When the same company says that it does not wish to accept risks that would cause revenue from its top 10 customers to decline by more than 10% it is expressing tolerance. Operating within risk tolerances provides management with greater assurance that the organization remains within its desired risk appetite, which in turn provides a higher degree of comfort that the company will achieve its objectives.

Risk appetite is the amount of risk an organization is willing to accept in pursuit of value. It is directly related to an organization's strategy and may be expressed as the acceptable balance between growth, risk and return. Risk appetite may be made explicit in organizational strategies, policies and procedures, and in control systems. It may also be implicit, needing to be derived from an analysis of organizational decisions and actions.

Risks are evaluated against the organization's appetite and tolerance for risk. This appetite is a balance between risk and return and must ultimately be a judgment that is made by the Board of Directors. This involves setting the parameters for whether particular risks should be accepted, rejected or managed in some way.

Risk and return

The whole notion of risk and return is important in considering risk appetite. Table 6.1 shows the effect of different risk appetites in the capital structure of a business.

Each column in Table 6.1 shows the same business in terms of total capital employed, income and profitability (before interest). The columns reveal the different returns on investment depending on the extent to which the capital structure is made up of debt or equity. In this example, the return on capital employed is a constant 20% (an operating profit of £20 000 on capital employed of £100 000), the return on equity (the shareholders' investment) increases as debt replaces equity. This improvement to the return to shareholders carries a risk however, which increases as the proportion of profits taken by the interest charge increases. If profits turn down, there are substantially more risks carried by the highly geared business.

Risk perceptions

One of the problems of risk appetite is that perceptions of, and attitudes towards risk vary significantly from person to person, organization to organization and even country to country. It has been argued (Bettis & Thomas, 1990) that we have very

Table 6.1   Risk and return – effect of different debt/equity mix

	100% equity £	50% equity 50% debt £	10% equity 90% debt £
Capital employed	100 000	100 000	100 000
Equity	100, 000	50 000	10 000
Debt	0	50 000	90 000
Operating profit before interest and tax	20 000	20 000	20 000
Interest at 10% on debt	0	5000	9000
Profit after interest	20 000	15 000	11 000
Tax at 30%	6000	4500	3300
Profit after tax	14 000	10 500	7700
Return on investment	14%	21%	77%

little knowledge about how managers in organizations perceive and take risks, or of the commonalities or differences between individual risk taking and risk taking by managers in the organizational context.

Weber and Milliman (1997) described risk preference as a personal trait on a continuum from risk avoiding to risk-taking, with risk factors being based on the magnitude of potential losses and their chances of occurring. They found that risk preference may be a stable personality trait, but the effect of situational variables on choice may be the result of changes in risk perception. These situational variables may exist at both national and organizational levels.

Uncertainty avoidance was one of the dimensions in the study of national cultural differences among IBM employees carried out by Hofstede (1980). The characteristic of uncertainty avoidance indicated the extent to which members of a society felt threatened by uncertainty and ambiguity. This characteristic was associated with seeing uncertainty as a threat, but compensated for by hard work, written rules and a belief in experts. In a comparative study of four cultures (American, German, Polish, and Chinese), Weber and Hsee (1998) found that the majority of respondents in all four cultures were perceived to be risk averse. These authors proposed a 'cushion hypothesis' because in some countries (notably China), collectivism cushions members against the consequences of negative outcomes. This in turn affects the subjective perceptions of the riskiness of options.

At the organizational level, Douglas and Wildavsky (1983) explained risk perception as a cultural process, commenting that each culture, each set of shared values and supporting social institutions, was biased toward highlighting certain risks and downplaying others. Adams (1995) also adopted a 'cultural theory' perspective and differentiated the formality of risk management and its concern with risk reduction, from the informal arrangements by which individuals seek to balance risks with rewards.

March and Shapira (1987) suggested that managers are focused on performance in relation to critical performance targets. They identified three motivations for risk taking by managers: managers saw risk taking as essential to success in decision making; managers associated risk taking with the expectations of their jobs rather than with any personal preference for risk; and managers recognized the 'emotional pleasures and pains' of risk taking. As a result of their research March and Shapira (1987) noted that both individual and institutionalized (i.e. taken for granted within the organization) risk preferences were important in understanding organizational responses to risk management.

Adams (1995) developed the notion of the 'risk thermostat' to illustrate how:

■ Everyone has a propensity to take risks;

■ The propensity to take risks varies from person to person;

■ The propensity to take risks is influenced by the potential rewards of risk taking;

■ Perceptions of risk are also influenced by experience of 'accidents' that cause losses;

■ Individual risk taking represents a balance between perceptions of risk and the propensity to take risks;

■ Accident losses are a consequence of taking risks.

Figure 6.1 shows the risk thermostat with cultural filters (the ellipses) that influence each of the above factors. In this model, the propensity to take risks is a result of balancing behaviour between the rewards available and the perceived danger.

Risk and organizational culture

Risk culture is the set of shared attitudes, values and practices that characterize how an organization considers risk in its day-to-day activities. This may be determined in part from the organizational vision and/or mission statement and strategy documents but will be mainly derived from an analysis of organizational practices, in particular the rewards or sanctions for risk-taking or risk-avoiding behaviour.

There are three ways in which risk and organizational culture can interact:

■ Where a major shock or crisis occurs, for example, a fire in a critical manufacturing site, in which culture is changed towards risk management before any processes are altered.

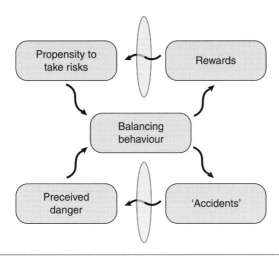

Figure 6.1   The risk thermostat with cultural filters.
Source: Adams (1995, p. 15).

■ Where corporate governance changes are accepted as a result of legislation or regulation but without any accompanying cultural change. Processes are implemented but culture may change only very gradually and over a long period of time.

■ Where compliance is not crucial (such as for a small, privately owned business), but where those in control can see benefits in risk management and this leads to a gradual change in both process and culture.

In his acclaimed book, Beck (1986, 1992 in translation) argued that we live in a *Risk Society* (the title of his book) and that all risk was socially constructed (i.e. the result of not only individual perceptions but shared beliefs and understandings held by social groups including professions, organizations, etc.) Many risks are not objectively identifiable and measurable but subjective and qualitative. For example, the risks of litigation, economic downturns, loss of key employees, natural disasters, loss of reputation are all subjective judgments. Risk is therefore to a considerable extent socially constructed and responses to risk reflect that social construction. Under a social construction perspective, risk can be thought about by reference to:

■ the existence of internal or external events;
■ information about those events (i.e. their visibility);
■ managerial perception about events and information (i.e. how they are perceived); and

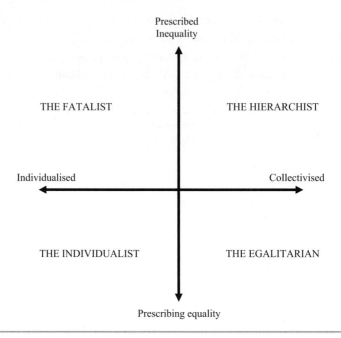

Figure 6.2   The four rationalities.
Source: Adams (1995, p. 35).

■ how organizations establish tacit/informal or explicit/formal ways of dealing with risk.

Adams presented four rationalities of risk, shown in Figure 6.2.

In his four rationalities, Adams identified four distinctive worldviews that have important implications for risk. These were:

■ Fatalists who have minimal control over their own lives and belong to no groups that are responsible for the decisions that rule their lives. They are resigned to their fate and see no point in trying to change it. Managing risks is irrelevant to fatalists.

■ Hierarchists inhabit a world with strong group boundaries with social relationships being hierarchical. Hierarchists are always evident in large organizations with strong structures, procedures and systems. Hierarchists are most comfortable with a bureaucratic risk management style using various risk management techniques.

■ Individualists are enterprising, self-made people, relatively free from control by others, but who strive to exert control over their environment. Entrepreneurs in

small–medium enterprises fit into this category. Risk management to individualists is typically intuitive rather than systematic.

■ Egalitarians have strong group loyalties but have little respect for externally
imposed rules. Group decisions are arrived at democratically. Egalitarians are
more commonly found in public sector and not-for-profit organizations where values are oriented to social concerns. Egalitarians are most comfortable in situations
of risk sharing through insurance, hedging or transfer to other organizations.

Collier et al. (2007) carried out an extensive research project into risk management
in organizations. The research found that fatalists were those who do not see risk
management as being important or having any consequences. This group comprised
only 7% of the respondents. Individualists agreed that risk management was about
positive consequences but disagreed or were neutral about its negative consequences,
perhaps reflecting them as a risk-seeking group (14% of respondents). Hierarchists
disagreed or were neutral in relation to positive consequences but agreed in relation
to negative ones. This was the risk-avoiding group (36% of respondents). The egalitarians were risk aware, being balanced between risk management's role in achieving
both positive and avoiding negative consequences (43% of respondents). The Collier
et al. research suggested that this might be the group that would embed risk in culture and decision-making. This research has important implications as it reflects the
differences between individuals and groups in how they see risk, their impact on the
organizational risk appetite and the controls that are put in place in response to risk.

Embedding risk in culture

The research by Collier et al. (2007) based on survey responses identified a trend in
risk management from it being considered tacitly in the past to it being considered
formally in the present and with the expectation that in the future there would be
a more holistic approach to risk being used to aid decision-making, with risk more
embedded in organizational culture. The research findings are shown in Figure 6.3.

The results in Figure 6.3 may be a reasonable expectation, or merely an aspiration,
or it may reflect some unease in the respondents that risk management practices in
use do not appear to connect to organization or business problems or contribute as
much to decision-making as they consider necessary or desirable. If the latter is so
then the picture may represent a somewhat idealized one.

However, there are examples of risk being used in decision-making. The International Loss Prevention Manager of a Fortune 500 chemical engineering company
explained how his company had embedded risk in their culture:

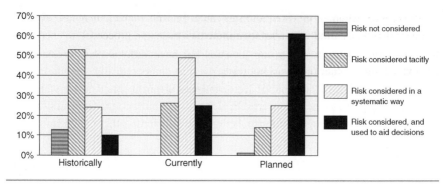

Figure 6.3   Trends in risk management.
Source: Collier et al. (2007).

"We have a very strong culture of risk management, as a company we for about 30 or 35 years focused very strongly on safety. That's only one risk arena of course, but safety has been held very publicly to be more important than profits, more important than turnover, more important than many other things – more important in anything in fact in our company. And the guy at the top says that every time he starts a major report. As a consequence of that approach we have a world-class safety record and we are certainly the leader, the best, in the chemicals business worldwide."

"Inevitably there are direct savings as a result of not having injuries, there are also indirect savings. Our incident management system looks at everything that happens. It may be a spanner dropping on a workman's head. He may be wearing a hard hat – he should be. There may be a property implication, if that spanner falls into a piece of machinery or arcs some electrical equipment or something like that. Now there's a direct benefit from having fewer injuries . . . I don't know that it has a direct impact on shareholders, but I think they like the story and frankly, if a company has the best safety record in the business as a shareholder you would probably like to be associated with that company."

"It seems to me that most of the risks that face us are associated with people or the activities of individuals or groups. External risks exist of course, earthquakes and storms, but you can do much more to control behaviour than you can to control the weather or seismic activity . . . I think that is generally embedding in culture, in people that you need to have a responsibility for the safety of colleagues and that you need to do things carefully and check with the right people that you're managing, that you're negotiating the right terms in contracts and that you're running the plant safely."

The company had a sophisticated approach to enterprise risk management but was adamant that this started with a safety culture as a base and proceeded to encompass wider areas of the business. The safety culture was well accepted so the identification and evaluation of other risks was not resisted.

References

Adams J. 1995. *Risk*. London: UCL Press.

Ansoff HI. 1988. *The New Corporate Strategy*. New York: John Wiley & Sons.

Anthony RN. 1965. *Planning and Control Systems: A Framework for Analysis*. Boston, MA: Harvard Business School Press.

Beck U. 1986. *Risk Society*. London: Sage, (1992 in translation).

AJ Berry, J Broadbent, D Otley (eds). 2005. *Management Control: Theories, Issues and Performance*. London: Palgrave Macmillan.

Bettis RA, Thomas H. 1990. *Risk, Strategy and Management*. London: JAI Press.

Chenhall RH. 2003. Management control systems design within its organizational context: findings from contingency-based research and directions for the future. *Accounting, Organizations and Society* 28:127–68.

Collier PM, Berry AJ, Burke GT. 2007. *Risk and Management Accounting: Best Practice Guidelines for Enterprise-wide Internal Control Procedures*. Oxford: Elsevier.

Daft RL, Macintosh NB. 1984. The nature and use of formal control systems for management control and strategy implementation. *Journal of Management* 10:43–66.

Douglas M, Wildavsky A. 1983. *Risk and Culture: An Essay on the Selection of Technological and Environmental Dangers*. Oxford: University of California Press.

Hofstede G. 1980. *Culture's Consequences: International Differences in Work Related values*. Beverly Hills: Sage Publications.

Kaplan RS, Norton DP. 2001. *The Strategy-Focused Organization: How Balanced Scorecard Companies Thrive in the New Business Environment*. Boston, MA: Harvard Business School Press.

March JG, Shapira Z. 1987. Managerial Perspectives on Risk and Risk Taking. *Management Science* 33:1404–18.

Mintzberg H, Waters JA. 1985. Of strategies, deliberate and emergent. *Strategic Management Journal* 6:257–72.

Otley D. 1999. Performance management: a framework for management control systems research. *Management Accounting Research* 10:363–82.

Porter ME. 1980. *Competitive Strategy: Techniques for Analyzing Industries and Competitors*. New York: Free Press.

Quinn JB. 1980. *Strategies for Change: Logical incrementalism*. Homewood, Ill: Irwin.

Simons R. 1990. The role of management control systems in creating competitive advantage: new perspectives. *Accounting, Organizations and Society* 15:127–43.

Simons R. 1995. *Levers of Control: How Managers Use Innovative Control Systems to Drive Strategic Renewal*. Harvard Business School Press: Boston, MA.

Weber EU, Hsee C. 1998. Cross-cultural differences in risk perception, but cross-cultural similarities in attitudes towards perceived risk. *Management Science* 44:1205–17.

Weber EU, Milliman RA. 1997. Perceived risk attitudes: relating risk perception to risky choice. *Management Science* 43:123–44.

Chapter 7

Identifying, Assessing and Estimating Risk

As we saw in Chapter 4, in the COSO model, risk assessment encompasses how risks are analyzed in terms of their likelihood and impact. This assessment is then used as a basis for determining how those risks should be managed. In the IRM risk management process, risk assessment comprises risk analysis and risk evaluation. Risk analysis takes place through processes of identification, description and estimation of risk. Risk evaluation is then used to make decisions about the significance of risks to the organization and how those risks should be treated.

In this chapter, we look in detail at the processes for identifying, describing and estimating risk and introduce the likelihood/consequences matrix. In Chapter 8 we look at the evaluation, treatment and reporting of risk.

Methods of identifying risk

Risk identification aims to determine an organization's exposure to uncertainty, which requires knowledge of the organization's objectives, its product/services, markets and the legal, political, economic, social and technological environment in which it operates. Risk identification needs to be methodical to ensure that all significant activities within the organization have been identified and all risks flowing from those activities defined. Risk identification involves perceiving hazards, identifying failures and recognizing adverse consequences as well as recognizing opportunities in the organizational environment, which it may want to take advantage of.

The organization may adopt either a top down (management knows best) or a bottom up (operatives know best) approach to identifying risk, or a combination of these methods. The intention is to identify as many risks as possible, so the widest possible sources (in terms of persons, past experiences and methods) can be used. Examples of methods of identifying risk are:

- questionnaires/surveys;
- interviews and focus groups;

- brainstorming;
- workshops;
- stakeholder consultations;
- industry benchmarking;
- checklists;
- scenario analysis;
- incident investigation;
- auditing and inspection; and
- business process analysis.

As we saw in Chapter 5, rather than list many hundred of risks, the categorization of risks in a meaningful way will aid in this process.

Risk description

The purpose of risk description is to enable risks that have been identified to be more fully explained, understood and communicated. A structured format can be used to facilitate the description and subsequent assessment of risk. Table 7.1 gives an example of the information that could be recorded for each risk identified.

This process is more than writing a sentence or two. As Table 7.1 shows, it is about describing who is affected, what the likely impact of the risk eventuating might be, what the appetite for this risk is, how it could possibly be treated, etc. No decisions are being made here, what is important is that all available facts are recorded to enable subsequent decisions.

Risk estimation

Risk estimation is concerned with estimating the likelihood of an event's occurrence and the possible consequences, on the basis of the risk description. Estimation can be quantitative, semi-quantitative or qualitative. Various methods may be used to assess the likelihood and severity of each risk once they are identified and described. Examples include:

- information gathering
  Undertaking a market survey, or research and development to obtain more information.

Table 7.1   Risk descriptions

	Explanation	Example
Name of risk	Identifies risk	Computer failure
Scope of risk	Qualitative description of the events, their size, type, number and dependencies	Risk of inability to process customer orders, deliveries and invoices due to hardware failure
Nature of risk	For example strategic, operational, financial or regulatory – used for later categorization (see Chapter 5)	Operational
Stakeholders	Stakeholders and their expectations	Customers, Business Units, Finance department, Bankers
Quantification of risk	Likelihood	Low likelihood as computer system is new
Risk tolerance/appetite	Loss potential and financial impact of loss	Impact significant and could result in loss of customers and reduced profitability
Risk treatment and control mechanisms	Primary means by which the risk is currently managed; level of confidence in existing controls	Off-site backup of data files is carried out daily; no hardware backup available
Potential action for improvement	Recommendations to reduce risk	Obtain assurance from hardware supplier that alternative reliable site is available. Test alternative provision
Strategy and policy developments	Identification of function responsible for developing strategy and policy	IT Department to prepare disaster recovery plan in event of loss of IT hardware, liaise with suppliers over alternative replacement equipment and test that facility

Adapted from Institute of Risk Management (2002). A Risk Management Standard.

■ business continuity planning
Creating and testing a practical plan for how an organization will recover and restore partially or completely interrupted critical functions within a predetermined time after a disaster or disruption (see Chapter 20).

■ soft systems analysis
Soft systems analysis is less concerned with tangible, quantifiable information and is more concerned with feelings, attitudes, perceptions of individuals and groups and how conflict emerges and is treated.

■ Probability or statistical analysis
Managers may gauge the probability (or likelihood or chance) of some event occurring by assigning a range of numeric probabilities. For example, a business may consider a range of estimated weekly sales figures and assign to each a probability:

Sales level (£)	Probability (%)
90 000	10
100 000	50
110 000	30
120 000	10

Calculating the probability results in a probability-weighted estimate of £104 000 even though there is no expected level of sales of £104 000.

■ computer simulations, for example Monte Carlo
Computer simulations of scenarios enable a consideration of actions against alternative events. The Monte Carlo technique uses probability distributions of different variables to simulate a wide range of events.

■ decision trees
uses a graph or model of decisions and their possible consequences, including chance event outcomes and resource costs. A decision tree is used to identify the strategy most likely to reach a goal.

■ root cause analysis
This method investigates the cause of incidents by working backwards and considering all possible causes, continually asking 'Why?'

■ fault tree/event tree analysis
Fault tree analysis (FTA) and event tree analysis (ETA) are systematic methods to encourage better understanding of how a particular condition could arise, allowing causes and outcomes of events to be identified. This is a graphical technique that uses logic diagrams to identify causes (the fault tree) and consequences (the event tree) of potential failures.

■ failure mode and effect analysis (FMEA)
FMEA is systematic brainstorming aimed at finding out what could go wrong with a system or process by breaking it down into its component parts. Under FMEA, for each component of a system, the effect of its failure is identified, together with the consequential failure on the rest of the system. The likelihood and consequence of failure can then be estimated. FMEA and fault tree/event tree analysis are used in complex manufacturing, such as the automotive industry.

■ human reliability analysis (HRA)
HRA aims to identify failures due to human interaction. Processes are broken down into decision points at which correct or incorrect performance can result.

■ sensitivity analysis
This is used to ask 'what if?' questions to test the robustness of a plan. Altering variables one at a time identifies the impact of that variable.

■ cost–benefit and risk–benefit analysis
Cost–benefit analysis is a technique that compares the advantages and disadvantages which would result from particular choices. Each advantage and disadvantage is assigned a monetary value, taking probabilities into account and often utilizing discounted cash flow techniques. Risk–benefit analysis balances the expected benefits that would arise from a particular choice with the expected risks. This type of analysis was reportedly used in the UK by Railtrack to determine whether investments in train braking systems should be made to avoid collisions on the rail network.

■ real option analysis
The uncertainty inherent in investments is usually accounted for by risk-adjusting probabilities so that cash flows can then be discounted at the risk-free rate. The real options approach forces decision makers to be more explicit about the assumptions underlying their cash flow projections.

■ Delphi method
This is a group technique for aggregating the opinions of a number of experts. Questionnaires may be completed independently, and these are then circulated anonymously between the panel members. The process is repeated several times to achieve a convergence of opinion.

■ SWOT (strengths, weaknesses, opportunities and threats) or PESTLE (political, economic, social, technological, legal and environmental) analysis
A detailed analysis of internal and external factors, often used at the early stages of strategic planning.

■ HAZOP (Hazard and Operability Studies)
A brainstorming technique commonly used in oil and chemical industries. It uses terms such as 'none', 'more than', 'less than', etc. to identify problems in systems design.

Many of the quantitative methods are reductionist in nature (e.g. FMEA, FTA/ETA, HAZOP, root cause, HRA), that is, although the methods provide a formal structure for estimating risk, they assume linear cause–effect relationships rather than holistic or whole system relationships. Many methods rely on the assignment of probabilities and the estimation of alternative cash flows. However, many methods are subjective and rely on individual perceptions of risk (e.g. soft systems analysis, brainstorming, cost–benefit and risk–benefit analysis, Delphi, etc.). Others are a mixture of quantitative and qualitative approaches, with subjective judgments reflected in probabilities (e.g. Monte Carlo simulations, sensitivity analysis).

Research by Collier et al. (2007) found that the risk management methods in highest use at the corporate or enterprise level were the more subjective ones (intuition, hindsight, judgment and experience), with quantitative methods used least of all. The degree to which these methods were observed to be effective in helping respondents' organizations to manage risk was highly correlated with their degree of use, as might be expected. If a method was not perceived as effective it was unlikely to continue in use. An exception was that there was less confidence in experience, intuition, hindsight and judgement with only 48% of respondents believing that these were the most effective methods, compared with the 70% of respondents who used those methods. It appeared from interview responses to the Collier et al. research, that while quantitative methods of risk management were used, these were evident at lower organizational levels where they were appropriate to functional specialties, rather than at the whole of enterprise level, where the methods used were more subjective. Two interviews with risk managers explain the subjectivity of much of enterprise risk management:

> "It is very difficult to get a solid database on which to start doing quantitative analysis you know, the world changes and all the factors change, so it is very difficult to start putting figures on. I think intuitive at the moment is certainly the move we're making . . . I think it's very intuitive, in that you learn as you go along and the only way you can do that is on past experience and therefore the more experience you can tap into, the better your intuition can become . . . There is a use for impact/probability because it enables you to provide a pictorial representation of where you think the risks are. Now if you are looking at busy directors, if you give them [that] one page pictorial view, it focuses their minds. Then you get more time to discuss the risks, rather than giving them reams of paper." Group Risk Manager, FTSE company, Financial Services.
>
> "At one end of the spectrum you have the pure downside risks of the more or less traditional insurance kind of areas. At the other end of the spectrum you have got really what is all around risk and opportunity . . . the big decision about going into a new territory, a merger, a new product, etc. – the really big ones – they are going to be very risk oriented decisions which will still not be very

analysable because that's the very nature of entrepreneurship where you have to have a risk management framework but it's about decision making ... But there's a whole big raft in the middle between those two extremes, where you can use particular analysis tools, where particularly your management accountants have a key role in looking at different outcomes and different modelling and those type of issues." Risk Manager, telecommunications PLC with UK and US listings.

Risk estimation: the likelihood/consequences matrix

Whichever method of estimating risk is used, the most common way of presenting those risks is through the likelihood/impact matrix. This process is commonly called risk mapping. The likelihood or probability of occurrence may be high, medium or low. Similarly, impact or consequences in terms of downside risk (threats) or upside risk (opportunities) may be high, medium or low.

Figure 7.1 shows a simple risk matrix on which risk categories can be plotted in terms of their (high/medium/low) likelihood and impact. The diagonal line indicates the organizational risk appetite and those risks above the line are the significant risks facing the organization which need some form of treatment. By considering the likelihood and impact (i.e. severity) of each of the risks (or risk categories) it is possible for organizations to prioritize the key risks.

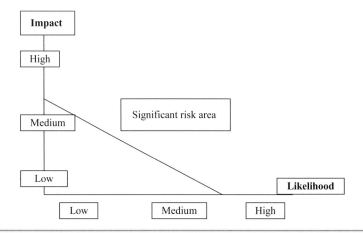

Figure 7.1   Risk matrix.
Source: Collier PM, Agyei-Ampomah S. *Management Accounting Risk and Control Strategy, P3 Study Guide*. London: Elsevier.

Table 7.2　Measures of likelihood and consequence

Likelihood (or probability)	Explanation	Example of quantification
Almost certain	Expected to occur	Frequently
Likely	Will probably occur	Monthly
Moderate	Could occur at some time and may be difficult to control	Once per year
Unlikely	Not expected to occur	Once in 5 years
Remote	May occur only in rare or exceptional circumstances	Once in 25 years
Impact (or consequence)		
Extreme	Would threaten the survival or viability of the business unit, have extreme political or community sensitivity or result in major impairment of reputation	Over £10 million
Very high	Would threaten the continued operation of the business unit or have significant impact on achieving business objectives or have significant political or community sensitivity or result in significant impact on reputation	Between £5 and £10 million
Medium	Would lead to significant review and change to the business unit or have a moderate impact on achieving business objectives or a moderate political or community sensitivity or a moderate impact on reputation	Between £1 and £5 million
Low	Would threaten efficiency or effectiveness of some aspect of the business, although this could be dealt with internally, or have a minimal impact on achieving business objectives or low political or community sensitivity or little impact on reputation	Between £100 000 and £1 million
Negligible	The consequences are dealt with by routine operations	Below £100 000

	Low likelihood	Medium likelihood	High likelihood
High consequences	Failure of information systems	Subcontractors fail to meet commitments	Government intervention in markets
	Serious accident	Failure of project planning system	Entry of new competitor
Medium consequences	Loss of certificates or licences	Insufficient capacity leads to delays	Management overload
	Shortcomings in succession planning	Excess capacity leads to losses	Poor Employee morale leads to resignations
Low consequences	Supplier failure	Profit shortfall Cost overruns	Inadequate R&D Legal claims

Figure 7.2   Likelihood/consequences matrix.
Source: Collier PM, Agyei-Ampomah S. *Management Accounting Risk and Control Strategy, P3 Study Guide*. London: Elsevier.

An alternative format for a likelihood/consequences matrix is shown in Table 7.2. For many organizations a 3×3 matrix of high/medium/low will suit their needs (as in Figure 7.2), while for others a 5×5 matrix (or even 7×7) may be more suitable.

Whatever the size of the matrix, care needs to be taken to avoid placing risks in the middle category so it is useful to define what is meant by 'high', 'medium' and 'low' in terms of likelihood and impact. This can be done either in terms of a quantified financial impact, or the number of times an event may occur. Table 7.2 shows one way in which criteria can be assessed using a 5×5 matrix.

In Table 7.2, likelihood is defined in terms of frequency, with impact defined in terms of a financial value. While there is considerable subjectivity in making these estimates, the result is an ability to prioritize the most significant risks. This is essential in terms of evaluating, treating and reporting risk, the subject of the next chapter.

Reference

Collier PM, Berry AJ, Burke GT. 2007. *Risk and Management Accounting: Best Practice Guidelines for Enterprise-wide Internal Control Procedures*. Oxford: Elsevier.

Chapter 8

Risk Evaluation, Treatment and Reporting

In the previous chapter we looked at how risks are identified, described and estimated using a likelihood and consequences matrix. This is an essential first step in evaluating the significance of risks and making decisions about how those risks can be avoided, mitigated, transferred or accepted, and the regular reporting to management and the Board about those risks.

Risk evaluation

Risk evaluation is used to make decisions about the significance of risks to the organization. When risk analysis (identification, description and estimation) has been completed, the risks faced by the organization need to be compared against its risk appetite and the array of opportunities and exposures faced by the organization. Risk evaluation is then concerned with making decisions about the significance of risks to the organization and whether those risks should be accepted or whether there should be an appropriate treatment or mitigation.

Risk treatment

Risk treatment is the process of selecting and implementing measures to modify the risk. This may include risk control/mitigation, risk avoidance, risk transfer, risk financing (e.g. hedging, insurance), etc. Risk treatment, also called risk response, involves decisions as to whether particular risks should be avoided, reduced, transferred or accepted.

Risk response may be:

- *Avoidance*: action is taken to exit the activities giving rise to risk, such as a product line or a geographical market, or a whole business unit. These are high-risk events.

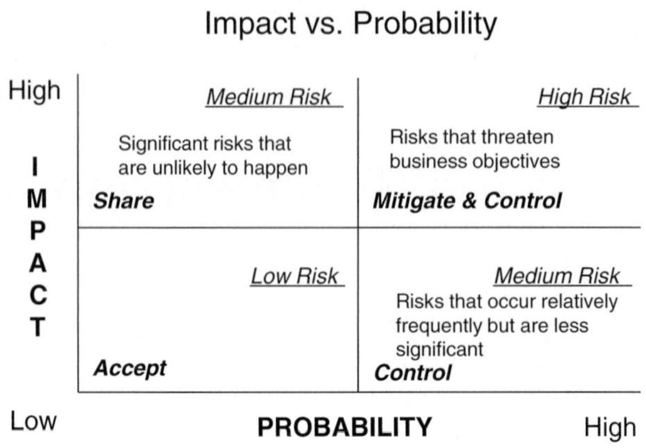

Impact vs. Probability

Figure 8.1 Risk mapping and response.
Source: COSO (2004) Enterprise Risk Management – Integrated Framework.

■ *Reduction*: action is taken to mitigate (i.e. reduce) the risk likelihood or impact, or both, generally via internal controls. These risks occur more frequently but have less impact.

■ *Sharing:* Action is taken to transfer a portion of the risk through, for example, insurance, pooling risks, hedging or outsourcing. These are significant risks, although they occur rarely.

■ *Acceptance*: no action is taken to affect likelihood or impact. These have low impact even when they do occur, which may be frequent.

Each response needs to be considered in terms of its effect on reducing the likelihood and/or impact of the risk. Risk response also needs to consider the costs and benefits of alternative risk responses.

The risk map or likelihood/consequences matrix (see Chapter 7) enables an organization to prioritize risks (from high through medium to low) and to determine an appropriate risk response (or risk treatment) depending on the likelihood and impact of the risk. Figure 8.1 shows the COSO ERM approach to risk response on the basis of the risk map.

Risk response involves:

■ Setting a policy defining the organization's attitude to a particular risk within its risk appetite and the objectives of the risk response;

■ Assigning individual accountability for the management of the risk, with the nominated person having the expertise and authority to effectively manage the risk;

- The management processes currently used to manage the risk;
- Recommended business processes to reduce the residual risk (after the application of controls, see below) to an acceptable level;
- Key performance measures to enable management to assess and monitor risk;
- Independent expertise to assess the adequacy of the risk response;
- Contingency plans to manage or mitigate a major loss following the occurrence of an event.

Methods of risk treatment

There are many methods of treating risk, and some are described in more detail in subsequent chapters. Following are some general approaches to risk treatment. Internal controls are used for risk reduction, to mitigate risks, while portfolio, hedging and insurance are methods of sharing risks, that is risks are transferred to third parties.

Internal control

Internal control is the whole system of financial and other controls established to provide reasonable assurance of effective and efficient operation; internal financial control; and compliance with regulation. Internal controls include accounting controls (e.g. budgets) but include quantitative controls (non-financial controls such as measures of quality) as well as qualitative (e.g. personnel) controls. Control encompasses all of the processes used by managers to ensure that organizational goals are achieved and procedures adhered to, and that the organization responds appropriately to changes in its environment. Controls are put in place in response to identified risks in order to reduce the likelihood or impact of risk. Internal control is dealt with in detail in Chapter 9 and in the various risk applications in Part C.

Portfolio

The assumption that capital markets are efficient leads to the view by investors that unsystematic risk (i.e. that which does not pertain to the whole market but is company-specific) can be managed by diversification through a portfolio approach to investments, or by the use of derivatives (see below and Chapter 12) to transfer systematic risk to third parties.

In establishing a portfolio approach to risk management, management and the Board recognize the diversity of possible risks and responses and the effect on the organization's risk tolerance. The basic principle of portfolio theory is that it is less risky to have diverse sources of income through a portfolio of assets or investments. The portfolio approach to risk management enables risk to be spread over a wider range of investments, thereby reducing the impact of an adverse event in any one business area on the whole business. Spreading investments can be achieved through a combination of market expansion or diversification.

However, this approach ignores the impact of organizational failure on the company itself and its stakeholders. A crisis in one organization may result in a crisis in other organizations and to loss of employment, or unavailability of products or services to consumers. It may also lead to a decline in social welfare and trust in markets. Enterprise risk management is concerned with the identification, evaluation, treatment and management of risk at the individual enterprise level, so it is less concerned with investment decisions in capital markets. However the portfolio approach is relevant in spreading risk across different business units, geographic or product markets.

Hedging

A hedge is a transaction to reduce or eliminate an exposure to risk. Hedging protects assets against unfavourable movements in an 'underlying' while retaining the ability to benefit from favourable movements. The most common 'underlyings' for which hedging takes place are in relation to changes in interest rates and foreign exchange fluctuations (but also exist for commodities, stocks and bonds). The instruments bought as a hedge tend to have opposite-value movements to the underlying and are used to transfer economic and financial risks within financial markets. This form of risk treatment is described in detail in Chapter 12.

Insurance

Insurance involves protection against hazards by taking out an insurance policy against an uncertain event. Insurance involves payment of a premium to an insurer, who will pay the sum assured to compensate the loss suffered by the insured. An insurer is able to offer such cover on the basis of probabilities assigned to particular events and the pooling of risks by many insured parties. The premium cost will be influenced by the extent of risk management carried out by the insured in order to prevent or mitigate risks from eventuating such as fire prevention precautions. This form of risk treatment is described in detail in Chapter 21.

Although insurance is still widely used, large organizations have reduced their reliance on it as managers have recognized that insurance often does not meet organizational needs cost-effectively. Risk reduction and risk sharing, and in some cases risk acceptance may be more appropriate responses.

The risk register

Once risks are identified, described, estimated using one or other quantitative or qualitative technique, and mapped according to their likelihood and consequence, most organizations record their risks in a risk register. This may contain as much information as may be considered useful for monitoring purposes. Examples of data to be included in a risk register are:

- Risk number (a unique identifier)
- Risk category (see Chapter 5)
- Description of risk
- Date risk identified
- Name of person who identified risk
- Likelihood
- Consequences
- A monetary value, if such can be allocated to the risk
- Interdependencies with other risks

The risk register will be updated with the risk treatment (or response) decided by management or the Board, including the responsible manager and the method of monitoring the risk and the effectiveness of the risk response. This will enable risk reporting (see below) and monitoring by management and the Board (see Chapter 9).

Risk reporting

Risk reporting is the provision of information to management and the Board that will explain the method of risk management, and how risks are identified and assessed. Although the risk register will contain all risks, only the highest risks (in terms of likelihood and consequence) will be reported at each organizational level (from business unit to corporate Board). For each identified risk, the risk response will also be recorded. Risk reports should show both the gross risk and the net risk to demonstrate the cost effectiveness of those controls.

- *Gross risk* involves the assessment of risk before the application of any avoidance, controls, transfer or other management response.

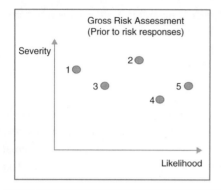
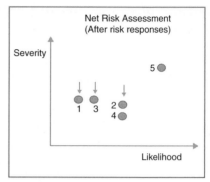

Figure 8.2   Gross and net risk assessments.
Source: Association of Insurance and Risk Managers (2001) *A Guide to Developing a Risk Management Process*, p. 18

■ *Net risk* involves the assessment of risk, taking into account the application of any avoidance, controls, transfer or management response to the risk under consideration.

An example of risk assessment using gross and net risk assessments is shown in Figure 8.2 which shows how the likelihood and/or impact of risks eventuating has been reduced through risk treatment.

The residual (or net) risk is that which remains after avoidance, reduction, sharing and acceptance responses have been implemented. A comparison of gross and net risk enables a review of the effectiveness of risk treatment and the cost-effectiveness of that risk treatment. Effective risk treatment enables Boards to consider:

■ The nature and extent of risks facing the organization;
■ The extent and categories of risk which it regards as acceptable for the organization to bear;
■ The likelihood of risks materializing;
■ The costs and benefits of risk responses;
■ How well the existing risk treatment techniques have reduced the overall exposure to the organization (or increased the opportunities available to it).

Reporting needs to address:

■ The control systems in place for risk management.
■ The processes used to identify and respond to risks.

■ The methods used to manage significant risks.

■ The monitoring and review system.

Risk reporting includes:

■ A systematic review of the most significant risks.

■ A review of the management responses to the significant risks.

■ A monitoring and feedback loop on action taken and variance in the assessment of the significant risks.

■ An 'early warning system' to indicate material change in the risk profile, or circumstances, which could increase exposures or threaten areas of opportunity.

■ The inclusion of audit work as part of the communication and reporting process.

Risk reporting completes the feedback loop of setting objectives (risk appetite), estimating and evaluating risk, putting in place risk responses, and measuring performance (the effectiveness of risk treatment through monitoring and reporting).

Case study: risk in a retail chain

XYZ group (the name has been changed to preserve anonymity) had over 400 retail stores and sales in excess of £1 billion per annum. The group had been subject to significant adverse publicity several years earlier when senior managers had been charged with fraud following the reporting of inflated profits and the misleading of auditors over supplier documentation. Following a change of top management, the company had made a significant investment in risk management and internal control.

Risk management was part of the internal audit function. The internal auditor/risk manager said that the motivation for risk management was to 'establish best practice in corporate governance'. The process commenced with a brainstorming by the internal audit team of 'risk drivers' to identify what could go wrong and what controls could be put in place to address risks. The internal audit team held interviews with all managers to determine a measure of the effectiveness of these controls on a scale from 1 to 5. The threat of inadequate controls was identified and recommendations were made for improvement. Although risks and controls were documented in a risk map, the internal auditor/risk manager did not see value in a formal risk register for hundreds of individual risks but rather saw risk management at a more aggregated level for the most significant risks.

A Risk Management Group (RMG) met every 2 months, comprising all senior business managers. The risk maps given by the internal audit team to the RMG showed the monetary value of what they called a 'fundamental control breakdown'. For each risk (e.g. supply chain failure) the 'mitigating factors' (i.e. controls) were identified. From the monetary value of a control breakdown was deducted the monetary value arising from controls implemented to give a 'residual risk' (i.e. the net risk after controls were implemented) to which was assigned a probability, although it was admitted that these values were subjective. The whole process was a 'top down' one, emphasizing a concern for 'high level' risks. The big risks identified through this process were in relation to the supply chain and individual suppliers, people management, the cost base, key business processes, retail property management, market share, product offering and pricing, brand management, and information systems and business continuity.

The audit committee of the Board comprised four non-executive directors, and was attended by the external auditors, the chief financial officer and the internal auditor/risk manager. The audit committee used the information provided by the RMG to monitor progress in relation to the risk maps. The risk maps were the main driver of the annual internal audit plan which was agreed by the audit committee, the RMG and individual business managers. Results of audits were provided to the RMG and audit committee where the value of the report was greater than £250 000.

At the time of interview, the internal auditor/risk manager wanted to implement a risk intelligence report to provide early warning of risks, by looking at key performance indicators to identify what the business should be concerned with. He also wanted to introduce a risk marketing plan to help communicate risk and to pass on the responsibility for risk to other managers within the business. The internal auditor/risk manager expected it to take another 2 years to establish risk management in the organization, to introduce more 'bottom up' involvement and to embed risk at the cultural level.

Case study: risk management in the Metropolitan Police Service

Risk management models cannot always follow the 'text book' standard, but need to be developed in a way that achieves ownership by managers. A case in point is the Metropolitan Police Service (MPS) which polices London and employs 45 000 people. The MPS Business Risk Management Team (BRMT) tried to introduce a risk register in each of its 33 commands, in a process that would record high-level strategic business risks and escalate them to each level within the organization up to a corporate risk register.

Procedures were written and training provided, but the BRMT faced resistance. Risks identified tended to be very operational and expressed in terms of failing to meet a target. They were generally shown to have a single cause and a single control.

The process was seen as bureaucratic and a waste of time by users. Consequently, the BRMT developed its own corporate risk register. They found that the complexity of outcomes the MPS is expected to deliver and its sheer size and reactive (to crime) culture blocked any meaningful adoption. This was not because of the risk management process, but because of the tools – the risk register – that were being used. There was also confusion about the distinction between 'upside' and 'downside' risk.

The BRMT developed two alternative approaches that found greater acceptance within MPS: the 'Bow Tie' and the 'Butterfly'. The 'Bow Tie' took a risk event as the focus, and looking backwards, identified the causes of the event and the preventive controls that could be put in place. Looking forwards from the event, consequences of the event and mitigating controls were identified.

The 'Bow Tie' was subsequently developed into a 'Butterfly' model which had at its centre an opportunity or project. The (backwards) causal direction applied preventive controls for organizational weaknesses and threats and harnessing controls to take advantage of strengths and opportunities. (The forward) consequences were split into positive outcomes with enhancing controls and negative outcomes with mitigating controls.

The new approach focused more on the controls rather than scoring a risk. Control became important because it represented the degree to which the organization was tolerably or intolerably exposed to causes and consequences.

The full MPS report of their risk management implementation is available from http://www.alarm-uk.org/PDF/ALARM%20publication%20of%20MPS%20article%2011-9-07%20_2_.pdf.

Chapter 9

Internal Control and the Manager's Role in Enterprise Risk Management

Every manager has at least part of his/her role associated with the identification, assessment and reporting of risk. Sometimes this will be in relation to risks specific to their functional responsibilities, for example currency hedging for treasury managers or credit risk for accounts receivable managers. At other times the management of risk will be generic, for example occupational health and safety applies to all managers. In addition to these risk management functions, each manager also has a wider responsibility under *enterprise* risk management (ERM) in terms of his/her awareness of environmental, regulatory, technological or similar changes affecting the organisation, whether or not it relates to their specific functional responsibility. At the enterprise level, risk management is about embedding a risk culture in the organisation (see Chapter 6). This broader responsibility becomes more important at senior management levels and is most important at the Board level, when directors need to take a much broader and longer-term view of risks that may not yet have emerged. The manager's role in ERM depends on the organisation's strategy for managing risk.

Risk management strategy

A risk management framework needs to be established in every organisation, reflecting its policy and guidelines in relation to identifying, assessing, evaluating, treating and reporting risk. Particular roles and responsibilities need to be established with clear responsibilities assigned to:

- The Board, or its audit committee (see Chapters 2 and 23),
- A risk management group (see below),
- The chief risk officer (see below),
- Internal audit (see Chapter 24),
- External audit (see Chapter 24),
- Line managers and
- Employees, through the organisation's culture.

Every organisation should develop a risk management strategy that encompasses:

■ the risk appetite and tolerance of the organisation, that is the level of risk it finds acceptable (see Chapter 6);

■ the risk assessment and evaluation processes the organisation practises (Chapter 7);

■ its preferred options for risk treatment (Chapter 8, e.g. retention, avoidance, reduction, transfer);

■ who is responsible in the organisation for risk management; and

■ how reporting and monitoring processes will take place.

Effective risk management requires

■ management commitment;

■ integration with the strategic planning process;

■ the use of a consistent language and framework;

■ acceptance of risk management as a continuous and evolving process;

■ organisation-wide ownership with a supportive culture;

■ that risk management be embedded in organisational processes.

The Chartered Institute of Management Accountants & International Federation of Accountants (2004) report '*Enterprise Governance: Getting the Balance Right*' presented a number of case studies. There were four key corporate governance issues that underpinned success and failure:

■ Culture and tone at the top;

■ The chief executive;

■ The board of directors;

■ Internal controls.

In the case of success, a virtuous circle was based on good governance being taken seriously because it benefited the organisation, not just because it was required by the law or codes of practice. In the case of failure, poorly designed executive remuneration packages distorted behaviour in the direction of aggressive earnings management and, in some cases, fraudulent accounting as occurred at Enron and WorldCom.

However, the cases found that whilst good corporate governance was necessary, it was insufficient for success. Whilst bad governance can damage an organisation, good governance cannot on its own ensure success. The CIMA/IFAC report identified four key strategic issues that underpinned success and failure:

- Choice and clarity of strategy;
- Strategy execution;
- Ability to respond to sudden changes and/or fast moving market conditions;
- Ability to undertake successful mergers and acquisitions (M&A).

Unsuccessful M&A was the most significant issue in strategy-related failure.

The case studies in the CIMA/IFAC report identified the conformance role of the audit committee and the absence of any Board-level equivalent body whose aim was to ensure adequate oversight of the performance dimension. A recommendation of the report was the establishment of a strategy committee of the Board to undertake regular reviews of strategy and to better inform the full Board's discussions about strategic decisions.

The Risk Management Group

Whilst the Board will have an audit committee (or a separate risk committee, see Chapter 23) to oversee enterprise risk management from a governance perspective, management should have a Risk Management Group to provide assurance to the Board that risk management processes are effective. The Risk Management Group will advise the Board (and/or audit and risk committees) on risk management strategy and processes and will be the body which implements the Board's strategies and policies.

The Risk Management Group should include:

- Chief risk officer (see below)
- Internal auditor
- Chief information officer (responsible for IT)
- Chief executive or chief operations officer
- Line managers representing each business unit
- Functional managers responsible for areas with high-risk exposure, for example health and safety, environmental protection, quality control, insurance, etc.

The Risk Management Group may also include the Chief Financial Officer and/or legal counsel.

Risk Management Groups will often be duplicated within each business unit. Each group will have responsibility for the risk identification, assessment and evaluation process through to recording in the risk register for their business unit and reporting risks and risk treatment (consistent with organisational policy) to higher levels of management and ultimately to the Board.

Chief Risk Officer

The chief risk officer (CRO) or risk manager works with other managers in establishing and maintaining effective risk management throughout the organisation. The effectiveness of the CRO and enterprise risk management will be based on how well the CRO is able to instill a risk-aware culture throughout the organisation and delegate the detail of risk management to each organisational level. This is more an internal championing and consulting role for the CRO, which is unlikely to be effective if risk management is centralised.

The risk management process is about managing, rather than eliminating a risk. This is most effectively done through adopting a risk culture. Like the CFO and CIO for their respective roles of finance and information, the CRO has cross-functional responsibility for risk. She/he is responsible for developing and implementing a risk strategy, providing the overall leadership and strategic direction for ERM, establishing the framework in which ERM takes place, developing policies and procedures, clarifying with the Board of Directors the organisational risk appetite, implementing methods for the identification and assessment of risk, risk recording through risk registers, monitoring of risk events and their consequences, coordinating risk mitigation strategies and risk reporting.

One of the main functions of the Board, the Risk Management Group and the Chief Risk Officer is to establish a system of internal controls which effectively manage the risk.

Internal control

An internal control system includes all the policies and procedures (internal controls) adopted by the directors and management of an entity to assist in achieving their objectives of ensuring, as far as practicable, the orderly and efficiently conducting a business, including adherence to internal policies, the safeguarding of assets, the prevention and detection of fraud and error, the accuracy and completeness of the accounting records, and the timely preparation of reliable financial information (Chartered Institute of Management Accountants, 2005).

An internal control system comprises the control environment and control procedures. The control environment is the overall attitude, awareness and actions of directors and management regarding internal controls and their importance to the entity ... [it] encompasses the management style, and corporate culture and values shared by all employees (Chartered Institute of Management Accountants, 2005). The control environment provides the context for the whole set of control procedures.

The Institute of Internal Auditors (IIA) describes the control environment as the attitude and actions of management and the Board regarding the significance of control within the organisation. The control environment provides the discipline and structure for the achievement of the primary objectives of the system of internal control. The control environment includes: integrity and ethical values, management's philosophy and operating style, organisational structure, assignment of authority and responsibility, human resource policies and practices, and competence of personnel (The Institute of Internal Auditors Inc., 2008 – The Glossary).

There are some important aspects of control that can be derived from these definitions:

■ Control is not limited to financial control but extends to operational and other forms of control;
■ Control is linked to organisational goals and environmental change;
■ Control is not only a set of procedures, but also a set of values or attitudes which need to be embedded in the culture of the organisation.

COSO model of internal control

COSO's *Enterprise Risk Management – Integrated Framework* (Committee of Sponsoring Organizations of the Treadway Commission (COSO), 2004) states that internal control is an integral part of enterprise risk management. This is described in COSO's *Internal Control – Integrated Framework* (Committee of Sponsoring Organizations of the Treadway Commission (COSO), 1992) which is encompassed within the ERM framework (see Chapter 4).

The COSO internal control framework contains five elements:

■ Control environment (see above).
■ Risk assessment: identifies the risks of failing to meet objectives in relation to financial reporting, compliance and operational objectives.
■ Control activities: the policies and procedures that help ensure management directives are carried out and objectives are achieved. These include both accounting and non-accounting controls.
■ Monitoring: the need for management to monitor the entire control system through specific evaluations.
■ Information and communication: capturing relevant internal and external information about competition, economic and regulatory matters and the potential of strategic and integrated information systems.

In September 2007 COSO produced a discussion document furthering its *Internal Control – Integrated Framework* (Committee of Sponsoring Organizations of the

Treadway Commission (COSO), 2007).[1] The discussion document provides guidance on monitoring internal control systems, arguing strongly that ineffective monitoring leads to control breakdown. This can happen if processes or risks change and controls do not adapt to those changes, or where previously effective controls cease to operate as they were originally designed.

The COSO discussion document recommends that monitoring of controls takes place through a structure that includes:

- a control baseline or starting point,
- a change-identification process,
- a change-management process, and
- control reconfirmation through seeking various sources of evidence.

The report discusses different types of information that can be used in monitoring, depending on the importance of the controls, and the underlying likelihood and significance of the risks the controls relate to.

Controls can be segregated into three types:

- Financial controls
- Controls that are quantitative but not financial
- Controls that are qualitative.

Financial controls

There are various accounting methods by which control is exercised. The main ones which will be covered here are:

- Financial ratios
- Budgets
- Budgetary reporting (variance analysis)
- Capital investment appraisal.

Financial ratios are calculated by dividing one figure by another, with the source of the figures being information presented in Income Statements and Balance Sheets. Ratios are interpreted by reference to their (improving or worsening trend) and by benchmark comparisons to similar organisations and industry averages. Ratios exist for profitability, liquidity (cash flow), gearing (borrowing), asset efficiency, and there are also shareholder-based ratios. Targets are usually set and monitored by the Board and senior management for the financial performance needed to maintain shareholder

---

[1] http://www.coso.org/Publications/COSO_Monitoring_discussiondoc.pdf.

value and the confidence of capital markets which is reflected in the share price. By monitoring ratios, the Board exercises control over financial performance.

Whilst ratios consider historical performance, budgets are concerned with expected future performance. Budgets provide:

- a forecast of future events, a short-term picture of the desired financial results resulting from the chosen strategy,
- a motivational target to which managers are expected to strive; and
- a standard for business unit and management performance which is then evaluated.

Budgets provide a control mechanism through both the feed forward and feedback loops. In feed forward terms, budgets can be reviewed in advance, to ensure that they are consistent with organisational goals and strategy. If they do not contribute to goals, changes can be made to the budget before it is approved. Using feedback, variations between the budget and actual performance can be investigated and monitored and corrective action can be taken for future time periods.

Although the tools of budgeting and cash forecasting are well developed and made easier by the widespread use of spreadsheet software, the difficulty of budgeting is in predicting the volume of sales for the business, especially the sales mix between different products or services and the timing of income and expenses. Consequently, sensitivity analysis is applied, sometimes using probabilities, reflecting various optimistic, conservative and pessimistic levels of confidence, to determine the effects of variations on the budget.

However, in their study of budgeting and risk Collier and Berry (2002) found that whilst the process of budgeting did involve the application of some quantitative techniques, the final budget was most commonly a single-point estimate based on subjective judgments about the likely organisational level of activity.

Budgetary control or variance analysis involves comparing actual performance against plan, investigating the causes of the variance and taking corrective action to ensure that targets are achieved. Variance analysis can be carried out for each responsibility centre, product/service and for each line item. Organisations can use variance analysis in a number of ways to support their business strategy, most commonly by investigating the reasons for variations between the budget and actual costs, even if those costs are independent of volume. These variations may identify poor budgeting practice, lack of cost control or variations in the usage or price of resources that may be outside a manager's control.

Capital investment or capital expenditure means spending money now in the hope of getting it back later through future cash flows. Most investment appraisals consider decisions such as: whether or not to invest; whether to invest in one project or one piece of equipment rather than another; and whether to invest now or at a later time. Capital investment decisions are made in relation to new production facilities, new product launches, and mergers and acquisitions. There are three main methods of evaluating investments: accounting rate of return; payback and discounted cash flow (DCF). For any project, investment appraisal requires an estimation of future incremental cash flows, that is, the additional cash flow (net of income less expenses) that will result from the investment, as well as the cash outflow for the initial investment. This is a form of long-term budgeting. Whilst the detail of these methods is outside the scope of the book, the limitations of the techniques are the inability to predict future cash flows and the discount rate used to convert future cash flows into present values.

Budgets and capital investment are forms of control exercised through the necessity for Board (or at least senior management) approval, whilst variance analysis provides the opportunity for the Board or senior management to monitor actual performance compared to plan and seek explanations for performance not in accordance with that plan.

Controls also exist over financial reporting (see Chapter 10), and the main accounting functions including accounts receivable, inventory, payroll, and accounts payable.

Non-financial controls

There are many kinds of non-financial controls that rely on measurement, including:

- Performance measurement through 'key performance indicators';
- Quality systems: measuring and monitoring errors and wastage;
- Project management: establishing detailed plans with budgets, timeframes and quality expectations (see Chapter 17).

Johnson and Kaplan (1987) criticised the excessive focus on financial performance measures, the limitations of which include their focus on short-term profitability. Financial measures are lagging indicators, providing information about performance after it has happened. By contrast, non-financial measures (which are quantitative but expressed in non-monetary terms) are leading indicators of performance. They inform an organisation about what is happening now, and give a good indication of what the likely future financial performance will be.

The development of the *Balanced Scorecard* by Kaplan and Norton (1992, 2001) has received extensive coverage in the business press and is perhaps the best-known framework for non-financial performance measurement. It presents four different perspectives (including the financial) but complements traditional financial indicators with measures of performance for customers, internal processes and innovation/improvement. Appropriate performance measures are identified for each category together with targets.

■ Customer measures provide information about customer satisfaction, repeat business, reputation, etc.

■ Process measures provide information about process efficiency, quality, cycle time, rework, wastage, etc.

■ Innovation and growth measures provide information about research activity, employee training and morale, etc.

These measures are grounded in an organisation's strategic objectives and competitive demands. Kaplan and Norton (2001) argued that meeting short-term financial targets should not constitute satisfactory performance when other measures indicate that the long-term strategy is either not working or not being implemented well.

Qualitative controls

There is also a wide variety of non-financial qualitative controls. Some of these are:

■ Formal structures: the organisational chart with its hierarchy of management;

■ Personnel controls: recruitment, training and socialisation, supervision and performance appraisal processes;

■ Informal structures: the organisational culture;

■ Rules, policies and procedures: embedded in manuals or corporate policies and in computer systems;

■ Physical controls: physical access to offices, computers, etc.;

■ Strategic plans: strategies direct behaviour and define the boundaries in which the organisation operates;

■ Incentives and rewards: reinforcing desired behaviour.

These controls influence behaviour by requiring certain policies and procedures or standard instructions to be followed. Qualitative controls ensure that behaviour is legally correct, co-ordinated and consistent throughout the organisation; is linked to objectives and is efficient and effective.

Internal audit and enterprise-wide risk management

As risk management became more widespread and took on the mantle of enterprise risk management, the role of internal audit, previously seen as part of the system of internal control, became transformed into a broader process designed to provide objective assurance on the effectiveness of that system, with the Institute of Internal

Auditors becoming the predominant body, rather than the accounting profession. Risk-based approaches have also been adopted by external auditors, particularly those subject to Sarbanes-Oxley requirements in relation to the specific risk of mis-reporting in financial statements.

The Institute of Internal Auditors defines internal auditing as an independent, objective assurance and consulting activity designed to add value and improve an organisation's operations. It helps an organisation accomplish its objectives by bringing a systematic, disciplined approach to evaluate and improve the effectiveness of risk management, control and governance processes (The Institute of Internal Auditors, Inc., 1999).

The core role of internal audit is to provide assurance that the main business risks are being managed and that internal controls are operating effectively. Internal audit differs from external audit in that it does not focus only on financial reports and financial risks but extends to a more holistic review of risk and control. However, internal and external auditors need to work closely together to provide the Board with the assurance it needs to satisfy corporate governance requirements.

Internal audit has shifted from a focus on systems and processes to a risk-based approach. The objective of risk-based internal auditing (RBIA) is to provide assurance to the board that:

- The risk management processes which management has put in place are operating as intended. This includes all risk management processes at corporate, divisional, business unit and business process levels.
- These risk management processes are part of a sound design.
- The responses that management has made to risks which they wish to treat are adequate and effective in reducing those risks to a level acceptable to the Board.
- A sound framework of controls is in place to mitigate those risks which management wishes to treat.

RBIA begins with management's approach to the risks that may prevent the business objectives from being achieved. Internal audit assesses the extent to which a robust risk management process is in place. An RBIA approach enables internal audit to link directly with risk management. Figure 9.1 shows the risk-based internal auditing approach.

The RBIA approach developed by the Institute of Internal Auditors also suggests that the internal audit approach is related to the level of risk maturity in the organisation. Figure 9.2 shows the different levels of risk maturity and the appropriate internal audit approach consistent with each level.

The Institute of Internal Auditors believes that internal auditors should not set the risk appetite, impose risk management processes, give the assurance on risk that

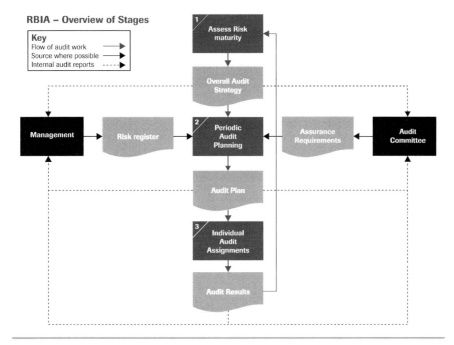

Figure 9.1   RBIA overview of stages.
Source: This diagram is taken from 'An approach to implementing Risk Based Internal Auditing', reproduced with the permission of the Institute of Internal Auditors – UK and Ireland (©The Institute of Internal Auditors – UK and Ireland Ltd., 2005).

is the role of management, make decisions about or implement risk response, or be accountable for risk management. However, internal auditors do provide advice to management and the Board, and challenge or support management decisions in relation to risk management.

Figure 9.3 would illustrate that well.

Internal auditors are specialists in systems for risk management and control, but managing individual risks is the role of line managers. Internal auditors assess how risks are identified, analysed and managed and give independent advice on how to embed risk management practices into business activities. Internal auditors can provide advice to the board in relation to:

- The identification of key risks
- The effectiveness of processes to identify and analyse threats to the business
- The controls in place to manage the most important risks
- The culture in relation to risk and control

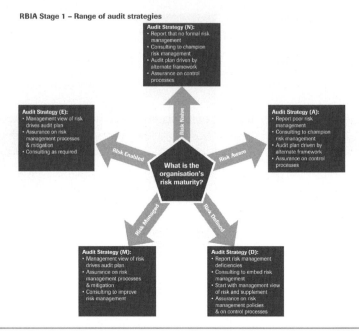

RBIA Stage 1 – Range of audit strategies

Figure 9.2   RBIA stage 1 – audit strategies.
Source: This diagram is taken from 'An approach to implementing Risk Based Internal Auditing', reproduced with the permission of the Institute of Internal Auditors – UK and Ireland (©The Institute of Internal Auditors – UK and Ireland Ltd., 2005).

- The adequacy and reliability of financial and non-financial reporting
- The effectiveness of management in directing and controlling the business
- The degree of compliance with legislation
- The safeguarding of business assets
- The control of change including systems development.

The relationship between the risk management and internal audit functions in an organisation is a two-way one. Risk management will inform the priorities for the internal audit plan. However, the risk management system will itself need to be audited, in order to ensure that it can be relied on.

Risk-based internal control and risk-based internal audit

There is a strong need to integrate risk management, internal control and internal audit so that both control systems and audit processes are based on the assessment and

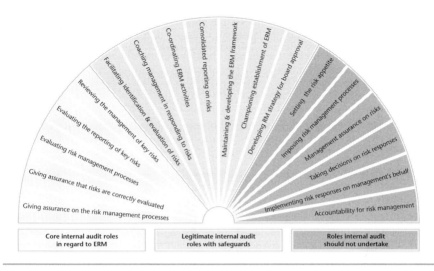

Figure 9.3

Source: This diagram is taken from 'Position Statement: The Role of Internal Audit in Enterprise-wide Risk Management', reproduced with the permission of the Institute of Internal Auditors – UK and Ireland (©The Institute of Internal Auditors – UK and Ireland Ltd., 2004).

evaluation of risks. In the traditional management control paradigm in organisations, risk management is but one additional form of control, along with other financial, non-financial and qualitative controls. In this paradigm, it is added as another suite of controls emanating from the risk register and following decisions about risk retention, avoidance, reduction, and transfer.

A more sophisticated risk management paradigm sees all management controls as being related to risk assessment, whether accounting-based, non-financial or qualitative. The risk management paradigm recognises that many controls are historically based or politically derived and exist where there is little or no likelihood or impact of risk. As such, controls need to go through a lifecycle of development and growth as the likelihood and consequence of new risks are identified and decline and their eventual removal as old risks fade away. Equally, audit should be based on risk assessments, with greater audit attention going to the highest likelihood and impact risks, as well as auditing the risk management process itself.

A risk-based approach to control is evident in many modern business enterprises and the methods they use to assess, mitigate and monitor the risks that are specific to their business models. For example, a risk-based approach to control was evident in the Just-in-Time environment described by Berry and Collier (2007). They report an automotive sequencer of parts which was required by its contract to deliver components to its customer's assembly line within a 2-h window. The organisation managed risk through strong technological and human links with suppliers and logistics providers. However, any failure within the supply chain which would result in stopping the customer's assembly line and incurring significant penalties to the assembler (low likelihood but high consequence) was mitigated by the use of helicopters to fly in missing parts. The controls put in place were specifically related to the identification and assessment of risk by the business in line with its business model and the context in which it operated. We revisit these issues in Part D.

References

Berry AJ, Collier PM. 2007. Risk management in supply chains: processes, organisation for uncertainty and culture. *International Journal of Risk Assessment and Management* 7:1005–26.

Chartered Institute of Management Accountants. 2005. *CIMA Official Terminology: 2005 Edition*. Oxford: Elsevier.

Chartered Institute of Management Accountants, International Federation of Accountants. 2004. *Enterprise Governance: Getting the Balance Right*.

Collier PM, Berry AJ. 2002. Risk in the process of budgeting. *Management Accounting Research* 13:273–97.

Committee of Sponsoring Organizations of the Treadway Commission (COSO). 1992. *Internal Control – Integrated Framework*.

Committee of Sponsoring Organizations of the Treadway Commission (COSO). 2004. *Enterprise Risk Management – Integrated Framework*.

Committee of Sponsoring Organizations of the Treadway Commission (COSO). 2007. Internal Control – Integrated Framework: Guidance on Monitoring Internal Control Systems.

Johnson HT, Kaplan RS. 1987. *Relevance Lost: The Rise and Fall of Management Accounting*. Boston: Harvard Business School Press.

Kaplan RS, Norton DP. 1992. The Balanced Scorecard – Measures That Drive Performance. *Harvard Business Review*: Jan.–Feb. 1992.

Kaplan RS, Norton DP. 2001. *The Strategy-Focused Organization: How Balanced Scorecard Companies Thrive in the New Business Environment*. Boston, MA: Harvard Business School Press.

The Institute of Internal Auditors, Inc. 2008. 247 Maitland Avenue, Altamonte Springs, Florida 32710-4201 USA. [Reproduced with permission. 1999. The *Definition of Internal Auditing*, 2008. The *International Standards for the Professional Practice of Internal Auditing*.]

The Institute of Internal Auditors – UK and Ireland Ltd. 2004. *Position Statement: The Role of Internal Audit in Enterprise-wide risk management* 2005. *An approach to the implementation of Risk Based Internal Auditing*.

Part C. Risk Applications in Organisations

In Part C, we consider many different aspects of enterprise risk management, from its concern with financial reporting, decision making and hedging (chapters 10, 11 and 12) to information systems risk (chapter 13), health and safety (chapter 14), and credit risk (chapter 15). We consider the broader aspects of strategy and business risk (chapter 16) to the narrower examples of project risk (chapter 17) and fraud and theft (chapter 18). We look at risk in relation to the environmental and regulatory change (chapter 19) and at business continuity (chapter 20) and insurance (chapter 21). We also give a summary of risk in the banking industry (chapter 22).

Each of these risk applications is important in its own right, but for enterprise risk management, each is a piece of the jigsaw that at senior management and Board level needs to be fitted together and be evaluated in terms of the relative importance of each piece. Based on the organisation's risk appetite and risk strategy, each application and its assembly into a coherent enterprise risk management framework will inform the development of appropriate risk treatment and reporting.

Chapter 10

Risk and Financial Reporting

Financial reporting by companies has become increasingly prescriptive in terms of what has to be disclosed for the benefit of shareholders and other stakeholders in the company. This is so in the financial statements themselves and in the Operating and Financial Review, in which various risk disclosures need to be made for the benefit of investors.

Accounting standards

Accounting standards reflect the basic accounting principles that are generally accepted by the accounting profession and which are a requirement under the UK Companies Act as essential for reporting financial information or under US Generally Accepted Accounting Principles (GAAP). Historically, each country has had its own set of accounting standards. The move towards the harmonization of accounting standards between countries through the work of the International Accounting Standards Board (IASB) has been a consequence of the globalization of capital markets, with the consequent need for accounting rules that can be understood by international investors. The dominance of multinational corporations and the desire of companies to be listed on several stock exchanges have led to the need to rationalize the different reporting practices in different countries.

International Financial Reporting Standards (IFRS) are published by the IASB. The predecessors of IFRS were called International Accounting Standards (IASs). The term International Financial Reporting Standards (IFRSs) includes both the newer IFRSs and the older IASs

The objectives of the IASB are to develop, in the public interest, a single set of understandable and enforceable global accounting standards that require high quality, transparent and comparable information in financial statements and other financial reporting to help participants in the various capital markets of the world and other users of the information to make economic decisions; to promote the use and rigorous application of those standards; and to work actively with national standard-setters to bring about convergence of national accounting standards in each country and IFRSs.

The Sarbanes-Oxley Act of 2002 is the main legislation affecting companies listed in the United States. The United States has a Financial Accounting Standards Board which has not yet adopted IFRSs. The United States equivalent of accounting standards is GAAP. However, the IASB and FASB have agreed in principle to develop a common conceptual framework to underlie published financial statements. At the time of writing, the Securities and Exchange Commission seems to be leaning toward giving US companies the option of switching to international financial reporting standards rather than mandating conversion as it prepares to release its road map for convergence late in 2008.

The main rules in relation to disclosure of information in financial reports of an entity (this is the term used for a listed organization) are contained within IAS1: Presentation of Financial Statements and IFRS7: Financial Instruments (IFRS7 is described later in this Chapter).

IAS1 prescribes the basis for presentation of general purpose financial statements to ensure comparability both with the entity's financial statements of previous periods and with the financial statements of other entities. It sets out overall requirements for the presentation of financial statements, guidelines for their structure and minimum requirements for their content. An entity shall present a complete set of financial statements (including comparative information) at least annually. A complete set of financial statements comprises:

(a) a statement of financial position as at the end of the period (a 'Balance Sheet');

(b) a statement of comprehensive income for the period (an 'Income Statement', previously called a 'Profit and Loss account');

(c) a statement of changes in equity for the period;

(d) a statement of cash flows for the period;

(e) notes, comprising a summary of significant accounting policies and other explanatory information; and

(f) a statement of financial position as at the beginning of the earliest comparative period when an entity applies an accounting policy retrospectively or makes a retrospective restatement of items in its financial statements, or when it reclassifies items in its financial statements.

Behind accounting standards sits a *Framework for the Preparation and Presentation of Financial Statements*. The Framework defines the objective of financial statements to provide information about the financial position, performance and changes in financial position of an entity that is useful to a wide range of users in making economic decisions. Financial statements prepared for this purpose meet the common needs of most users. However, financial statements do not provide all the information that users may need to make economic decisions since they largely portray the financial effects of past events and do not necessarily provide non-financial information.

Operating and Financial Review

In the United Kingdom, the Accounting Standards Board published a *Reporting Statement: Operating and Financial Review* (OFR) in 2006. The reporting statement is a voluntary statement according with 'best practice' principles for listed companies. The OFR (although different companies may use a different terminology) is intended to complement and supplement financial statements by being forward-looking, providing details of strategy including key performance indicators.

The OFR should provide information to enable shareholders '*to assess the strategies adopted by the entity and the potential for those strategies to succeed*' (Accounting Standards Board, 2006:13) including:

- The nature of the business, description of the market, the competitive and regulatory environment, and the organization's objectives and strategies;
- The development and performance of the business in the last year and in the future;
- The resources, principal risks, uncertainties and relationships that may affect long-term value;
- Description of the capital structure, treasury policies and objectives and liquidity of the business in the last year and in the future.

The OFR should include the objectives of the business, the Board's strategies for achieving those objectives, financial and non-financial performance measures used to monitor progress towards achieving objectives, the main trends that the Board considers as likely to affect future prospects, a description of the principal risks and uncertainties facing the business and the Board's approach to managing those risks. As can be seen from this partial list, the OFR explicitly requires the directors to comment on objectives, risk and risk management in a way completely consistent with the enterprise risk management approach.

Risk disclosure in the United Kingdom

Prior to the OFR guidelines, a study by Solomon et al. (2000) found that little guidance was available in the Combined Code as to what information about risks UK-listed companies should disclose in their annual reports. They suggested a framework for corporate risk disclosure comprising:

- The voluntary or mandatory nature of disclosure.
- Investors' attitudes towards risk disclosure.

- Forms of risk disclosure, that is reported separately or grouped.
- Disclosure preference, that is whether all risks had equal importance.
- Location of disclosure, in the OFR, or elsewhere.
- Level of risk disclosure, whether current levels were adequate or whether increased disclosure would help decision-making.

Solomon et al. surveyed institutional investors during 1999. They found that almost a third of institutional investors agreed that increased risk disclosure would help their portfolio decision-making. They also found that institutional investors saw a strong link between corporate governance reform and risk disclosure. Solomon et al. recommended that the current voluntary ('comply or explain') framework be retained.

Linsley and Shrives (2006) studied risk disclosure in 79 UK company annual reports. They found a significant association between the number of risk disclosures and company size. However, they found no association between risk disclosures and measures of risk using financial ratios. There were few monetary assessments of risk but companies did disclose forward-looking risk information. Linsley and Shrives concluded that the dominance of general statements of risk management policy and a lack of coherence in risk narratives implied that stakeholders would be unable to adequately assess the risk profile of a company from its annual report.

Appendix A in this chapter contains extracts from HMV Group plc Annual Report and Accounts for 2007. HMV's Annual Report reveals that, like most listed companies, increasing attention is now given by companies to risk disclosure. Risk disclosure takes place in the OFR (HMV calls this a 'Business and financial review' which describes the risks it faces), the corporate governance statement (explaining the role of the audit committee and the Board's approach to internal control), and the Directors' report (which discloses details of financial risks and hedging activity, described in Chapter 12). Risk is also mentioned in the external audit report and in the notes to the accounts.

Sarbanes-Oxley Act

For companies listed in the United States, the introduction of the Sarbanes-Oxley Act in 2002 was the legislative response to the financial and accounting scandals of Enron and WorldCom and the misconduct at the accounting firm Arthur Andersen. Its main aim was to deal with core issues of transparency, integrity and oversight of financial markets. Sarbanes-Oxley (or SOX) introduced the requirement to disclose all material off-balance sheet transactions. The Act requires the certification of annual and quarterly financial reports by the chief executive and chief financial officer of all companies with US securities registrations, with criminal penalties for knowingly making false certifications.

SOX, in particular sections 302 and 404, take an approach that is limited to internal control over financial reporting. SOX requires the CEO and CFO to give assurances regarding the effectiveness of internal controls. Section 404 of Sarbanes-Oxley requires companies to state that management has the responsibility for establishing and maintaining an adequate internal control structure and procedures for financial reporting; and to make an assessment of the effectiveness of the internal control structure and procedures for financial reporting.

SOX is reported to have increased both management compliance costs and audit costs in US-listed corporations. In 2006, COSO published *Internal Control over Financial Reporting – Guidance for Smaller Public Companies* (Committee of Sponsoring Organizations of the Treadway Commission (COSO), 2006),[1] which provided 20 basic principles that would help ensure compliance with the Sarbanes-Oxley requirements for internal control over financial reporting. Consistent with COSO's internal control framework, the principles cover the control environment, risk assessment, control activities, information and communication, and monitoring.

The Sarbanes-Oxley legislation focuses more on the role of the audit committee than on the responsibilities of the Board. However, there are no provisions relating to the internal audit function or its role in risk and control. An independent Public Company Accounting Oversight Board has been established in the US with responsibility for setting standards for auditing, quality control and independence. Under SOX, external auditors are required to report on management's assessment. By contrast, in the United Kingdom and most other countries, there is no requirement for auditors to express a view publicly on the effectiveness of a company's internal controls.

The US Securities and Exchange Commission (SEC) has identified the Turnbull guidance contained within the Combined Code on Corporate Governance as a suitable framework for complying with US requirements to report on internal controls over financial reporting, as set out in Section 404 of the Sarbanes-Oxley Act 2002 and related SEC rules.

Disclosure of risk in financial instruments

Although the use of financial derivatives and hedging of foreign currency and interest rate exposure is covered in Chapter 12, a brief coverage of the rules pertaining to financial disclosure is appropriate in this chapter.

---

[1] http://www.coso.org/Publications/erm_sb/SB_EXECUTIVE_SUMMARY.PDF.

The objective of IFRS7: Financial Instruments is to require entities to provide disclosures in their financial statements that enable users to evaluate:

(a) the significance of financial instruments for the entity's financial position and performance; and

(b) the nature and extent of risks arising from financial instruments to which the entity is exposed during the period and at the end of the reporting period, and how the entity manages those risks.

Under IFRS7, disclosures are both quantitative and qualitative. The qualitative disclosures describe management's objectives, policies and processes for managing those risks. The quantitative disclosures provide information about the extent to which the entity is exposed to risk, based on information provided internally to the entity's key management personnel. Together, these disclosures provide an overview of the entity's use of financial instruments and the exposures to risks they create.

IAS 39 Financial Instruments: Recognition and Measurement, requires that all financial assets and financial liabilities, including derivatives, are to be recognized on the Balance Sheet at fair market value. This means that financial instruments such as swaps, which may have been off-balance sheet previously, would have to be recognized. Changes in the fair market values of financial instruments are recognized in the Income Statement for the period. IAS 39 also provides for different treatments in accounting for those derivatives used for hedging, and those derivatives used for trading purposes. For hedge accounting to be used, there must be a highly effective hedging relationship between the derivative instrument and the underlying exposure it is required to offset. However, as the fair values of financial instruments fluctuate from one period to another, this could lead to increased volatility of reported earnings, and hence increased share price volatility as investors incorporate earnings information into share price valuation. The 2007–2008 'subprime' mortgage crisis in the United States and its flow-on effects has called into question the whole notion of fair value reporting because of the volatility in capital markets.

Generally, gains and losses associated with transaction and translation risks appear in the financial statements of a company. However, those associated with economic exposure do not appear in the financial statements, as they are more subjective and hence difficult to measure. Translation risk does not affect the cash flows of the entity, but nevertheless attracts considerable treasury attention. It relates to the situation in which, for the purposes of preparing a balance sheet for publication, overseas assets and liabilities are translated at current rates into the currency of the country in which the entity is domiciled, for example, into sterling for a UK-registered company. If sterling has weakened, overseas assets and liabilities will be translated into higher sterling figures; if sterling has strengthened, then they will be translated into smaller sterling figures.

Role of the audit committee in relation to financial statements

The audit committee should review the significant financial reporting issues and judgments made in connection with the preparation of the company's financial statements, interim reports, preliminary announcements and other related statements. Although it is management's responsibility to prepare financial statements, the audit committee should consider significant accounting policies, any changes to those policies and any significant estimates and judgments. Management should inform the audit committee of the methods used to account for significant or unusual transactions where the accounting treatment is open to different approaches. Taking the advice of the external auditors, the audit committee should consider whether the company has adopted appropriate accounting policies and made appropriate estimates and judgments. The audit committee should review the clarity and completeness of disclosures made in the financial statements.

Although Sarbanes-Oxley legislation privileges risk in relation to financial reporting mis-statements, accounting standards generally, and the Operating and Financial Review in particular place a significant emphasis on disclosure of risk in a company's annual report.

Case study: Royal Dutch/Shell

In January 2004, the Anglo-Dutch company announced that it had removed 3.9 billion barrels of oil and gas from its 'proven' reserves in its balance sheet. This represented one-fifth of the company's proven reserves. The announcement by Shell resulted in a fall in its share price, which reduced its market capitalization by £2.9 billion. In responding to criticism after the announcement, the Chairman said 'The group has made, and is continuing to make, significant enhancements to the internal controls surrounding the booking and reporting of reserves at all levels of the organization' (reported in The Times, 6 February 2004). The announcement led to the forced resignation of the chairman, Sir Philip Watts, and his deputy for exploration and production. The resignations followed an internal report from the group's audit committee to its board. New chairman Jeroen van der Veer was reported as saying 'The reason they went was because the board believed, based on the facts of the audit committee, that a change in the leadership was necessary . . . The work on the reserves recategorization is continuing so I am not going to speculate if there was anything illegal' (reported in The Sunday Times, March 7, 2004).

In August 2004, the Financial Services Authority fined the Royal Dutch/Shell group of companies £17 million for committing market abuse and breaching stock exchange listing rules. The fine was a result of the 'unprecedented misconduct' in relation to misstatements of proven oil and gas reserves, despite indications and warnings between 2000 and 2003 that these reserves were false or misleading.

The US Securities and Exchange Commission (SEC) provides clear guidelines on what constitutes proven reserves: a reasonable certainty that the reserves can be delivered. These rules appeared to have been broken and the SEC launched an investigation. Following the ruling, the US Securities & Exchange Commission fined Shell US\$ 120 million (£65 million). A class-action lawsuit in the US against Shell by investors was settled in 2008 for US\$ 352 million.

Appendix: Extracts from HMV Group plc Annual Report and Accounts 2007

Source: http://www.hmvgroup.com/files/1172/HMV_R_A_2007.pdf

Extracted from HMV's 'Business and financial review' (i.e. the OFR, see earlier in this chapter)

Risks and uncertainties

The Board has a policy of continuous identification and review of key business risks and uncertainties. It oversees the development of processes to ensure that these risks are managed appropriately and operational management are delegated with the tasks of implementing these processes and reporting to the Board on their outcomes. The key risks identified by the Board are as follows:

Competition

The Group operates in extremely competitive markets. In recent years there have been significant changes in retail trends and consumer behaviour. In particular, the growth of Internet retailing and the increase in the range of books, CDs and DVDs offered for sale by supermarkets has, and will require, the Group to adapt and invest in new strategies to remain competitive. Actions taken by competitors as well as the Group to maintain their respective competitiveness have placed pressure on the Group's product pricing, margins and profitability which, in the future, could have an adverse impact on the Group's business and financial condition.

Growth of digital entertainment

Physical entertainment media is a key driver of footfall to the Group's stores and of online customers to its various Internet sites. Technological advances and changing consumer preferences have given rise to new methods of digital delivery, both legal and illegal, of music, film, electronic games and books, thereby reducing the purchase of physical media formats. The Group has responded to these challenges by the launch of its own websites and continued investment to grow these businesses, however further unforeseen technological developments could have a further adverse impact on the Group's future profitability and cash flows.

Seasonality

The business of the Group is highly seasonal with the Christmas season being the most important trading period in terms of sales, profitability and cash flow. Lower than expected performance in this period may have an adverse impact on results for a full financial year.

External factors

Retail markets are sensitive to economic conditions and can also be affected by external factors such as an act of terrorism or war or an outbreak of a pandemic disease, which could reduce the number of customers visiting the Group's stores causing a decline in revenue and profit.

Failure of supply

The Group has agreements with key suppliers and an interruption or loss of supply of core category products from these suppliers would affect the Group's ability to trade.

Damage to reputation or brands

The HMV and Waterstone's brands are material assets of the Group and maintaining their reputation is key to the success of the Group. Failure to protect these brands, an event that materially damaged the reputation of these brands and/or a failure to sustain their appeal to customers could have an adverse impact on the financial performance of the Group.

Information Technology systems

The Group relies on a number of important IT systems, both for its stores and its Internet sites. Any significant system performance problems could affect the Group's ability to trade as well as its profitability.

Key personnel

The performance of the Group depends on its ability to continue to attract, motivate and retain key head office and store staff. The retail sector is very competitive and the Group's people are frequently targeted by other companies for recruitment.

Retail store network

Retaining a portfolio of good quality real estate, in prime retail areas and at commercially reasonable rates remains critical to the performance of the Group. All of the Group's stores are held under operating leases, and consequently the Group is exposed to the extent that any stores become unviable as a result of rental inflation. Where a store location becomes surplus to requirements, the Group's policy of occupying prime, highly marketable locations serves to limit such lease exposure.

Strategic initiatives

On March 13, 2007, the Group communicated the outcome of a strategic and operational review, which included a number of key initiatives necessary to turn around the financial performance of the Group over a three-year period. A failure of one or more of these initiatives could have an adverse impact on the profitability and cash flows of the Group.

Extracted from HMV's Corporate governance statement

Audit Committee

The Audit Committee, as at the end of the financial year, comprised Christopher Rogers (Chairman), Lesley Knox, Roy Brown and Mark McCafferty. Mr Rogers was appointed to the Committee on October 1, 2006 and the other Committee members were all appointed to the Committee on April 23, 2002. The Chairman, Chief Executive Officer, Group Finance Director, the Head of Internal Audit, and the external auditors were invited and attended meetings of the Audit Committee. Christopher Rogers, Chairman of the Committee, is a qualified Chartered Accountant, and Finance Director of Whitbread plc, and thus, has recent relevant financial experience. The Board believes that the other Committee members have relevant experience to serve on this Committee. The Committee is required to meet a minimum of three times a year and members' attendance at the Committee can be found on page 28 (of the Annual Report). Both the Head of Internal Audit and the external auditors have direct access to the Chairman of the Committee outside the formal Committee meetings.

The main duties of the Committee are as follows:

(i) monitoring the integrity of and reviewing the financial statements;
(ii) the appointment of and the review of the effectiveness and independence of the external auditors;
(iii) approval of the scope of the Company's risk management programme and review of the risk management process;
(iv) reviewing the operation and effectiveness of the internal audit function; and
(v) to oversee the establishment and maintenance of good business practices throughout the Group.

During the period under review, the Committee met on three occasions in order to review a wide range of financial matters, including annual and half year profit figures, financial statements, trading statements and other regulatory information disclosed to the public, to conduct a review of the internal audit function and to receive regular reports from internal audit.

Internal control

The Board attaches considerable importance to, and acknowledges its responsibility for, the Group's system of internal control and risk management and carries out regular reviews of their effectiveness. A system of internal control is designed to manage rather than eliminate risk of failure to achieve business objectives and can only provide reasonable and not absolute assurance against material misstatement or loss. The Audit Committee reviews the effectiveness of the risk management process and significant risk issues are referred to the Board for consideration. The Board confirms it has reviewed the Group's system of internal controls including financial, operational and compliance controls as well as risk management, and that these accord with the guidance on internal controls set out in the Internal Control: Revised Guidance for Directors on the Combined Code, issued by the Financial Reporting Council in October 2005, and that such controls have been in place during the year under review and up to the date of approval of the Annual report and Accounts and that there are satisfactory ongoing processes for identifying, evaluating and managing the significant risks faced by the Group. The systems of internal control and the processes used by the Board to review the effectiveness of those systems include:

Group

■ an internal audit function, which carries out a programme of audits covering the management of significant corporate risks and reports directly to the Audit Committee and the Board on the effectiveness of key internal controls;

■ detailed risk registers, which describe the significant risks and control strategies in each area of the business and which are reviewed annually;

■ a comprehensive system of financial reporting, which includes an annual budget process, monthly reporting with rolling forecasts, and half year and annual reporting to enable the Group to meet its public financial reporting requirements;

■ regular performance monitoring, with remedial action taken where necessary;

■ regular Board meetings, with a formal schedule of matters reserved to the Board for decision;

■ established procedures for planning, approving and monitoring major projects;

■ a policies and procedures manual, which sets out, inter alia, authority limits and guidelines for capital expenditure, which include annual budgets and appraisal and review procedures. All operating businesses have to confirm compliance with the manual on an annual basis;

■ certain centralized functions, that are staffed by appropriately qualified individuals who draw on external professional advice. These functions include finance, tax, treasury, management information systems, legal, company secretarial and internal audit; and

■ clearly defined organizational structures and appropriate delegated authorities.

Audit committee

■ approving the scope of the annual Group risk management programme;

■ reviewing the results of the risk identification process;

■ providing input on risks and internal controls into the annual Board strategy discussions;

■ reviewing the effectiveness of the risk management process and discussing significant risk issues with the Board;

■ considering reports from internal and external audit on the system of internal control and any material control weaknesses;

■ reviewing the internal audit and external audit work plans; and

■ at the year end, before producing the Statement of Directors' Responsibilities in the Annual Report and Accounts, the Board, through the Audit Committee, considers reports generated from the internal and external auditors on any major problems that have occurred during the year.

HMV's Annual Report also includes a detailed health and safety report (see Chapter 14).

Extracted from the Directors' report

The Business and Financial Review on pages 12–23 (of the Annual Report, see extract above) contains details of the performance of the Group during the year, likely future developments and the principal risks and uncertainties facing the Group.

Financial instruments

The Group's Treasury Department is principally responsible for managing the Group's funding arrangements and certain financial risks, described below, to which the Group is exposed. Treasury manages these risks using policies approved by the Board.

Liquidity risk

The Group has committed bank facilities currently comprising a multi-currency revolving credit facility of £260 million and a £ 80 million term facility, which together with cash on deposit provides sufficient funding for the Group's operations. The adequacy of the funding arrangements is reviewed regularly. On April 28, 2007, the Group had undrawn committed bank facilities plus cash available to it totalling £163.0 million.

Interest rate risk

With reported net debt of £130.2 million on April 28, 2007, and with the Group being in a net cash position in the third quarter (as was the case in the previous year), the Group currently considers that there is limited interest rate exposure and thus there are no requirements for interest rate hedging. The net exposure will continue to be monitored throughout the year.

Counter party risk

Treasury deposits any cash balances that arise with counter parties that have a strong credit rating, with an agreed limit for each counter party, so as to limit the risk of loss arising from a failure. Counter parties include AAA-rated liquidity funds and various banks.

Foreign exchange risk

The Group uses forward foreign exchange contracts to hedge the foreign exchange risk of imports where volumes are significant. However, the Group's operating businesses generally source the majority of their products from suppliers within their country of operation and so the foreign exchange exposure is small. The Group is also exposed to foreign currency translation risk through its investment in overseas subsidiaries. This is partially hedged by local debt, but the Group does not hedge the remaining exposure. Generally, the Group does not hedge any net translation exposure of overseas earnings, although it may in certain circumstances implement hedges to secure short-term financial objectives.

Extracted from the audit report

We review whether the Corporate Governance Statement reflects the Company's compliance with the nine provisions of the 2006 Combined Code specified for our review by the Listing Rules of the Financial Services Authority, and we report if it does not. We are not required to consider whether the Board's statements on internal control cover all risks and controls, or form an opinion on the effectiveness of the Group's corporate governance procedures or its risk and control procedures.

Extracted from the Note to the accounts

Note 2: Accounting policies

Key sources of estimation uncertainty

The key sources of estimation uncertainty that have a significant risk of causing material adjustment to the carrying amounts of assets and liabilities within the next financial year are the measurement and impairment of goodwill and the measurement of defined benefit pension obligations. The Group determines whether goodwill is impaired on an annual basis and this requires an estimation of the value in use of the cash-generating units to which the goodwill is allocated. This involves estimation of future cash flows and choosing a suitable discount rate. Measurement of defined benefit pension obligations requires estimation of future changes in salaries and inflation, as well as mortality rates, the expected return on assets and the selection of a suitable discount rate.

Note 26: Financial Instruments

Cash flow hedges

The Group uses derivative instruments in order to manage foreign currency exchange risk arising on expected future purchases of internationally sourced products in the Group's subsidiaries. Treasury policies recommend covering up to 6 months in advance on forecast exposures using derivative products comprising of forward foreign currency contracts and currency options, although the Group has not used currency options during the year. In all cases the implementation of these derivative instruments has been negotiated to match expected purchases and they therefore qualify for hedge accounting. The fair value of cash flow hedges in place at April 28, 2007 is £nil (2006: £nil).

References

Committee of Sponsoring Organizations of the Treadway Commission (COSO). 2006. Internal Control over Financial Reporting – Guidance for Smaller Public Companies.

Linsley PM, Shrives PJ. 2006. Risk reporting: A study of risk disclosures in the annual reports of UK companies. *British Accounting Review* 38:387–404.

Solomon JF, Solomon A, Norton SD. 2000. A conceptual framework for corporate risk disclosure emerging from the agenda for corporate governance reform. *British Accounting Review* 32:447–78.

Chapter 11

Risk and Financial Decision-Making

While Chapter 10 was concerned with the disclosure of risk-related information in financial reports to external interested parties (shareholders and other stakeholders), managers use various financial tools and techniques that influence, and are influenced by risk in relation to internal decision-making. Many of these decisions are concerned with strategy, future plans, profitability analysis and the performance evaluation of business units.

In this chapter we consider risk in the use of financial techniques for decision-making: capital investment, budgeting and business unit performance evaluation.

Strategy and capital investment

The difficulty for businesses in the twenty-first century is that they are faced with almost continual risk and uncertainty in economic conditions, technology, competition, and consumer demand. Organizations must continually adapt to technological and market change, making investments that anticipate rather than react to external changes. The absence of strategic capital investments can lead to reactivity and following market and technology trends, always behind the industry leader, which is likely to lead to a steady erosion of market share. Capital investment is an essential component in delivering business strategy and can be crucial in enabling a business to be competitive amidst turbulent business conditions.

However, the formulation of strategy in many organizations can be divorced from the capital investment decision-making and the annual budgeting cycles, as organizations focus on meeting short-term financial targets. Consequently, the issue of translating strategy formulation into implementation is problematic unless resource allocations for new and replacement capital investment follows strategy.

One of the most important elements of strategy implementation is capital investment decision-making, because investment decisions provide the physical infrastructure (buildings, production plant and office equipment, computer systems, etc.) through which organizations produce and sell goods and services. Even for public and third sector organizations, the issue is the same, even though their products and services may not be sold.

Investment appraisal

Capital investment or capital expenditure (often abbreviated as 'cap ex') means spending money now in the hope of getting it back later through future cash flows. The process of evaluating or appraising potential investments is to:

- generate ideas based on identifying opportunities or solutions to problems;
- research all relevant information;
- consider possible alternatives, including the 'do nothing' option;
- evaluate the financial consequences of each alternative;
- assess non-financial aspects of each alternative;
- obtain approval;
- prepare an implementation plan and implement the proposal;
- control implementation by monitoring actual results compared to plan.

There are three main types of investment:

- new facilities for new product/services;
- expanding capacity to meet demand;
- replacing assets in order to reduce production costs or improve quality or service.

These are inextricably linked to the implementation of business strategy. Most investment appraisals consider decisions such as:

- whether or not to invest;
- whether to invest in one project or one piece of equipment rather than another;
- whether to invest now or at a later time.

In capital investment decisions, enterprise risk management recognizes the risk of not achieving strategic goals through failing to invest, or inappropriate investment decisions, the risk of not understanding market needs sufficiently well, the risk of not properly evaluating alternatives, for example through bias in decision-making, the risk of poor predictions of financial and non-financial consequences of the decision, and poor implementation. While there is always a risk of making the wrong decision, there is also a risk of doing nothing and being left behind, technologically or in the marketplace.

There are three main methods of evaluating investments:

- Return on investment (ROI).

■ Payback.

■ Discounted cash flow (DCF).

A detailed understanding of each is beyond the scope of this book, but while the first is concerned with profits, the second and third are concerned with cash flows from an investment. For any project, investment appraisal requires an estimation of future incremental cash flows, that is the additional cash flow (net of income less expenses) that will result from the investment, as well as the cash outflow for the initial investment and any additional working capital requirements. The return on investment method is a simple calculation of the accounting profit divided by the investment value. However, cash flow is usually considered to be more important than accounting profit in investment appraisal because it is cash flow that drives shareholder value. The payback method calculates the number of years the organization will take to recoup its investment through future cash flows. In the discounted cash flow method, the time value of money is taken into account by discounting future cash flows by a risk-adjusted cost of capital from which is deducted the investment value to determine whether the project is viable (i.e. where the present value of future cash flows exceeds the original investment).

The risks inherent in any of these methods are the difficulty of predicting future cash flows and ascertaining the risk-adjusted cost of capital. The cost of capital is the cost of equity and debt funds to the organization, a result of weighting interest rates on borrowings and dividend and expected share price changes on equity, and adjusting the weighted average cost of capital to provide an additional margin requirement for investments which have a higher risk.

Budgeting

Anthony and Govindarajan (2001) described budgets as an important tool for effective short-term planning and control. They saw strategic planning as focused on several years ahead, while budgeting focused on a shorter time frame, typically only a single year. Strategic planning therefore precedes budgeting and provides the framework within which the annual budget is developed. A budget is a 1-year slice of the organization's strategic plan. Anthony and Govindarajan also differentiated the strategic plan from the budget, on the basis that strategy was concerned with products and services while budgets were more concerned with allocating resources to business units and holding business unit managers accountable for their performance.

A budget is a plan expressed in monetary terms covering a future time period (typically a year broken down into months). Budgets are based on a defined level of activity, either expected sales revenue (if market demand is the limiting factor) or capacity (if that is the limiting factor). Budgets may be rolling, that is additional months are added each month to the budget so that there is always a 12-month forward forecast for the organizations. Budgets can also be re-forecast part way through a year, for example quarterly or six-monthly, to take into account changes since the last budget cycle, resulting in a common distinction made by organizations between budget and forecast.

The purposes of budgeting are to:

■ implement strategy by allocating resources in line with strategic goals;
■ co-ordinate activities and assist in communication between different parts of the organisation;
■ motivate managers to achieve targets;
■ provide a means to control activities; and
■ evaluate managerial performance.

There are several methods of budgeting. Incremental budgets are the most common as they do not question earlier historical (or political) resource allocations. They take the previous year's budget as a base and add (or subtract) a percentage to give the next year's budget. Priority-based budgets are more common in government and the third sector where resources are allocated in line with strategic priorities, for example to deliver a particular service through a programme in a particular area. Zero-based budgeting identifies the costs that are necessary to implement agreed strategies and achieve goals, as if the organization had no prior history. This method has the advantage of regularly reviewing all the activities that are carried out to see if they are still required, but has the disadvantage of the cost and time needed for such reviews. It is also very difficult to develop a budget which ignores current resource allocations.

Whichever method of budgeting is used, there are two approaches that can be applied. Budgets may be top–down or bottom–up. Top–down budgets can ignore the problems experienced by operational managers, who will have a better appreciation of capacity limitations and market demand. However, operational managers may not appreciate the considerable pressure Boards face to achieve the level of performance expected by the stock market. The aggregation of a bottom–up budget may be inadequate in terms of growth or 'bottom-line' profitability. Consequently, most budgets are the result of a combination of top–down and bottom–up processes. By adopting both methods, budget-holders are given the opportunity to bid for resources (in competition with other budget-holders) within the constraints of the shareholder value focus of the business.

A typical budget cycle will have the following sequence:

1. Identify objectives.
2. Forecast economic and industry conditions, including competition.
3. Develop detailed sales budgets by market sectors, geographic territories, major customers and product groups.
4. Prepare production or purchasing budgets to satisfy the sales forecast and maintain agreed levels of inventory.
5. Prepare non-production expense budgets.
6. Prepare capital expenditure budgets.
7. Prepare cash forecasts and identify financing requirements.
8. Obtain board approval of profitability and financing targets.

Modelling budgets and forecasts

Within the budget cycle there will be many disparate views about economic and industry conditions, competitor strength, customer retention, pricing and volume combinations, capacity levels and likely future performance, as well as the effect of targets on motivation. This will be a consequence of individual risk perceptions and risk appetites, not just that determined at the enterprise level. How well these factors can be understood and modelled using a spreadsheet will depend on the knowledge, skills and time available to the business. Typically, budgets either at the corporate or business unit level will contain a number of subjective judgements of likely future events and a number of simplifying assumptions about product/service mix, average prices, cost inflation, etc.

Assigning probabilities to different scenarios (e.g. different levels of sales) or sensitivity analysis can be used to see the effect of alternative forecasts, from the optimistic to the pessimistic. Table 11.1 shows the effect of assigning probabilities to different scenarios. Table 11.2 shows the effect of sensitivity analysis.

The application of probabilities in Table 11.1 results in an average budgeted profit, even though the probability-weighted sales and profit forecast do not tie in with any of the optimistic, most likely or pessimistic forecasts.

The application of scenario analysis in Table 11.2 shows the effect of any of the optimistic, most likely or pessimistic forecasts being achieved. This provides more decision-useful information than probability weightings. Only the optimistic forecast will generate a profit. Consequently, an enterprise risk management approach is likely to proactively put in place strategies and controls that will ensure the achievement of the optimistic scenario. By contrast, the probabilistic method may lead to a more reactive approach that is accepting of the weighted average forecast profit.

Table 11.1   Effect of probabilities

Budget	Optimistic ($)	Most likely ($)	Pessimistic ($)	Probability–weighted ($)
Sales forecast	1 200 000	1 000 000	900 000	
Probability	35%	50%	15%	
	420 000	500 000	135 000	1 055 000
Gross margin (25%)				263 750
Overhead expenses				250 000
Operating profit				1 3750

Table 11.2   Effect of sensitivity analysis

Budget	Optimistic ($)	Most likely ($)	Pessimistic ($)
Sales forecast	1 200 000	1 000 000	900 000
Gross margin (25%)	300 000	250 000	225 000
Overhead expenses	250 000	250 000	250 000
Operating profit	50 000	0	−25 000

Collier and Berry (2002) studied the budgeting process in four organizations. They categorized budgets as Risk Modelled, Risk Considered or Risk Excluded. Collier and Berry found no evidence of risk modelling through input–output or cause–effect relationships and there was no evidence of the use of sensitivity analysis or probabilities. Rather, while the process of budgeting was found to be risk considered in which a top–down budgeting process reflected negotiated targets, the content of budget documents was Risk Excluded, being based on a set of single point estimates, in which all of the significant risks were excluded from the budget itself.

Collier and Berry found that the separation of budgeting and risk management had significant consequences for the management of risks as the process of budgeting was separate from the content of budget documents. This has implications for risk management in the achievement of strategic objectives.

Budgets, capital investment and risk

As for capital expenditure decisions, the enterprise risk management approach will recognize both the power and limitation of budgets. Budgets are often the most highly visible method of internal control used by organizations, continually monitoring whether sales, costs, profitability and cash flow targets are being achieved.

As for capital investment decisions, there are many risks in budgeting, even for the short-term period of a single year. Errors can be made in understanding the cause–effect relationships behind past performance; understanding market trends, seasonal factors, and current competitor activity; understanding the drivers of business costs and the ability of managers to exercise cost control. There have been many studies that reveal the bias in budgets and the problems of aggregating bottom–up budgets into corporate-level ones (Berry & Otley, 1975; Lowe & Shaw, 1968; Otley & Berry, 1979).

Compared with the traditional budgetary control model, the 'Beyond Budgeting' movement (Hope & Fraser, 2003) has two fundamental differences. First, it is a more adaptive way of managing. In place of fixed annual plans and budgets that tie managers to predetermined actions, targets are reviewed regularly and are based on relative performance improvement compared with world-class benchmarks and prior periods. Second, the 'beyond budgeting' model enables a more decentralized way of managing. In place of the traditional hierarchy and centralized leadership that lie behind traditional budgeting, 'beyond budgeting' proponents argue that it enables decision-making and performance accountability to be devolved to line managers and a culture of personal responsibility.

There are 12 principles (six for processes and six for leadership) that govern the Beyond Budgeting Model.[1] The first six principles relate to managing with adaptive processes. The model has similarities to the strategy-focused approach of Kaplan and Norton (see Chapter 6) in that it is based on goals, rewards, continuous planning, controls that are based on performance measurement, resource allocations that are consistent with plans, and co-ordination. The principles explicitly remove fixed targets, the annual budgeting process and any comparison of actual performance against plans.

The six principles of devolved leadership focus on the transfer of power from a remote Head Office to operating managers and their teams, giving them the authority to use their judgment and initiative to achieve results without being constrained by a predetermined plan or agreement. Beyond Budgeting implicitly takes a risk-based approach whereby the inability to predict unpredictable events in the annual budget cycle is seen as removing any value in that process. It is replaced by a more flexible and dynamic approach. There are risks in such an approach, not least being the reputational effect that would follow publicity that an organization had abandoned its annual budgeting cycle (although an interesting case study of the abandonment of budgeting by Svenska Handelsbanken is contained in Wallander (1999).

---

[1] See the beyond budgeting website at http://www.bbrt.org/bbprinc.htm.

Performance evaluation of business segments

While capital investment and budgeting are forward-looking processes, a further aspect of strategy implementation is improving and maintaining the performance of different segments within the business. The analysis of performance and profitability can be considered in relation to:

- products or services,
- customers, and
- business units.

While profit reports for products/services are sometimes produced (and then typically only at the level of sales less variable costs), traditional financial reporting within organizations usually centres on business unit managers and is used for evaluating the performance of those managers.

Product or service profitability is important in order to determine which products or services should be expanded and which contracted or abandoned. This is especially important where products/services are sold in different market segments at different prices, or where some products are high volume and others are low volume, but are produced using the same facilities. Similarly, understanding customer profitability is important as some customers drive such demands that cause cost to be incurred, that their lack of profitability needs to be addressed through pricing or abandonment decisions (a good example here is the distinction made by banks between the profitability of business and personal branch-based banking).

While organizations can usually relate variable costs to sales revenue, the accounting problem of allocating overhead costs (which over several decades have been increasing in proportion to total costs in capital-intensive and knowledge-based industries) involves often arbitrary methods to allocate common costs over products/services/customers which can result in problematic judgments about product/service/customer profitability. Judgments about profitability are fraught with risk because poor accounting judgments can lead to inappropriate short-term and even strategic decisions to abandon product/services, markets, or customers.

The decentralization of businesses has reduced the power of the head office with its functional structure (marketing, operations, distribution, finance, etc.). Instead, many support functions are now devolved to business units, which may be called subsidiaries (if they are legally distinct entities), divisions, departments etc. For simplicity, we will use the term divisionalization although the principle applies to any business unit structure.

Divisionalization allows managers to have autonomy over local aspects of their business unit, but those managers are then accountable for the performance of those business units to head office. Divisionalized business unit managers may be responsible for costs (cost centres), 'bottom line' profit (profit centres), or profit and investment (investment centres). Whichever form is taken, it is called a responsibility centre.

Divisionalization makes it easier for an organization to diversify, while retaining overall strategic direction and control. Divisionalization can take place functionally (departments responsible for marketing, production, distribution, finance, etc.) or by products or geographic areas. Performance improvement is encouraged by assigning managerial responsibility for divisional performance, typically linked to executive remuneration (bonuses, profit-sharing, share options, etc.).

Solomons (1965) highlighted three purposes for financial reporting at a divisional level:

1. To guide divisional managers in making decisions.
2. To guide top management in making decisions.
3. To enable top management to appraise the performance of divisional management.

However, the risks involved in divisionalization can be significant. Business unit managers have autonomy and can act contrary to the interests of the enterprise. This is an agency problem that requires the implementation of sufficient controls and incentives to ensure that business unit managers pursue corporate strategy. Managers must comply with corporate policies and achieve financial and non-financial targets, not just in the short-term budget period but also in the long-term. This can only be done by safeguarding the organization's physical, human and knowledge resources, and its reputation, market share, quality, etc. which may be inconsistent with the pressure for short-term profits. Enterprise risk management relies heavily on individual business unit managers to manage risks within their sphere of responsibility and to report the relevant risks upwards to the corporate level. Enterprise-wide risk management requires that controls be put in place to ensure that business unit managers are acting in the best interests of the enterprise and that risk management is being carried out effectively by each business unit and that significant risks are being communicated upwards. There will therefore be considerable reliance by the Board on controls and the internal audit function in relation to business units.

Solomons (1965) identified the difficulties involved in measuring managerial performance. Absolute profit is not a good measure because it does not consider the investment in the business and how long-term profits can be affected by short-term decisions such as reducing research, maintenance and advertising expenditure. These decisions will improve reported profits in the current year, but will usually have a detrimental long-term impact, which creates a significant risk to the organization. The individual manager, who may well have moved on to another business unit or organization will not have to bear the consequences of those past decisions.

The performance of divisions and their managers can be evaluated using two methods: return on investment or residual income. Return on investment (ROI) is the profit achieved on the capital employed. However, a problem with this approach is whether a high rate of return on a small capital investment is better or worse than a lower return on a larger capital. For example:

	Division A	Division B
Capital invested	£ 5 000 000	£ 10 000 000
Operating profit	£ 1 000 000	£ 1 500 000
Return on investment	20%	15%

Division B makes a higher profit in absolute terms but a lower return on the capital invested in the business.

However, Solomons (1965) also argued that a decision cannot be made about relative performance unless we know the cost of capital. The residual income (RI) approach calculates the profit remaining after deducting the notional risk-adjusted cost of capital from the investment in the division. The RI approach is similar to the Economic Value Added (EVA^{TM}) approach developed by consultant Stern Stewart to assess shareholder value in the stock market. Using the same example:

	Division A	Division B
Capital invested	£ 5 000 000	£10 000 000
Operating profit	£ 1 000 000	£1 500 000
Less cost of capital at 15%	£ 750 000	£1 500 000
Residual income	£ 250 000	Nil

As the cost of capital is 15% in the above example, Division A makes a satisfactory return but Division B makes no return at all. Division B is not contributing to shareholder value while Division A is creating it. The aim of managers should be to maximize the residual income from the capital investments in their divisions. However, Solomons (1965) emphasizes that the RI approach assumes that managers have the power to influence the amount of capital investment, something which is often not the case.

As we saw for capital investment decisions and the use of the discounted cash flow technique, determining a risk-adjusted cost of capital is not straightforward and can be very subjective, especially where different decisions are considered to be more or less risky than others. And as we have seen in terms of profitability decisions, cost allocations by accountants can distort judgements about business unit as well as product and customer profitability. Equally difficult is where a capital investment is shared by more than one business unit.

An additional complication is the transfer price in many organizations where divisions buy and sell from other divisions in the same organization. Often, the transfer price is arrived at through political negotiation rather than an equitable sharing of costs and revenues and this can lead to decisions which may be in the interests of one division but not in the best interests of the organization as a whole. A central risk for business unit managers is therefore the extent to which what they are held accountable for is actually controllable by them or whether it is more influenced by corporate decisions over which managers have little or no control. Enterprise risk management needs to consider the effect of judgments about (and incentives for) business unit performance on the whole organization as well as on each business unit.

Financial techniques are usually a critical part of making decisions, whether an organization is concerned with capital investment, the annual budget or the evaluation of business unit performance. While these tools are valuable, care must be taken in recognizing the risks and limitations inherent in these techniques. In particular they involve subjective estimates and assumptions that prevent the financial results of their application not being accepted at face value.

References

Anthony RN, Govindarajan V. 2001. Management Control Systems. Boston, Mass: McGraw Hill-Irwin.

Berry AJ, Otley DT. 1975. The aggregation of estimates in hierarchical organizations. *Journal of Management Studies* May:175–93.

Collier PM, Berry AJ. 2002. Risk in the process of budgeting. *Management Accounting Research* 13:273–97.

Hope J, Fraser R. 2003. *Beyond Budgeting: How Managers can Break Free from the Annual Performance Trap*. Boston, MA: Harvard Business School Press.

Lowe EA, Shaw RW. 1968 October. An Analysis of Managerial Biasing: Evidence from a Company's Budgeting Process. *Journal of Management Studies* :304–15.

Otley D, Berry A. 1979. Risk distribution in the budgetary process. *Accounting and Business Research* 9:325–7.

Solomons D. 1965. *Divisional Performance: Measurement and Control*. Homewood, IL: Richard D. Irwin.

Wallander J. 1999. Budgeting – an unnecessary evil. *Scandinavian Journal of Management* 15:405–21.

Chapter 12

The Management of Financial Risk

The financial environment in which companies operate has undergone substantial change in recent times, including increased globalization and changes in the regulatory environment of financial and capital markets. The ability of companies to successfully raise funds in global capital markets, and thus expand their worldwide operations has also brought increased uncertainty. Not only do companies have to be alert to their international competitors' strategies, and technological, market and management innovations, but they also have to think about the risks associated with currency volatility, interest-rate changes and the legal, political, social and economic climate in countries where they do business. Therefore, risk management has become an area of increasing importance in financial management.

Financial risk

Companies are exposed to various types of risks in the course of their business operations that affect their profitability, cash flows and/or cost of capital. These risks can be classified as:

- Firm-specific risks: these risks are specific to the particular activities of the company such as fire, legal action and fraud. These risks can often be managed through internal controls and insurance contracts.
- Market-wide risks: these risks are associated with the economic environment in which all companies operate, where changes in interest rates, currency exchange rates and commodity prices affect all companies. These risks cannot be managed effectively through internal controls and are in the main managed using derivative contracts.

Financial risk management is largely a process of changing the methods of financing within a company, largely to address market-wide risks. Most companies are actively managing their exposures to the risk of changes in commodity prices, interest rates and currency movements in line with their objectives, risk exposure, and risk appetite.

Risk management of financial risk

As for other risk management approaches, financial risk management involves identifying the type of risks the company is exposed to in the course of its business. For example, changes in the price of oil will be of concern to an airline; a manufacturer who sources raw materials from, or sells into other countries will be concerned about changes in currency exchange rates relative to its home currency; and companies with high levels of debt will be concerned about increasing interest rates.

Quantification of risk exposure is important to understand the extent and significance of that exposure. This can be done by measuring the impact of the risk factor on the value of the company or on income, costs, cash flow, or cost of capital. Several different techniques can be employed including regression analysis, simulation analysis and Value at Risk.

Once its financial risks have been identified and quantified, the company then has to decide whether to hedge each of the significant exposures, that is to transfer the risk elsewhere. The decision to hedge needs to be made within the context of the company's objectives, its risk exposure and risk appetite, and its perception of changes in commodity prices, currency rates and interest rate movements. Therefore, the company's strategies for managing the exposures may include one or more of the following:

- Accept the risk and doing nothing. There is a trade-off between risk and return, but this will depend on the risk exposure and the company's risk appetite.
- Manage the risk using internal (operating) hedging techniques. As many exposures offset each other, internal hedging strategies can be used (explained later in this chapter).
- Manage the risk using external (derivative) hedging techniques. There are a wide range of derivative products that can be used to manage or reduce risk exposure (explained later in this chapter).

Once a decision has been made to manage the exposure, there needs to be proper monitoring and reporting to ensure that the risk is being managed in line with the company's risk management strategy.

The Treasury function

The Treasury department or the corporate treasurer has responsibility for managing financial risk. Treasury is concerned with the relationship between the business and its financial stakeholders, which include shareholders, lenders and taxation authorities.

A separate treasury function is more likely to develop the appropriate skills, and enable economies of scale, for example in reducing interest rates on borrowings. The main functions of the treasurer are:

- Banking: managing relationships with banks.
- Liquidity management: working capital and cash management. The treasurer will need to ensure that the business has the liquid funds it needs, and invests any surplus funds.
- Funding management: identifying suitable sources of funds, the cost of those funds, the extent and type of security required, and management of interest-rate risks.
- Currency management: providing the business with forecasts of exchange rate movements, which in turn will determine the procedures adopted to manage exchange rate risks. This function also covers any dealing in the foreign exchange markets.

The authority and responsibility associated with the treasury function must be carefully defined and monitored by the Board. This becomes even more important as the range of derivative instruments increases. The board and senior managers need to be aware of which risks are being carried by the business, which are being mitigated through hedging, etc. Companies are required to disclose in their annual reports information about their treasury policies, and their use of derivatives and other financial instruments (see Chapter 10).

The treasurer needs to examine the various products and select the most cost-effective product that is appropriate for the company's exposure and risk preference.

Derivatives

A derivative is an asset whose performance is based on the behaviour of an underlying asset (commonly called underlyings, for example shares, bonds, commodities, currencies, exchange rates). Derivative instruments include options, forward contracts, futures, forward rate agreements and swaps.

The common reasons for using derivatives are to hedge risks, to speculate or to lock in an arbitrage profit. The Board of an organization will need to determine their objectives and risk appetite in deciding how the use of derivatives would meet their needs. From an enterprise risk management perspective, there are many opportunities to make gains through the use of derivatives but also the risk of substantial losses. Derivatives provide a form of insurance against changes in commodity prices, exchange rates and interest rates that would otherwise affect business profitability.

However, Boards also need to ensure that any exposure is within their tolerance for risk and that losses sustained will not materially affect the core business.

■ *Hedging* involves the reduction or elimination of financial risk by passing that risk on to someone else. The person that takes on the risk acts as a speculator, and in the financial markets it is the trader or dealer in a financial institution who is the other party to the hedging activity. The corporate treasurer will normally be involved only in hedging activities and will not be a speculator or an arbitrageur.

■ *Speculation* occurs where a view is taken of likely market movements and the speculator hopes to make a profit by pre-judging the direction in which currency will move. A classic example of this would be buying a foreign currency and hoping that the currency will appreciate. The speculator takes on risk by buying the currency because he or she does not know whether the currency will appreciate or depreciate.

■ *Arbitrage* is the simultaneous purchase and sale of a security in different markets with the aim of making a risk-free profit through the exploitation of any price difference between the markets.

In relation to risk management, a business that hedges avoids or reduces risk by passing it on to others; a speculator looks for and takes on risks; and an arbitrageur is risk-neutral. This chapter is concerned with hedging as a method for the mitigation of risk.

Hedging

A hedge is a transaction to reduce or eliminate an exposure to risk. Hedging protects assets against unfavourable movements in the 'underlying' while retaining the ability to benefit from favourable movements. The financial instruments bought as a hedge tend to have opposite-value movements to the underlying and are used to transfer risk. There are potential benefits from corporate hedging. It can reduce the variability of the company's cash flows and therefore the probability that the company will encounter financial distress. If hedging reduces the probability of financial distress, it would also likely increase the company's debt capacity and lower the cost of borrowing. This may in turn lead to the acceptance of capital investment projects that may have been otherwise rejected and the availability of funds to take on the investment. Risk-averse managers will also prefer to hedge to protect their jobs.

However, there are also arguments against hedging. If shareholders hedge their investment risk by holding a diversified portfolio, then further hedging by the company may harm rather than enhance shareholders' interests. The costs associated with derivative products such as brokerage fees and commissions may discourage managers from actively managing their exposures. Senior management may lack the necessary expertise to monitor and evaluate the cost and benefits of the range of hedging methods and instruments available (a problem faced by financial institutions like Barings and Société Générale, described elsewhere in this book). The complexities associated with the tax and accounting consequences of derivative transactions may also discourage some companies from using these instruments.

Interest rate risk

Interest rate risk is a problem faced by all companies with borrowings. Given the volatility of interest rates, an awareness of the risks of interest rate movements is important. Interest rate risk can be defined as the risk to the profitability or value of a company resulting from changes in interest rates. Fluctuations in interest rates may affect different companies in different ways but almost every company is affected by changes in interest rates.

A company that borrows or invests surplus funds does so at either a fixed rate of interest or at a floating (variable) rate. Fixed rates provide certainty as interest payments or receipts are known regardless of future interest-rate movements. However, there are also risks associated with fixed-rate debts. For long-term debts the company risks being locked in to a high interest rate if interest rates fall during the life of the loan. A floating-rate borrowing (or investment) varies through the life of the loan (or investment). Floating rates are usually expressed as a margin over an agreed reference rate and are reset at regular intervals. For example, a floating interest rate may be quoted as LIBOR (the London Interbank Offer Rate) +3%. Changes in short-term interest rates can have a significant impact on the interest paid on a floating rate debt. While rising interest rates increase the cost of borrowing, falling interest rates reduce interest income from the investment. Thus, although a floating-rate debt provides some flexibility, the company may lose out if interest rates rise.

Companies face interest-rate risks from the interest-rate sensitivity of their debts and/or their investments. However, for non-financial services companies, the risks from interest-rate sensitivity of their debts would usually outweigh the risks from their investments. The impact of interest rates on the business will depend on the choice of funding: the mix between capital and debt; the mix between fixed and floating rate debt; and the mix between short-term and long-term debt.

There are a number of factors that need to be considered when deciding whether to use fixed-rate or floating-rate instruments:

- The expectation of future interest-rate movements. If interest rates were expected to fall, a floating rate would be more attractive to a borrower.

- The term of the loan or investment. Interest-rate changes would be easier to predict in the short-term than in the long-term.
- Differences between the fixed rate and the floating rate.
- The company's goals, risk management strategy and risk appetite.
- Current levels of debt and the current interest-rate exposure. A mix of fixed- and floating-rate instruments ensures diversification of interest rate exposure and acts as a natural hedge.

Internal hedging

Operating or internal hedging strategies for managing interest-rate risk involve restructuring the company's assets and liabilities in a way that minimizes interest-rate exposure. These methods include:

- Smoothing: The company tries to maintain a balance between its fixed-rate and floating-rate borrowing. The portfolio of fixed- and floating-rate debts thus provides a natural hedge against changes in interest rates.
- Matching: The company matches its assets and liabilities to have a common interest rate. If a company borrows to finance an investment and receives a floating interest rate from that investment, the loan should also be taken at a floating interest rate.
- Netting: The company aggregates all positions, both assets and liabilities to determine the net exposure. If a company has interest bearing investments of, say, £50 million and a loan of, say, £100 million, then the company would only hedge the net exposure of £50 million as the interest-rate risk on the investment would offset the risk on the loan.

External hedging

Four types of hedging for interest rates are considered here: interest rate swaps, forward rate agreements, futures, and options.

Interest rate swaps

An interest rate swap is the exchange of one stream of interest payments for another in the same currency. They could be used, for example to change future cash flows by converting floating-rate interest payments into fixed-rate interest payments and vice versa; or to enhance returns by taking a position on interest rates in the market.

Note that the motivation in the latter case is purely speculative and could therefore increase instead of reduce risk. The relative advantages of interest-rate swaps are that as an over-the-counter product, they can be customised to meet the company's needs in terms of amount and duration.

Forward rate agreements

A forward-rate agreement (FRA) is an agreement whereby a company can lock in an interest rate today for a period of time starting in the future. On the future date the two parties (the buyer and the seller) in the FRA settle and, depending on interest rate movements, one will pay an amount of money to the other representing the difference between the FRA rate and the actual rate. The buyer of the FRA pays fixed and receives floating rates, while the seller pays floating to receive fixed rates. A company will buy FRAs to hedge against rising interest rates (where it is a net borrower) and sell FRAs to hedge against falling interest rates (where it is a net investor).

Interest rate futures

Futures are standardized forms of FRAs. They are normally transacted with banks and other financial institutions, and are tailor-made to suit the dates and amounts that each individual company requires. However, interest-rate futures are traded on the stock exchange (not over-the-counter) and each contract is for a pre-specified amount and a pre-specified date. Interest rate futures may be short-term interest rate futures (shorts); or long-term interest rate futures (bond futures).

The underlying item for short-term interest-rate futures is a notional money market deposit (typically a 3-month deposit) or a standard quantity of money market instruments (e.g. $1 m of 90-day US Treasury bills). The underlying item for long-term interest-rate futures is a standard quantity of notional government bonds (e.g. £50 000 nominal value of notional 9% UK government bonds). The price of interest-rate futures increases if interest rates fall and the price falls if interest rates rise. As a result, short-term interest-rate futures can be used to lock in to an interest rate for short-term borrowing by selling futures. Companies expecting to invest or lend can lock in a short-term rate by buying futures.

Interest-rate options

An option is the right, but not the obligation, to carry out a transaction at some time in the future at a price set today. Swaps, FRAs and futures are all contracts which two parties agree to transact and which must be carried out even if circumstances change. An option, however, gives the buyer the choice of whether to transact or not. A company would generally buy an option from an option seller. An option is a form of insurance, and as such a premium is paid at the time the option is taken out, for the period of the option.

Foreign exchange rate risk

Exchange rates tell us how many units of one currency may be bought or sold for one unit of another currency. The spot rate is the exchange price for transactions for immediate delivery. The forward rate applies to a deal which is agreed upon now but where the actual exchange of currency is not due to take place until some future date. The exchange of currencies at the future date will be at the rate agreed upon now. Currency volatility is a major risk faced by companies doing business outside their home countries. There are a number of factors that influence a currency's exchange rate:

- Speculation. Speculators enter into foreign exchange transactions not because they have a need for the currency but with a view to profit from their expectations of the currency's future movements. If speculators expect a currency to devalue, they will short sell the currency with the hope of buying it back cheaply in the future.
- Balance of payments. The net effect of importing and exporting will result in a demand for or a supply of the country's currency.
- Government policy. Governments from time to time may wish to change the value of their currency. This can be achieved directly by devaluation, revaluation or through the use of foreign exchange markets.
- Interest-rate differentials. A higher rate of interest can create a demand for a particular currency. Investors will buy that currency in order to hold financial securities in the currency with the higher interest rate.
- Inflation rate differentials. Where countries have different inflation rates the value of one country's currency is falling in real terms in comparison with the other. This will result in a change in the exchange rate.

Exchange rate risk occurs as a result of either transaction risk or economic risk. Transaction risk occurs from the effect of changes in nominal exchange rates that affect a company's contractual cash flows in foreign currencies. It relates to contracts already entered into but which have yet to be settled. Thus, a company is subject to transaction risk whenever it imports goods from or export goods to another country which are paid at a later date, or where a company borrows or invests in a foreign currency or uses derivatives denominated in a foreign currency.

Economic risk refers to the degree to which the value of the firm's future cash flows can be influenced by exchange rate fluctuations. These are essentially the risks which affect a business before a transaction actually takes place, and are not therefore measurable. Even companies that trade only in their home country may be subject to economic risk if they face foreign competition within their local markets. Companies can lose competitiveness if their home currency appreciates against its major competitors. Economic risk involves the effect of exchange rate changes on expected future cash flows from the company's operations. It is sometimes referred to as competitive risk and it is an important risk, from the long-term perspective of the company.

Hedging exchange rate risk

Companies exposed to transaction risk can either accept the risk of exchange rate movements or they can take steps to protect their future cash flows from exchange rate fluctuation. If they have sold goods in other countries and are prepared to accept the risk of currency fluctuation they could, in addition to the profit on the sale of the goods, make a currency gain. This would happen if the rate of exchange had moved in their favour between the time that they delivered the goods and the time when they are paid. However, it could be that the rate of exchange moves the other way, giving them a currency loss, and the payment they receive when converted into their own currency may not cover their costs. It is to avoid this possibility that many companies seek to avoid the risks of currency movements by hedging. As for interest rate risk, hedging can take place internally or externally.

Internal hedging techniques

Internal hedging means using techniques available within the company or group to manage exchange-rate risks. These techniques do not operate through the foreign exchange markets and therefore avoid the associated costs. Internal hedging techniques include:

- Invoicing in the home currency: the company invoices in its own currency. The exchange rate risk is not avoided, but is transferred to the customer.

■ Bilateral and multilateral netting: a form of matching appropriate for multinational groups or companies with subsidiaries or branches in a number of overseas countries. Bilateral netting applies where pairs of companies in the same group net off their own positions regarding payables and receivables. Multilateral netting is performed by a central treasury department where several subsidiaries are involved and netting is carried out centrally. The process is based on determining a base currency, for example sterling or US dollars, so that the intra-group transactions are recorded only in that currency. Each company in the group reports its obligations to other group companies to a central treasury department, which then informs each subsidiary of the net receipt or payment needed to settle their foreign exchange intra-group positions.

■ Leading and lagging: changing the timing of payments in an attempt to take advantage of changes in the relative value of the currencies involved. Leading could, for example, be a requirement for immediate or short-term payment where the payee's currency, representing the basis for settlement, is weakening against the payer's currency. Lagging on the other hand, is an arrangement whereby the payee grants long-term credit or defers payment to another party in anticipation of exchange rate changes. This procedure is used mainly for settlement of intra-company balances, but it can also be used externally, for example, between two companies in different countries which carry on extensive trade with each other.

■ Matching: the use of receipts in a particular currency to match payment obligations in the same currency.

External hedging techniques

External techniques use financial markets to hedge foreign currency movements. These include the use of forwards, futures, options and swaps on currencies.

Forward markets

A forward contract is one in which one party agrees to buy 'something', and another party agrees to sell that same 'something' at a designated date in the future. In the case of a forward exchange contract, one party agrees to deliver a specified amount of one currency for another at a specified exchange rate at a designated date in the future. The specified exchange rate is called the forward rate. When an investor takes a position in the market by buying a forward contract, the investor is said to be in a long position. If the investor's opening position is the sale of a forward contract, the investor is said to be in a short position.

Futures

A company would sell currency futures to hedge receivables in a foreign currency, and buy currency futures to hedge foreign currency payments, assuming that the foreign currency is the underlying currency of the futures.

Currency swaps

A currency swap is the regular exchange of interest or cash flows in one currency for that of another currency. Unlike an interest rate swap, there is an exchange of principal at the beginning and at the end of the swap contract. Currency swaps are useful for medium-to-long-term hedging as futures, forward contracts and currency options are generally only suitable for hedging up to 1-year ahead.

In the context of global capital markets and global trade, managing financial risk for interest rates and currency exchange rates (as well as other underlyings) is an important part of enterprise risk management, as the risk of losses unconnected with trading can severely affect profitability and shareholder value. The extent to which an organization is involved in internal or external hedging strategies will depend, as for other risks, on its risk exposure and risk appetite. Managing financial risk needs to be a core focus of enterprise risk management, even though it may be managed by a specialist Treasury function. However, there needs to be close monitoring of the role of the Treasury department, to ensure its practices are consistent with the organizational risk management strategy and that it is not engaged in speculative activity.

Chapter 13

Risk and Information Systems

Information technology is the backbone of the modern business enterprise. The failure of a computer system can bring business to a stand-still but a poorly designed system can also result in loss of customers, fraud, hacking and ultimately to business failure. In enterprise risk management, protecting the organization's information system permeates all of its operations.

Information security

Information security is about protecting the information resource of an organization. The information security standard, ISO/IEC 27001:2005, is specifically risk-based and provides the most comprehensive guidance on the subject. The Standard recommends that organizations implement information security controls prioritized by, and in proportion to, the business and information risks they identify.

BS 7799-3:2006[1] gives guidance to support the requirements given in ISO/IEC 27001:2005 regarding all aspects of an information security management system. This includes assessing and evaluating the risks, implementing controls to treat the risks, monitoring and reviewing the risks, and maintaining and improving the system of risk controls. The focus of this standard is effective information security through an ongoing programme of risk management activities. This focus is targeted at information security in the context of an organization's business risks. The Standard provides a best practice checklist in relation to information security. The key elements include:

- *Security policy*: which defines security, allocates responsibility, and defines reporting mechanisms for suspected breaches.
- *Security organization*: a management structure should exist with roles defined and documented, covering authorization of hardware and software purchases, prevention systems for unauthorized access, and policies governing third party access to data.

---

[1] The Standard can be purchased at http://www.bsi-global.com/en/Shop/Publication-Detail/?pid= 000000000030125022&recid=3138.

■ *Asset classification and control*: an asset register of all hardware and software should be maintained. The owners of databases should also be catalogued.

■ *Personnel security:* security staff should be responsible for ensuring that systems are in place and monitored to minimize risks from error, fraud, theft or hacking.

■ *Physical and environmental security*: controls should be in place to restrict access to computer systems. Disposal of equipment, data files and printed reports should be carried out securely. Fire and flood protection should also be in place.

■ *Computer and network management:* systems and data should be protected against attack from viruses, malicious software, denial of service attacks, etc. Anti-virus software, intruder detection systems and firewalls (described further in Chapter 18) should be in place and policies should exist for the use of e-mail (including the treatment of spam email) and access to websites (including employee access and downloading of copyrighted and obscene material).

■ *Systems access controls:* physical access, passwords, and authentication of remote users should be documented and maintained with terminals protected by screen savers and time-outs.

■ *Systems development and maintenance*: all systems should be developed in accordance with standards, tested and documented with segregated areas of the system used for development, testing and live systems. Change control systems should be in place to control all development and maintenance work.

■ *Business continuity and disaster recovery:* a plan should exist to cover all information systems including backup, offsite fireproof storage and alternative hardware, software and building site requirements for recovery. Adequate insurance should be taken out.

■ *Compliance*: organizations should be aware of their legal and contractual obligations and comply with relevant legislation, for example Data Protection Act 1998; Computer Misuse Act 1990.

IT Governance

At the enterprise level, 'IT Governance' has emerged as the application of general governance principles to the information function, covering information strategy, information technology and information management. The IT Governance Institute,[2] the research arm of the Information Systems Audit and Control Association (ISACA), has published *IT Control Objectives for Sarbanes-Oxley*[3] to help bridge

---

[2]See http://www.itgovernance.co.uk/ and http://www.itgi.org/.

[3]Download available from http://www.isaca.org/Template.cfm?Section=Home&CONTENTID=32621& TEMPLATE=/ContentManagement/ContentDisplay.cfm.

the gaps between business risks, technical issues, control needs, and performance-measurement requirements. Emphasizing the importance of information technology in the design, implementation, and sustainability of internal controls over disclosure and financial reporting, the document is designed to reflect the latest thinking on this increasingly global topic. The primary focus of ISACA's guidance relates to IT controls in relation to financial reporting, which is critical to compliance with the requirements of the US Sarbanes-Oxley Act.

CobiT

An important tool for IT Governance is CobiT, Control Objectives for Information and Related Technology.[4] CobiT was developed by ISACA in 1996 and is now operated by the IT Governance Institute. CobiT is designed to help management balance risk and control investment in an unpredictable IT environment; and address concerns about performance measurement, IT control profiling, awareness and benchmarking.

The CobiT model views internal control as a process that includes policies, procedures, practices and organizational structures that support business processes and objectives. It addresses three audiences: management, users and auditors. It groups IT processes into four categories: planning and organization; acquisition and implementation; delivery and support; and monitoring. CobiT defines high-level 'Business Control Objectives' for the processes which are linked to business objectives and supports these with 'Detailed Control Objectives' to provide management assurance and/or advice for improvement. The Control Objectives are supported by Audit Guidelines. Figure 13.1 shows the CobiT framework.

The CobiT Management Guidelines use the principles of the *Balanced Scorecard* and define:

- Benchmarks for IT control practices, known as 'maturity models'. Using maturity models, the organization can benchmark itself against the best in the industry, international standards and the organization's own goals.
- Critical success factors for controlling IT processes.
- Key goal indicators determine (by feedback) whether an IT process has achieved its business requirements in terms of availability of information; absence of integrity risks and confidentiality risks; cost-efficiency; and confirmation of reliability, effectiveness and compliance.
- Key performance indicators use measures to determine (by feed forward) how well the IT process is performing in enabling the goal to be reached and are indicators of capabilities, practices and skills.

---

[4]Download available from http://www.isaca.org/Template.cfm?Section=COBIT6&Template=/TaggedPage/TaggedPageDisplay.cfm&TPLID=55&ContentID=7981.

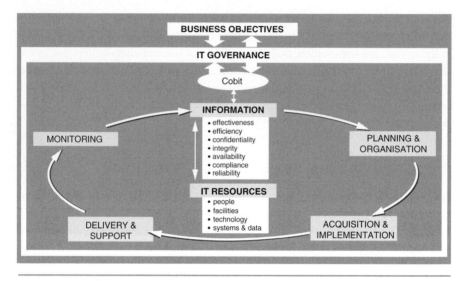

Figure 13.1   CobiT Framework.
Source: IT Governance Institute, COBIT Framework 4.1 Executive Summary, p. 28. Available from: http://www.isaca.org/AMTemplate.cfm?Section=Downloads&Template=/ContentManagement/ContentDisplay.cfm&ContentID=34172.

SAC and eSAC

Systems Auditability and Control (SAC) and, with the growth of e-commerce, its development into Electronic Systems Assurance and Control (eSAC)[5] was produced by the Institute of Internal Auditors Research Foundation[6] and is aimed at understanding, monitoring, assessing and mitigating technology risk and emphasizes internal control as a system, a set of functions, sub-systems, people and the interrelationships between all of these.

Risks in eSAC are defined as fraud, errors, business interruptions and inefficient and ineffective use of resources. Control objectives reduce these risks and assure information integrity, security and compliance. Information integrity is guarded by input, processing, output and software quality controls. Security measures include data, physical and program security controls. Compliance controls ensure conformance with laws and regulations, accounting and auditing standards and internal policies and procedures.

---

[5]Download available from http://usuarios.lycos.es/systemsaudit/ExecSumm-final.pdf.
[6]See http://www.theiia.org/research/research-reports/.

Under eSAC, internal controls have three components: the control environment; manual and automated systems; and control procedures. Control procedures can be classified as:

■ Preventive, detective or corrective;

■ Discretionary or non-discretionary;

■ Voluntary or mandatory;

■ Manual or automated;

■ Application or general controls.

Risk assessment for information systems

When performing an IT risk assessment, the effect of a risk-related event and the likelihood that a potential event will occur should be considered. Some of the factors (the following list has been adapted from ISACA's *IT Control Objectives for Sarbanes-Oxley* and CobiT) to consider when looking at impact and probability include:

■ A failure in reporting financial or non-financial information.

■ Implementation of an unapproved program change.

■ Lack of availability of the system or an application.

■ Failure to maintain the system or an application.

■ Failure in the integrity of information managed by the application, such as calculation accuracy, and completeness.

■ Volume of transactions running through the system or application.

■ Complexity of the technology and the application.

■ Volume and complexity of changes made.

■ Age of the system or application.

■ Past history of problems related to the system or application.

■ Custom in-house programming versus off-the-shelf packages.

Information system controls

Controls in relation to information systems can be classified as:

■ Security controls for the prevention of unauthorized access, modification or destruction of stored data;

- Integrity controls to ensure that data is accurate, consistent and free from accidental corruption;

- Contingency controls to ensure a back-up facility and a plan to restore business operations are maintained.

- General controls ensure the effectiveness of the information systems as a whole, to ensure appropriate use of computer systems and security from loss of data. General controls are considered in terms of controls over personnel, logical access (i.e. passwords, etc.), facilities and business continuity.

- Application controls are designed for each individual application, to prevent, detect and correct transaction-processing errors. Application controls are specific to each application but can be grouped into input, processing and output controls.

- Software control prevents making or installing unauthorized copies of software which may be protected by copyright and intellectual property legislation.

- Network controls have arisen in response to the growth of distributed processing and e-commerce. They prevent unauthorized access to data transmitted over networks and secure the integrity of data through firewalls, data encryption, authorization, virus protection, and the protection and detection of hacking.

Systems development risk

Organizations will frequently need to improve or change their information systems. As this is where risks can first emerge, it is important to have strong controls over systems development to avoid developing a computer system that does not meet user needs, is late or costs more than was estimated. Those involved in a computer implementation project are usually committed to its success, but may fail to recognize any warning signals. Often, cost escalation and delay are noticed but if the system does not work at all, there may be a fundamental risk to the business operations which are dependent on effective information systems.

One long-standing approach to systems design is the Systems Development Life Cycle (SDLC). An abbreviated version of the SDLC for systems development is based on:

- *Feasibility study*: identifying the needs and objectives of the system by identifying current problems and the technical, operational and economic feasibility of the proposed solution.

- *Systems analysis:* the processes necessary to generate the specification for the system through a methodical investigation of a problem and the identification and ranking of alternative solutions. This requires more detailed information than was contained in the feasibility study and will result in a tender specification and a choice between in-house and outsourced provision.

- *Systems design:* the conversion of specifications into a workable design including source data, input layout, file structure, reports, and interfaces with other systems, etc. Increasingly, computer-assisted software engineering (CASE) tools are used for systems analysis and design by many organizations.

- *Implementation:* the use of project management techniques for hardware, software, testing, documentation and training and conversion from existing systems.

- *Systems operation and maintenance:* maintenance involves the correction or enhancement of systems once they are in operation. There should also be a post-implementation review.

To mitigate risk, systems development projects need to include the following controls:

- At the feasibility study stage, there should be a clear understanding about the objectives of the new system, the deliverables, cost and expected time to completion.

- At the system design stage, there need to be rules with regard to data security and levels of authorization which need to be built into the system. At this stage, the auditor needs to review system documentation, interfaces with other systems, and ensure the acceptance of design by all in the project team, especially users.

- At the testing stage, there must be comprehensive testing by systems development staff, programmers, users and internal auditors. Auditors need to review the specifications, flowcharts, test data and operating instructions.

- At the implementation stage, there needs to be a review of training and documentation, file conversion and operational issues, for example staffing and supervision.

A steering committee is an important control to ensure that risks in systems development are minimized. The steering committee monitors the system implementation in comparison with the plan and ensures that specific deliverables are accepted at each stage of systems development. It has overall responsibility to ensure that the system meets requirements in terms of quality, time and cost. The steering committee should include the sponsor of the project who authorized it and is committed to its success; the project manager who has responsibility for the day-to-day delivery of the project; specialist IT staff with responsibility for delivering the project; user representatives with responsibility for accepting the system; and internal audit representatives with responsibility for ensuring the adequacy of internal controls and system testing in conjunction with users.

Systems development auditing

Internal auditors have an important role to play in ensuring that risks are adequately addressed by controls designed-in during the development phase, as it is more expensive to add controls once a system is operational. The auditors also need to ensure that financial and non-financial information is accurate and complete and suitable for its intended purpose. They need to identify potential problems in data collection, input, processing and output, ensure an adequate audit trail, and review the scope for possible fraud. Internal audit can only achieve these by working closely with the systems development team.

Systems implementation

An implementation plan will cover the process of changing over to the new system after it has been tested. To ensure accuracy of processing and results, there should be a period of parallel operation during which the new system is operated in conjunction with the existing system. This should continue until the new system is proven to work by reconciling outputs from both systems and ensuring that users are satisfied with the new system and are confident about discontinuing the existing system. If there is a changeover without parallel running, then testing prior to implementation becomes more important and additional monitoring may be needed during the early stages of implementation.

Particular care needs to be taken in converting data from existing systems. This needs to be properly planned and sufficient resources allocated to carry out the conversion. Adequate controls need to be implemented to ensure the consistency of data as they are transferred between systems, identifying any duplications and omissions.

The auditor may be required to sign off the system before implementation. This involves forming a professional opinion that the system meets user requirements; functions properly; has been developed with adequate built-in controls; is auditable; and that data has been converted completely and accurately.

The project team should carry out a thorough review of the new system after implementation to establish whether the system is operating as intended and to confirm that user needs are being satisfied. The internal audit team should ensure that the post-implementation review has been properly carried out by the project team.

Systems operation

Systems operation is a further area of risk for the enterprise. The Information Technology Infrastructure Library (ITIL)[7] is an internationally accepted best practice model in the public domain that guides business users through the planning, delivery and management of quality IT services. ITIL assists organizations to align their IT services with business requirements. ITIL is based on a core set of ten processes and one function. There are five processes targeted at service support and five processes focused on service delivery. The Service Desk function interfaces to all 10 processes to provide a single point of contact from customers to IT. The five service support processes and goals are:

- *Configuration management*: To identify, record and report on all IT components.
- *Incident management:* To restore normal service operation as quickly as possible and minimize any adverse impact on business operations.
- *Change management*: To ensure that standardized methods and procedures are used for efficient and prompt handling of all changes to minimize the impact of change-related incidents and improve day-to-day operations.
- *Problem management*: To minimize the adverse impact of incidents and problems on the business that are caused by errors in the IT infrastructure and to prevent recurrence of incidents related to these errors. Problem Management seeks to get to the root cause and initiate action to remove the error.
- *Release management:* Release Management takes a holistic view of any change to an IT service and ensures that all aspects of a release of new software or processes are considered together.

The five service delivery processes and goals are:

- *Service level management*: To maintain and improve IT service quality through a constant cycle of agreeing, monitoring and reporting to meet customer business objectives.
- *Availability management*: To optimize the capability of the IT infrastructure, services and supporting organization to deliver a cost-effective and sustained level of availability enabling the business to meet its objectives.
- *Capacity management:* To ensure that all the current and future capacity and performance aspects of the business requirements are provided cost-effectively.

---

[7] See http://www.itil-officialsite.com/home/home.asp.

■ *IT service continuity management*: To ensure that the required IT technical and services facilities can be recovered within required and agreed timescales. This is a systematic approach to the creation of a plan and/or procedures to prevent, cope with and recover from the loss of critical services for extended periods.

■ *Financial management:* To provide cost-effective stewardship of the IT assets and resources used in providing IT services.

The service desk function and goals are:

■ To provide a single point of contact for customers and an operational single point of contact for managing incidents to resolution.

■ To facilitate the restoration of normal operational service with minimal business impact on the customer within agreed service levels and business priorities.

Information technology is central to organizational functioning. Consequently risks arise in relation to system design, operation and access. Enterprise risk management needs to start with user and auditor involvement in systems design, building in controls to the design as well as auditability. A weak IT system is one of the biggest risks an organization can face. An example of this is provided in the case study of the Criminal Records Bureau in the United Kingdom.

Case study: Criminal Records Bureau

The objective of the Criminal Records Bureau (CRB) in the UK is to widen access to criminal records so that employers can make better-informed recruitment decisions, especially in relation to the protection of children and vulnerable adults. The CRB was a Public Private Partnership with Capita plc. Capita won the £400 million 10-year contract with the cheapest bid. Its responsibility was to operate a call centre, carry out data entry of CRB applications, collect fees, develop and maintain the IT infrastructure and issue criminal record disclosures to employers.

Planning for the CRB commenced in 1999 and live access began in March 2002, 7 months later than planned caused by problems in business and technical development and the decision to conduct more extensive testing prior to live operations. The implementation of the system was a calamity and led to a major investigation into weaknesses in the design and operation of the system.

The investigation identified significant weaknesses in the business assumptions made by Capita in establishing the system. In particular, the assumption that 70–85% of people would apply by telephone to a call centre or via the Internet was incorrect and not based on adequate research with potential users, 80% of whom preferred paper applications. The data entry screens had been designed for input from a telephone call, not from paper forms, and optical character recognition (OCR) systems did not have the capacity to handle the volume of paper applications that were subsequently received. Also, systems had been designed around receipt of individual applications and could not cope when batched applications were received from employers. The processes were also unable to cope with the volume of errors and exceptions on paper applications.

Information for this case came from the National Audit Office (2004) Report *Criminal Records Bureau: Delivering Safer Recruitment?* (HC266)[8]

Chapter 14

Risk Management for Health and Safety

Accidents and illness at work cause suffering to the injured people and their families and can cost organizations substantial sums of money. Good practice in health and safety is also required under many laws and regulations. Laws and regulations vary between countries, and while this chapter focuses on the United Kingdom, the principles are applicable in any country.

Health and safety is an integral aspect of enterprise risk management as it affects everyone in the organization as well as others who visit the organization. Health and safety requires leadership from the top of the organization and a culture that supports a concern for safety and health

Legislative framework

In the United Kingdom, the Health and Safety at Work Act 1974 sets out the duty of care on employers to ensure the health, safety and welfare of their employees while they are at work. The Management of Health and Safety at work Regulations 1999: Regulation 3 states that every employer shall make a suitable and sufficient assessment of

- the risks to the health and safety of his[1] employees to which they are exposed while they are at work; and
- the risks to the health and safety of persons not in his employment arising out of or in connection with the conduct by him of his undertaking.

In 2008 the Health and Safety Executive (HSE) became the single national regulatory body responsible for promoting the cause of better health and safety at work in the United Kingdom. Inspectors from the HSE or from the local authority carry out workplace inspections and enforce regulations. They investigate some

---

[1]The term 'his' is retained here as it is used in the legislation.

accidents and complaints but their main role is to help organizations understand their obligations.

There are numerous laws and regulations affecting health and safety generally, as well as specifically in relation to particular industries (e.g. construction), hazards (e.g. asbestos) and work practices (e.g. manual handling). Some of the most common regulations are:

■ All employers must be registered with the Health and Safety Executive or the local authority.

■ Personal Protective Equipment at Work Regulations 1992: every employer shall ensure that suitable personal protective equipment is provided to his employees who may be exposed to a risk to their health or safety while at work except where and to the extent that such risk has been adequately controlled by other means which are equally or more effective. Employers should provide appropriate personal protective equipment and training in its use to their employees wherever there is a risk to health and safety that cannot be adequately controlled by other means.

■ Reporting of Injuries Diseases and Dangerous Occurrences Regulations 1995 (RIDDOR) requires the reporting of deaths or major injuries, and injuries resulting in time off work of 3 days or more, certain diseases and certain dangerous occurrences (see below).

■ Health and Safety (First Aid) Regulations 1981: the number and type of first aid personnel should be based on an assessment of need.

■ Control of Substances Hazardous to Health Regulations 2002 (COSHH): employers must assess the risks to health from exposure to all substances hazardous to health.

■ Employers' Liability Compulsory Insurance Act 1969: All employers must take out insurance which provides compensation for injuries or illness caused on or off site. Employers must display their certificate of insurance in the workplace. The certificate must show that the employer has insurance cover for at least the minimum level required by the law. At the time of writing the minimum level of cover required is £5 million, although many employers take out insurance for larger sums.

■ A health and safety law poster must be displayed, or all employees must be given individual copies of the same information.

Because of the breadth of health and safety regulations, it is common practice for even small organizations to appoint someone competent (whether an experienced employee or an external adviser) to assist management to comply with their health and safety responsibilities.

Health and safety policy

A health and safety policy sets out an organization's general approach and objectives and the arrangements that are in place for managing health and safety. If an organization has five or more employees, the policy must be written. A written policy statement shows employees, and everyone else, the organizational commitment to health and safety. It should describe how management will implement and monitor health and safety controls. The policy should be reviewed regularly.

A health and policy statement would generally cover the following objectives[2]:

- to provide adequate control of the health and safety risks arising from work activities;
- to consult with employees on matters affecting their health and safety;
- to provide and maintain safe plant and equipment;
- to ensure safe handling and use of substances;
- to provide information, instruction and supervision for employees;
- to ensure all employees are competent to do their tasks, and to give them adequate training;
- to prevent accidents and cases of work-related ill health;
- to maintain safe and healthy working conditions; and
- to review and revise the policy as necessary at regular intervals.

Responsibilities of employers

Employers are responsible for protecting the health and safety of their staff and other people, such as customers and members of the public who may be affected by their work. The responsibility of employers is to:

- make the workplace safe and eliminate or control risks to health;
- ensure that plant and machinery are safe and that safe systems of work are followed;
- ensure that materials are moved, stored and used safely;
- provide adequate welfare facilities;
- give workers the information, instruction, training and supervision necessary for their health and safety;
- consult workers on health and safety matters.

---

[2] A policy template has been produced by the HSE which expands on the above objectives and can be downloaded from http://www.hse.gov.uk/business/policy-statement.pdf.

Every employer has overall responsibility for health and safety, although responsibility may be delegated for day-to-day tasks to someone else, for example a manager or supervisor. Employers must consult their employees. If a trade union is recognized which has a union-appointed safety representative, the employer must consult them on matters affecting the employees they represent. Otherwise, the employer must consult employees either directly or through an elected health and safety representative.

Employers must ensure that all plant and equipment that requires maintenance is identified, that the maintenance is carried out and that new or second-hand plant and equipment meets health and safety standards before it is purchased.

All employees must be given health and safety induction training when they commence work. This should cover basics such as first aid and fire safety. There should also be job-specific health and safety training depending on the duties of each particular job. Employers must also provide training if risks change and refresher training when skills are not frequently used.

Employers must also be able to show that health and safety is being monitored, for example by carrying out spot checks, and by investigating accidents or ill health.

Responsibility of employees

Employees also have legal responsibilities. Employees must:

- take reasonable care for their own health and safety and that of others who may be affected by what they do or do not do;
- co-operate with their employer in complying with health and safety requirements;
- correctly use work items provided by the employer, including personal protective equipment, in accordance with training or instructions; and
- not interfere with or misuse anything provided for employee health, safety or welfare.

Health and safety risk assessment

Just as risk assessment is a central part of estimating risk and the precursor to evaluating and treating risk for all enterprise-wide risks, so it is important in health and safety to protect employees and others and to ensure compliance with the law.

A health and safety risk assessment helps the employer focus on the risks that have the potential to cause real harm. In many instances, straightforward measures can readily control risks, for example ensuring spillages are cleaned up promptly so people do not trip, slip, or fall. For many risks, that means simple, cheap and effective measures to ensure employees and others are protected. The law does not expect employers to eliminate all risk, but they are required to protect people as far as is reasonably practicable.

The process of risk assessment for health and safety is similar to that for other forms of risk assessment;

1. Identify the hazards;
2. Decide who might be harmed and how;
3. Evaluate the risks and determine how those risks might be mitigated;
4. Record findings and risk treatment actions;
5. Review and monitor.

A hazard is anything that may cause harm, such as chemicals, electricity, working from ladders, etc. while risk is the likelihood that somebody could be harmed by the hazard, as well as how serious the harm to a person could be.

Hazards can be identified from a variety of sources: observation (walking around), and asking employees. Manufacturers' instructions on the safe use and maintenance of equipment are also helpful. Looking back at past records of accidents and near-misses also provides useful information.

The HSE identifies a number of specific hazards[3]:

- Slips, trips and falls;
- Manual handling resulting in sprains, strains and pains;
- Working at height;
- Hazardous substances, with asbestos particularly highlighted;
- Fire and explosion;
- Radiation;
- Using computers and display screens;
- Noise;
- Vibration;
- Electricity;
- High-pressure systems;
- Use of work equipment;
- Construction and maintenance;
- Transport;
- Stress.

---

[3]A usefull introduction to health and safety and risk assessment is available from the HSE at http://www.hse.gov.uk/pubns/indg259.pdf.

In conducting a risk assessment, hazards may not only affect employees but also a variety of other parties, either directly or indirectly: contractors, cleaners, the general public, customers and suppliers, visitors, and voluntary workers. There may also be particular requirements, for example for new or young workers, new or expectant mothers, and people with disabilities.

In assessing risk, employers need to consider the size of the organization; its history of accidents; the nature and distribution of the workforce; the remoteness of the site from emergency medical services; the needs of travelling, remote and lone workers; and employees working on shared or multi-occupied sites.

Risk response

Some risks may be avoided altogether, for example changing to a less hazardous chemical. Some risks may be mitigated through controls, for example providing guards on machinery; restricting fork lift truck access to defined corridors; issuing personal protective equipment (clothing, footwear, goggles, etc.); and providing welfare facilities (e.g. first aid and washing facilities for removal of any contamination). Employers' Liability Compulsory Insurance should be relied on as a last resort where all other methods of risk treatment have failed.

Risk reporting

As for other forms of risk, recording and reporting risks enables monitoring and corrective action. Most organizations will keep an accident book to record all such events. This will enable monitoring of trends, performance against targets and the benchmarking of data within the organization and with similar organizations and industry averages. Accident records also enable a review of existing risk management strategy and facilitate improvements. Specialist software is now available to make recording, analysis and reporting easier.

However, in the case of health and safety, there is also a legal requirement under RIDDOR[4] (see above) to report certain accidents and ill health. The information enables the HSE and local authorities to identify where and how risks arise, and to investigate serious accidents. The Incident Contact Centre (ICC) is a 'one-stop' reporting service for work-related health and safety incidents in the United Kingdom.

Employers must keep a record of any reportable injury, disease or dangerous occurrence. This must include the date and method of reporting; the date, time and place

---

[4]Reporting of Injuries Diseases and Dangerous Occurrences Regulations, 1995.

of the event; personal details of those involved; and a brief description of the nature of the event or disease.

Under RIDDOR, employers must report to the ICC:

- deaths;
- major injuries (e.g. fracture, dislocation, amputation, loss of sight, electric shock, etc.)
- over-3-day injuries – where an employee is away from work or unable to perform their normal work duties for more than 3 consecutive days;
- injuries to members of the public or people not at work where they are taken from the scene of an accident to hospital;
- some work-related diseases (e.g. poisoning, skin or lung diseases or occupational cancers; or where a doctor notifies the employer that an employee suffers from a reportable work-related disease);
- dangerous occurrences, where something happens that does not result in an injury, but could have done, that is a 'near miss';
- registered gas fitters must also report dangerous gas fittings they find, and gas conveyors/suppliers must report some flammable gas incidents.

An example of health and safety reporting is contained in the extract from HMV's 2007 Annual Report to shareholders (see below). As for IT systems (Chapter 13), people are one of the most valuable resources to any organization, and protecting them from accident or ill health while at work should be of fundamental concern for enterprise-wide risk management. Embedding a safety conscious culture in an organization is a good precursor to introducing an enterprise risk management culture that was described in Chapter 6.

Extract from HMV Group plc Annual Report 2007 on Health and safety

The Group complies with all laws of health and safety, and takes all possible steps to ensure that everyone in our stores and places of work is safe while there. We aim to minimise incidences of accident or incident while in our locations, and we are committed to preventing a reoccurrence of an accident or incident, should it happen. We are committed to a system of monitoring and recording our health and safety performance in order to enable us to improve continually.

HMV UK and Ireland introduced Safety, Health and Environmental (SHE) management software in 2005. Therefore, 2006/2007 was the second year that accurate

Reporting year	Number of accidents (total)	Number of RIDDOR reportable accidents
2004/2005	134 accidents in total	12 RIDDOR reportable
2005/2006	224 accidents in total	9 RIDDOR reportable
2006/2007	125 accidents in total	7 RIDDOR reportable

accident reporting figures were recorded. The number of total accidents reported during the year under review decreased by 45% and reportable RIDDOR accidents fell by 22%.

Sixty-one local authorities conducted inspections of HMV stores and no formal notices were served; 15 Chartered Institute of Environmental Health 1-day courses were conducted with 120 store managers, assistant managers and loss prevention staff attending, and all attained the required standard. Two in-store health and safety briefs were produced and delivered to stores, with subjects covered including manual handling and accident and risk assessments.

The Group's UK distribution centres received two health and safety audits over the course of the year conducted by the Risk and Safety Manager. An average audit mark of 95% was achieved, the pass mark being 80%. To date, Store Health and Safety Audits have been carried out in 218 stores, with 59% achieving the required pass mark.

In Waterstone's, a primary focus during the year was to integrate into the health and safety regime the acquired Ottakar's store estate and store managers, including arrangements for the reporting of accidents and changes to operating instructions.

Visits were carried out to all former Ottakar's stores to ensure that a suitable fire risk assessment was available and that any structural or management hazards were identified and action implemented. Over 200 Ottakar's store managers and assistant managers were provided with health and safety training to align them with practice in Waterstone's. These initiatives delivered to these stores significant improvements to health and safety standards. Total accidents reported to the Waterstone's health and safety team decreased to 200 from 207 in the prior year, despite the significant increase in store numbers following the acquisition of Ottakar's. This reflects improved standards across the business, albeit there is likely to have been some initial under-reporting of accidents from former Ottakar's stores.

Objectives for HMV UK and Ireland for 2007/2008 include: a further 20% reduction in all accidents; a 10% reduction in RIDDOR reportable accidents;

implementation of a car drivers' policy; implementation of a violence at work policy; delivery to all store-based loss prevention officers of training for defusing aggression and dealing with violence; improve reporting of violent incidents; complete physical risk assessments for all security offices and shoplifting detention areas.

Chapter 15

Credit Risk Management

Companies carry credit risk when they do not receive payment for their products or services prior to delivery. Customers take advantage of credit terms to improve their cash flow by delaying payment as long as possible, ideally until their goods or services are sold. Credit risk management is concerned with ensuring that customers meet their obligations by paying for goods and services provided and repaying loans and interest on any borrowings. Both need to take place within the agreed terms of trade or borrowing covenants. Effective credit management is an important component of enterprise risk management and essential to the long-term success of any organization that lends money or extends credit. Credit risk management involves credit policy and acceptance and collection processes. In this chapter we are primarily concerned with non-bank institutions, although the concepts are the same the language varies slightly. Chapter 22 addresses the banking and financial sector in more detail.

Credit policy

Every organization should have a credit policy which is explicit about the quality of customer/borrower the organization is prepared to do business with (which takes into account the organization's risk appetite), terms of trade, and in the case of lenders, interest rate policy (higher interest rates will typically be applied to higher rated risks) and the security for loans that the organization deems to be adequate. Credit policy may also extend to whether or not the organization allows settlement discounts, insures or factors its debts, and whether a retention of title clause applies (see later in this chapter for a discussion of these issues). The organization's credit policy establishes the risk culture of the organization in relation to credit risk.

A company's credit (or collections) department will administer the credit policy and will typically be separate from any sales or order fulfilment responsibility, carrying out credit acceptance and collection action. It will liaise closely with Treasury in relation to planned cash receipts.

Credit terms and settlement discounts

Businesses will offer customers credit terms as part of their standard conditions of trading. These terms may be for any period, from cash on delivery, to 7, 14, 30 days. Thirty days is most common for the sale of goods, typically 7 or 14 days for services. Where terms are expressed as net 30, this means the customer is expected to pay in full within 30 days of the invoice (or sometimes 30 days after the end of the month in which the invoice was issued, something which should be explicit in the credit policy and trading terms to avoid ambiguity). Sometimes, businesses will offer a settlement discount to encourage early payment. So terms of net 30, 2.5% 7 days may encourage customers to pay early (within 7 days) and so achieve a 2.5% saving, or alternatively delay payment which then must be made in full. Whatever the credit terms in use, these must be made very clear to customers.

Credit acceptance

The first stage of credit is determining which customers or borrowers should be extended credit. The most useful information is past experience by the organization or others about the payment history of a potential customer/borrower, as past defaults or current financial problems are the best indicator of potential bad debts or late payments in the future.

Credit acceptance decisions will be based on a combination of factors, with the precise factors depending on the amount of the likely exposure:

- A credit application form will show basic details of the customer/borrower, their assets and liabilities, sales and profit levels, etc.;
- Credit references provided by other parties;
- A credit report from a credit reference bureau;
- A company search to show registered office details, names of directors, and any adverse reports, etc;
- An internet search which might identify current issues affecting the applicant;
- Financial statements, preferably audited.

Credit analysis involves a wide variety of financial analysis techniques, including ratio and trend analysis as well as the creation of projections and a detailed analysis of cash flows. Credit analysis also includes an examination of organizational reputation, the available collateral to secure any loans and management ability.

The organization extending credit may allocate points to the available information in order to rate the credit worthiness of an applicant. Credit bureaux will carry out a similar process on behalf of the organization for a fee, but credit bureaux may well have access to more information about a credit applicant than an organization can obtain by itself. The organization or credit bureaux will usually carry out ratio analysis on financial data to ascertain trends and comparison to industry benchmark data.

The purpose of credit scoring is to measure the risk of extending credit in order to make a judgment about whether or not credit should be extended, the credit limits that should be applied, and whether any security should be obtained. Credit rating or credit scoring is the use of a mathematical model which measures the likelihood that a customer will repay (or not) their debt on time. Credit scoring often uses a database built using observations of a large number of customers, some of whom have defaulted on payment and most of whom will not have defaulted. Statistical techniques are then used to estimate the probability of default for a particular credit applicant based on historical data. The credit scoring model predicts the probability of default for new customers based on their characteristics compared with defaulting and non-defaulting customers. A scaling process is then applied to give a credit score which ranks customers by the degree of risk faced by a lender.

Decisions to extend credit need to be properly documented and approved by a manager with authority although the authority level may change with the amount of credit being extended.

Credit collection

The principal measure of the efficiency of credit collection is days' sales outstanding. This is calculated by dividing the amount owed to the company by the average daily sales, a calculation which can be done by anyone outside the organization based on annual published financial statements, or using more detailed internal data held by the organization on a more frequent basis. For example:

Trade receivables	£1,800,000
Sales	£12,000,000
Average daily sales	£12,000,000/365 = £32,877
Days' sales outstanding	£1,800,000/£32,877 = 54.7 days

The calculation of 54.7 days is then compared with the company's standard trading terms, which might be 30 days. This means that customers are, on average, taking almost two months to pay their debts. Credit collection action needs to be taken to reduce this figure.

The basic principle of credit collection is a thorough and ongoing process of collection action, becoming increasingly more serious, and always being fully documented. Common methods applying to credit collection include:

■ Making the terms of trading clear to customers when they first apply for credit to avoid uncertainty and dispute. It may be an advantage to have customers sign the terms of trading as having been read and understood;

■ Issuing invoices accurately and quickly: incorrect or late invoices give customers an excuse for delaying payment;

■ Issuing statements at the end of each month as both a reminder and to give customers the opportunity to identify any missing invoices;

■ Telephone calls, increasing in intensity, reminding customers that payment is due. Recording of customer responses (e.g. 'the cheque is in the post') enables each response to be followed up in subsequent telephone calls.

■ Letters, increasing in intensity, reminding customers of the organization's credit policy and that payment is due.

■ Use of credit collection agencies to take more action, including telephone calls, letters and ultimately legal action where necessary.

Customers who deliberately delay payment, generally due to their own cash flow problems, typically use a variety of excuses, for example:

■ An error in the invoice;
■ Pricing different to that quoted;
■ Shortfall in delivery;
■ Poor quality.

Consequently, part of the organization's risk management is to ensure that invoicing is accurate and agrees with the customer's purchase order and the acknowledgement of goods received (which should be signed for on receipt). The trading terms/conditions of sale should prescribe the procedure to be followed in the event of a dispute over quantity received, quality or price. Good practice is to require all customer disputes to be notified in writing within a short period of time, for example 7 days. Credit collection action then needs to be taken to ensure that all disputes are investigated and resolved quickly as customers may withhold payment of their whole account on the basis of an outstanding dispute for a small amount.

If collection of a debt becomes too difficult, a company may pass debt collection action to a collection agency. The company then accepts that in passing responsibility, the collection agency takes a share of the amount recovered as well as any legal costs incurred.

Legal action, bad debts and credit insurance

Where credit collection action has not proven effective, it is most likely that a default is probable, as the customers may well be delaying payments to many suppliers. A letter from a solicitor threatening legal action or issuing a default court summons for payment is likely to be the only remaining possibility.

Despite all action, some debts will never be recovered and have to be written off as bad debts. Companies will make provisions for doubtful debts in their accounting records to be reflected in their financial statements before this time. This ensures that their financial statements do not include assets where recovery of funds is uncertain.

Credit insurance may be taken out whereby an insurer, in return for a premium, pays a percentage of the defaulted customer's account to the insured company. This mitigates losses to some extent, but is an expensive form of reducing credit risk (insurance is covered in Chapter 21).

Factoring

One method of improving cash flows is to sell trade debts to a financier who pays the business a percentage of the invoice value. The financier charges an interest rate on the unpaid value of sales and retains security over those debts. This is a useful method where a company has good quality sales but a poor cash flow, but it is expensive, and there is normally recourse to the seller by the financier in the event of debts that are unpaid by customers.

Covenants

Protective covenants can be written into loan agreements. Covenants may:

- limit the borrower's ability to borrow further money;
- provide for monitoring e.g. regular reports and audits;
- allow the lender to call for repayment of the loan if specified events occur or when financial ratios (e.g. debt/equity or interest cover) fall below an agreed level.

A recent innovation to protect lenders and bond holders from the danger of default is the credit derivative (the principle of derivatives was covered in Chapter 12), most commonly a credit default swap. These financial contracts allow companies to buy protection against defaults from a third party. The third party receives a periodic fee as compensation for the risk it takes, and in return it agrees to buy the debt should a credit default take place. Credit default swaps are like an insurance policy, as they can be used by lenders to hedge against credit events such as a default. However, because there is no requirement to actually hold any asset or suffer a loss, credit default swaps can also be used for speculative purposes.

Retention of title

In the sale of goods, possession and ownership of the goods are most commonly simultaneous. Retention of title is the process whereby a seller retains title over the goods sold to a buyer, even after delivery takes place, until such time as the goods are paid for. To achieve retention of title, the contract of sales has to stipulate that although the goods are delivered to a buyer, ownership of those goods does not pass to the buyer until payment is made. However, to be effective, this particular aspect of the contract needs to be explicitly brought to the attention of the buyer. Retention of title allows the seller to physically recover the goods if the customer has not paid for them.

One of the most significant assets held by a company (except retail businesses) is the value of its receivables, the amounts owed by customers for goods or services sold but unpaid for. Credit risk is even more important for financial institutions who lend money to borrowers (see Chapter 22). Enterprise risk management looks at credit risk as a major risk facing an organization and credit control as a means by which the risk of non-payment or delayed payment is reduced through effective credit acceptance and collection processes, but also through other methods of mitigation where a credit risk does eventuate.

Chapter 16

Strategy and Business Risk

The category of business risk encompasses those risks which attach to the unique circumstances of a particular organization. Business risks will therefore vary between organizations within an industry and between industries. In this chapter we consider some common elements of business risk that are not dealt with in other chapters, both strategically and operationally.

Strategic risk

In their 2008 report 'Strategic business risk: 2008 – the top 10 risks for global business'[1] Ernst & Young reviewed 12 key business sectors in the global marketplace and identified the top 10 strategic risks faced by business. The report also highlighted the five fastest-growing threats that could have a significant impact over the next 3–5 years.

Ernst and Young defined strategic risk as a risk that could cause severe financial loss or which could undermine the competitive position of a particular company. They classified these risks as:

- macro threats emerging from the geopolitical and macroeconomic environment in which all businesses operate;
- sector threats which reshape specific industries; and
- operational threats that impact the performance of leading businesses in an industry.

These risks vary in their significance across industries. The top 10 risks identified in the Ernst & Young report are:

- Regulatory and compliance risk. The possibility of regulatory intervention in some sectors increases this risk, especially in highly regulated industries, for example banking, insurance, pharmaceuticals and biotechnology.

---

[1] http://www.ey.com/Global/assets.nsf/International/EY_Strategic_Business_Risk_2008/$file/EY_Strategic_Business_Risk_2008.pdf.

■ Global financial shocks. Examples like the US sub-prime mortgage crisis can lead to difficulties in raising capital, losses sustained from falling share prices, and the impact of a recession on demand.

■ Aging consumers and workforce. There are shifts in demand, and the emergence of new asset management products for aging consumers. There is also the impact of an ageing workforce, most notably in the US automotive industry which faces huge pension and healthcare costs for its employees.

■ The inability to capitalize on emerging markets. Saturated home markets lead to an increased focus on emerging economies, which also provide opportunities for lower cost production. The growth of China and India as competitors in world markets is significant.

■ Industry consolidation/transition. The inability to grow organically and the need to respond to global competitive pressure have led to merger and acquisition activity with size being seen as an important factor in negotiating for resources. Private equity has also removed businesses from stock markets and altered the model of investment returns.

■ Energy shocks. Lack of access to competitively priced long-term fuel supplies is a key risk in many industries. Assuring fuel stocks from the Middle East is of long-term importance to governments as well as industries.

■ Execution of strategic transactions. Transactions like mergers and acquisitions, and the rise of private equity investment vehicles undertaken in response to industry consolidation may not deliver the promised benefits because of people, process or technology limitations.

■ Cost inflation. The return to levels of high inflation due to regulation, labour availability, fuel and raw material prices, etc. is a major risk.

■ Radical greening. Increased environmental concerns over climate change and the impact of changed weather conditions. While 'going green' may be costly in the short-term, consumer preferences and regulation may require businesses to make necessary changes to their practices. Carbon trading will have an impact on many industries and represents a new product that can be traded in financial markets.

■ Consumer demand shifts. Changes in consumer preferences, population ageing, the growth of Indian and Chinese markets and internet distribution channels require a flexible industry response.

Enterprise risk management and business strategy

Integrating risk management into the business planning process is an important component of enterprise risk management and ensures that the organization is able to take advantage of emerging opportunities (the 'upside') while also being able to cope when something goes wrong (the 'downside'). The focus on risk and strategy is that enterprise risk management is primarily concerned with the failure to achieve business objectives. Hence, integrating risk management with strategy leads to a focus on the 'performance' rather than 'conformance' aspect of risk and corporate governance.

An organization's strategic plan, with its mission and vision statements, sets the strategic goals of the organization for the business cycle. It will identify future opportunities as well as the critical strengths and weaknesses of the organization. Strategic planning will identify the structures, systems and processes that will help the organization achieve its intended outcomes both in the short and long term. As part of the strategic planning process, the organization may re-evaluate its risk appetite as this will impact its goals and the risks it is willing to take to achieve those goals. Part of identifying goals and the means by which goals are to be achieved is the identification, assessment and treatment of all the risks to which it is exposed and which may impact on the achievement of the organization's objectives.

A risk management plan as part of the strategic plan helps to determine whether the risk minimization strategies adequately address the extent, likelihood and impact of the risks. Risk-based controls are then put in place to avoid the organization being exposed to risks beyond its risk appetite. However, too many controls may make it difficult for an organization to exploit the opportunities it will face. This is a risk of control itself. Internal audits will also play a role in helping ensure that strategic plans are being implemented, and that controls to mitigate risk are effective.

Strategic planning and risk management should not be separate activities. Strategies to manage risks and enhance opportunities should be incorporated into strategic plans and kept up-to-date. Both strategic and risk management plans will support specific projects and actions that provide the basis to take advantage of opportunities.

Asset risk management

The category of business risk also extends to the organization's assets, those things the organization owns which are necessary to deliver strategy. Asset risk has a particular meaning within the financial services sector but here we refer to it as risks in relation to the business infrastructure – its asset base. We have already dealt with information technology risk in Chapter 13 and credit risk management in Chapter 15. Here, we are concerned with the physical infrastructure of building, machinery and inventory.

Asset risk management is ensuring the protection of assets, improving asset reliability through maintenance, inventory, warranty, and planning functions associated with asset performance management. Asset management involves:

- Recording information about equipment and property in an asset register including its specification, date of acquisition, purchase cost, warranty information, service contracts, spare parts, and repair facilities. There should also be an ongoing review of the expected lifetime of assets and technological or market changes that could lead to obsolescence.

■ Preventive maintenance through regular inspections and breakdown maintenance that quickly and cost-efficiently leads to a return to operation, with learning transferred to subsequent usage and preventive maintenance programmes.

■ Ensuring compliance with regulatory standards by securing requisite approvals and satisfying industry-specific standards in relation to health and safety, environmental protection, quality, etc.

Inventory risk

A specific asset which poses considerable risk is inventory (or stock). Inventory consists of merchandize a business owns but has not sold. The risks associated with inventory include:

■ Obsolescence due to new technologies or improved quality or production methods leading to more cost-effective products.

■ Spoilage of perishables.

■ Damage to inventory due to accidents in storage or handling of goods.

■ Theft of goods.

Inventory turn is a measure of how quickly stock is sold (or from a different perspective, how many days inventory is held to satisfy sales orders). Inventory risk management involves minimizing the amount of inventory held, often through holding inventories 'just in time' to satisfy production requirements and anticipated demand. In earlier years, businesses held inventory 'just in case' it was needed, but this often resulted in significant inventory write-offs.

Organizations need to develop strategies that minimize their inventory holding to avoid too much working capital being tied up in inventory and to avoid obsolescence, spoilage, damage or theft, while ensuring that customer demand can be satisfied and production efficiencies maintained.

Supply chain and logistics risk management

A significant risk in meeting customer demand and maintaining production lies outside the organization and is in the hands of suppliers. Supply chain risks range from single logistic activities, which may be internal or external to the organization, to the whole supply chain or network. Organizations will often be reliant on a single supplier for a key product, especially with the growth of outsourcing. Organizations will often locate production facilities in different countries to take advantage of lower raw material or labour costs and will ship intermediate products around the world. Therefore, suppliers by their very nature can be more susceptible to incidents than the organizations which they supply. In a 'just in time' environment, the risk of supplier failure can have an immediate and significant impact on the organization.

A disruption to niche suppliers can have a pronounced ripple effect that impacts multiple organizations. The threats to the supply chain are many and varied, from a natural disaster to a fire, political instability, financial failure, equipment break-down or an industrial dispute. While uncommon, catastrophes such as the 1995 Kobe earthquake, Hurricane Katrina in New Orleans in 2005 and the Chinese floods of 2007–2008 can massively disrupt both supply and transportation systems.

Organizations should be fully aware of the risk of disruption not only to principal suppliers but also to 2nd or 3rd tier suppliers in the supply chain and the resulting impact on the organization's ability to continue operating. Organizations should also be aware of the risks associated with the transportation system, such as the failure of a trucking firm, theft of goods in transit, delays in ship berthing and unloading, etc.

The challenge for enterprise risk management is to extend risk management to a supply chain that may stretch around the world and encompass a large number of independent suppliers and transporters over whom the organization has little or no direct control. The risk of failure in the supply chain can easily lead to an inability to produce or sell product, loss of customers and reputation.

Supply Chain Risk Management has emerged as a fundamentally important element of enterprise risk management, a specific example of expanding the risk focus beyond the traditional organizational boundary. To effectively manage supply chain risks an organization needs to:

- Know the organization's critical activities so that critical suppliers (of both products and transportation services) can be identified;
- Estimate the potential impact of the loss of a supplier;
- Carry out a risk assessment to understand the potential risks which could affect the supplier.

Once this information has been obtained, decisions about risk mitigation can be made. This starts with preventive action. Globalization enables organizations to use facilities in safe locations, close to raw material supplies and a reliable workforce, with good transportation access. Globalization can increase rather than reduce access to alternative suppliers and transportation methods to fill gaps in the supply chain. It is important to ensure that alternate suppliers are not subject to the same risks, for example would suffer the same natural disaster or the same restriction of raw materials supply.

A supplier strategy should describe purchasing strategies that can be used to mitigate supplier risk. These could include:

- diversification (buying from more than one supplier);
- asking suppliers to carry additional inventory as a contingency;
- ensuring that the supplier has excess capacity; and
- establishing 'failure to perform' clauses that significantly penalize a supplier's failure to supply in accordance with the contract.

Those responsible for selecting and negotiating with suppliers must make 'risk aware' purchasing decisions, aware of which suppliers are critical to the organization and which are not. Purchasing of non-critical services can be made on a pure commercial basis, but decisions relating to critical suppliers should be risk-based. Buyers should be aware of the consequence of the loss of or disruption to a supplier so they can weigh this against the commercial value of the supplier.

Buyers need to understand the supplier itself and not just the product being supplied. This is usually carried out as part of the tender and negotiation process. In reviewing the supplier, the buyer should consider: the quality of all of the organization's products – not just those being supplied; their incident history; key personnel dependencies; financial stability; volume flexibility; and the quality of the business continuity plans that the supplier has put in place.

The risk management approaches that an organization takes, for example to prevent fire may be taken for granted in the home country but may not be so common in developing countries. Organizations may therefore want to transfer their risk management practices to key suppliers.

An important element of supply chain risk mitigation is recognizing the signs early and dealing with them quickly. After purchasing, the organization needs to monitor suppliers to ensure any problems are detected early. 'Near miss' incidents or any reduction in quality or late delivery should be investigated as they may identify a more serious problem which can be addressed earlier. Any negative press relating to the company should also be part of the monitoring process.

Good information transfer within the supply chain is also crucial, so that problems, should they arise, are immediately known and remedial action can be taken to reduce the impact of a failure within the supply chain (especially due to the knock-on effect of disruption in the 2nd or 3rd tier of a supply chain). Using internet-based technologies, organizations can transfer orders instantaneously to suppliers and track the movement of goods door to door using bar code scanning and global positioning systems. This is an important element of risk mitigation as it enables corrective action to be taken more quickly if likely delays are known earlier.

If supply chain disruption does occur, a quick response can help to minimize consequences. Using an aircraft rather than a ship may be more costly but if supply is ensured, this may be the only alternative. Business continuity planning (see Chapter 20) is crucial to quick recovery while insurance (Chapter 21) can provide compensation for losses during the interim.

Case study: Gamma Holding

Gamma Holding develops, manufactures and sells high-quality, innovative industrial and consumer-related textile products. The company operates in 42 countries, and employs approximately 7000 people. Its headquarters are located in The Netherlands and its shares are listed on the Euronext Amsterdam stock exchange. Gamma Holding's 'Risk Inventory' is shown in Table 16.1.[2]

Enterprise risk management requires both a strategic and operational perspective on business risk, the risk that is specific to the business. Risk management needs to be integrated with strategy to reinforce the performance dimension. Risks also need to be addressed in the implementation of strategy through risk management of assets (both infrastructure and inventory) and the supply chain and logistics. Putting effective controls in place for business risk ensures that opportunities can be grasped, customer demand can be satisfied and production efficiencies maintained.

---

[2]This list has been adapted from http://www.gammaholding.com/en/Corporate_Governance/Risk_management/Risk_inventory?session=tbp87bda7jof29p15qg7cfd591.

Table 16.1   Gamma Holdings risk inventory

Type of risk	Description	Measure(s) of control
Market risks	Increasing competition	Some of the markets in which the business units operate are characterized by increasing competition from low-wage countries. Particularly in market segments with low margins, Gamma Holding must continually monitor costs in order to retain attractive market positions and to be able to achieve further growth. Against this background, both production and fabrication activities have been relocated to low-wage countries over the past 2 years. In addition, Gamma Holding is trying to stay ahead of the competition by focusing strongly on the market and the customer. Innovation is key in this regard, and the development of new materials and products is stimulated. Gamma Holding wants to focus more on strengthening marketing and sales and intensifying product and process innovations. Furthermore, cooperation is increasingly important, not just with suppliers and customers, but also within the group. These three elements – cost reduction, market and customer focus, and innovation – offer opportunities to enhance Gamma Holding's distinctive identity as a niche player vis-is competitors. The aim is to deliver distinctive quality and service with production capacity that allows a flexible response to the needs and wishes of customers and the market.

Table 16.1　(*Continued*)

Type of risk	Description	Measure(s) of control
	Fewer suppliers and higher prices of raw materials	Gamma Holding manufactures high-quality products for specific applications, which must meet the stringent requirements of customers and end-users. Consequently, the raw materials that Gamma Holding uses for its products must comply with strict specifications. However, the chemicals industry, which supplies such raw materials, is made up of a limited number of players in a market that is in a constant state of flux of consolidation and disposal. In order to retain access to these raw materials with the right specifications, Gamma Holding is continually strengthening its ties with its suppliers. It is also constantly on the lookout for new suppliers in emerging markets who, after a thorough testing period, can supply such raw materials. Gamma Holding also has to contend with rising prices of energy and raw materials. This trend has mainly been fuelled by the sharp rise in the price of oil. By having various business units join forces in the field of purchasing and continually seeking out alternative raw materials, this risk is limited wherever possible. In addition, Gamma Holding is constantly exploring ways to make energy consumption more efficient and effective. In this regard, investments have been made and energy-saving projects launched.

Table 16.1   (*Continued*)

Type of risk	Description	Measure(s) of control
	Political and economic instability	New growth markets not only present opportunities, but also involve risks. One of these is the political and economic instability of the countries in which Gamma Holding establishes operations. A sudden change of government or a lengthy political crisis can affect the economy of a country. This can hamper business activity and thus impact Gamma Holding's profitability. Gamma Holding has made the strategic choice to shift production to low-wage countries. Therefore, each decision to relocate production is preceded by a risk analysis, which identifies not just political risks, but geographical ones too, and weighs them up against the total risk profile of the group. Also in markets where Gamma Holding has had a presence for a longer period of time, political and economic stability is a constant focus of attention. For example, throughout the years, Exotic Fabrics has continually had to contend with unstable situations in Western Africa. These risks are taken into account when valuing the respective assets.

Table 16.1   (*Continued*)

Type of risk	Description	Measure(s) of control
Operational risks	Fire and business damage	On behalf of the operating companies, Gamma Holding has drafted a normative set of requirements for the implementation of measures in the field of fire and business damage. A central Technical Risk Manager assesses, on location, the risk profile of the companies and advises the management and the Executive Board on technical and organizational improvements. The policy formulated and the improvements implemented by the operating companies have led to a significant improvement in the risk profile and thus to lower premiums for the group. Increasingly, Gamma Holding's production and assembly locations are being combined. This leads to significant efficiency improvements, but at the same time reduces the number of alternatives within the group to transfer similar types of production in an emergency. Accordingly, in order to minimize process disruption, the entire business process has a high level of technical security. Moreover, Gamma Holding is constantly looking for alternative facilities to which it can turn, both inside and outside the group.

Table 16.1   (*Continued*).

Type of risk	Description	Measure(s) of control
	Management risk	Gamma Holding attaches great importance to well-balanced and effective management teams within all its operating companies, also in view of the considerable demands the strategic plan makes on the employees. A shortage of personnel with the right competences at the right place can lead to a decline in Gamma Holding's performance and to the company quickly falling behind the competition. Another risk is the dependence on key employees and the safeguarding of know-how. In this respect, human resource management will be intensified within Gamma Holding over the coming years.
	Increasing environmental regulation	Throughout the world Gamma Holding is increasingly being confronted with new environmental legislation and regulations. Furthermore, the use of certain raw materials, which are essential for the production process, is being questioned as a result of, among other things, European regulations. For instance, the first effects of REACH, the new regulations governing chemicals that came into force on June 1, 2007, were felt. On the basis of this, a number of suppliers are simplifying their product offerings, which can lead to changes in specifications for raw materials. In this context, Gamma Holding – in close consultation with the respective raw-material suppliers – is conducting additional acceptance tests and analyses in order to rule out the possibility of specification changes that could have an adverse effect on its products. In addition, Gamma Holding, as a responsible corporate citizen, is constantly seeking ways to reduce the amount of environmentally harmful raw materials used in the production process.

Chapter 17

Project Risk and Contract Risk

Organizations are faced with continual change and the need for flexible response to those changes. Enterprise risk management has been seen to encompass all aspects of an organization's ongoing activities as well as its strategic planning. Two areas where risk management needs to be more focused are in relation to project management and contract management, where single item and short-term events may need specific risk management attention.

Project management

A project is a carefully defined set of activities that together are intended to achieve specified goals. Project management is concerned with planning, organizing, and managing resources to bring about the successful completion of a specific project with its unique goals. A project may be defined for a wide range of alternative purposes, from a construction project, to development of a new computer system, launching a new product, or the takeover of a competitor. Each project is finite, with defined commencement and completion dates, and its own budget. As such, it is different from an ongoing process or operation that is embedded within routine organizational operations.

The management of ongoing operations and projects can be quite different, with the latter requiring quite specific project management skills. While enterprise risk management is applicable, there are specific aspects of managing project risk that are covered in this chapter. Hence managing project risk is like managing business risk (see Chapter 16) but is much narrower in its focus, although the risks may be significant.

The primary objective of project management is to achieve the project goals to the required scope, quality, time and budget. Project risk management is an essential component in the successful management of any project, whether small or large, short-term or long-term. Customers (either internal or external to the organization) dictate many elements of scope, quality, time and cost and once determined are contained within a contract, specification or agreement. Risk is managed by the project team, using the same techniques of risk assessment, estimation, treatment and monitoring that apply for other risks at the enterprise level.

Project risks

The risks associated with a project can be:

■ Inherent, following from the scope of the project and its objectives;
■ Acquired, resulting from the organization itself, and the approach, technology, methods, tools, techniques, skills and experience that are applied to the project;
■ Contextual, resulting from events or circumstances outside the project boundary but which impact on the project.

The overall project scope and the approach to its execution carry inherent risks. The project scope includes all the processes that are required to complete the effort and achieve the project goals. The actual execution covers project activities such as change management.

Changes in the business environment (including regulatory action, technological change, competitor activity, etc.) will also impact the project. The internal processes put in place to manage the project will also be important, especially the support of the project sponsor, resourcing of the project team and the commitment of external partners and suppliers. Legacy systems and procedures that are incompatible with the project may also impact its success.

The risk of a project is likely to be increased if there is a:

■ lack of mature project management methods and processes;
■ poor track record of project delivery;
■ history of problems with budget, schedule, status and overall project success, or solutions that have not achieved the expected benefits.

Risk is also increased where there are changes to the project after its commencement. Change management processes are therefore crucial because agreeing, documenting and implementing change avoids misunderstandings between parties, delays, cost overruns or quality or specification failures resulting from the integration of work already done or agreed to be done with the change required.

Assessing and managing risk is a key element of project management. All projects have risks and cost-effective management of risk is essential if a project is to achieve its business outcomes. These typically include cost, schedule, quality and satisfying the specification of the customer.

Project risk management

Project risk management is a process that must start from the inception of the project, and continue until the project is completed and its expected benefits realized. It provides a holistic view of project risks, identifies potential problems and builds processes to help the service provider monitor and manage those risks.

This means risk must be addressed when the project's scope and justification are first documented. Initially, a brief risk assessment should be done when proposing a new project. Any identified high-risk factors should be analyzed to determine whether actions could be undertaken to eliminate, reduce or transfer the risk before the project commences. This may require adjustments to the proposed project's scope, goals, timelines or resources.

Once a project is approved, a project risk management plan should be developed for all risks that were not eliminated during the project proposal process. This should include a description of the risk, the impact of the risk on the project, what actions can be taken to assist in reducing the risk and a contingency plan. The project manager and project team must seek the assistance of the project sponsor to manage risk in line with risk appetite for the project, which will be based on the organization's risk appetite and the risk appetite that has been determined for a particular project, which may vary from project to project.

Effective management of project risks requires:

- Commitment from senior management and the project sponsor throughout the project.
- Communication and consultation with internal and external stakeholders at every stage of the project risk management process. Risks perceptions may vary and it is important to reflect and reconcile these perceptions.
- Effective project management. The project must ensure that there are plans and processes for managing project risks. The project team should have a good understanding of the risks that the project may face and of appropriate methods for managing those risks.
- Risk ownership. Each identified risk must be assigned to a nominated person who is best able to manage the risk.
- Effective risk management. The use of available tools and techniques can significantly increase the effectiveness of the risk management process.

One of the main areas where risk can be shared is between the party commissioning the project and the party executing the project, as the perceived risk surrounding a project that is to be carried by each party will tend to inflate budgets and timeframes.

Risk can change as the project progresses. It is possible for a project initially assessed as low risk to quickly escalate into a high-risk project. Any alteration of project risk factors must be built into the project risk management plan.

Sound project risk management increases the likelihood of project success for the customer in terms of delivering the outcome in accordance with the specification, on time and on budget. It also increases the likelihood that the project will be profitable to the service provider with the positive reputation from a successful project more likely to lead to more work. The effective management of risk will usually require a balance to be struck between the scope and quality of the project's deliverables and the extent to which they satisfy the needs of the business, the time-scale for the project, and the cost of the project.

Project risk management process

A project risk management process includes the following processes:

- Agree the project specification.
- Define the risks associated with a project and how those risks will be managed.
- Determine whether and how risks will be accepted, mitigated, transferred or avoided.
- Plan the resources and skills required (people, physical resources, expertise, etc.) using appropriate project management techniques.
- Assemble a project team with the requisite skills and experience and appoint a project manager.
- Communicate the project plan.
- Identify each action needed to deliver the project and delegate to the project team members.
- Delegate the key responsibilities for project risk management within the project team.
- Continually monitor project progress and adjust plans as necessary.
- Undertake a continual review of risks and the effectiveness of controls and risk mitigation activities.
- After project completion, evaluate the project for any learning that can be transferred to future projects.

Project control

Project control is that part of project management that keeps it on-track, on-time, and within budget. Project control begins at the inception of the project with planning and ends after completion of the project with a post-implementation review. Each project should be assessed for the appropriate level of control needed to mitigate risk. Too much control is too time consuming and can lead to a failure to take advantage of opportunities, while too little control carries the risk of not meeting specification, quality, timeframe or budget. If project control is not implemented correctly, the cost to the business will be seen in financial loss, the remediation of errors, penalties, insurance claims, and reputational damage.

Various standards and methods exist to help with project management and in doing so, to manage risk. *BS 6079-3:2000 Project management. Guide to the management of business related project risk*[1] provides guidance on the identification and control of business related risks encountered when undertaking projects in the industrial, commercial and public or voluntary sectors. It is written for project sponsors and project managers who are responsible to higher levels of authority for one or more projects of various types and sizes.

Projects in Controlled Environments (PRINCE-2)[2] is a standard method for project management, designed to provide a framework covering all the disciplines and activities required within a project. The focus is on the Business Case which describes the rationale and business justification for the project. The Business Case drives all the project management processes, dividing the project into manageable and controllable stages from initial project set-up through to completion.

A number of project management tools are also available to reduce project risk. These include:

■ Gantt charts. These show the start and end dates of each element of a project. They can also show the dependencies between activities and the current progress compared to plan.

■ Program Evaluation and Review Technique (PERT) is a method that analyses the tasks necessary to complete a project, and the time needed to complete each task. This is an event-oriented technique rather than based on start and end dates. It is used more in research and development projects where time, rather than cost, is the major factor.

■ Critical Path Method (CPM) is a mathematically based algorithm for scheduling a set of project activities with interdependent activities. CPM calculates the longest path of planned activities to the end of the project, and the earliest and latest that each activity can start and finish without delaying the project, that is the path that is 'critical' to completion. It is commonly used in construction, software development, and engineering.

---

[1] Available for purchase from http://www.bsi-global.com/en/Shop/Publication-Detail/?pid= 000000000019994545.

[2] See http://www.prince2.org.uk/home/home.asp.

Microsoft Project is an example of project management software which creates critical path schedules, and displays processes in a Gantt chart. Members of a project team can have different access levels to different levels of the projects.

Contract management

Common contracts include those covering the sale of goods or services, the purchase of goods or services, employment and borrowing. Many contracts adopt standard terms and conditions while others are customised for more complex matters such as for large-scale construction or joint ventures, or with complex specifications such as the rights to intellectual property. Contract management includes:

- negotiating the terms and conditions of contracts made with customers, suppliers, partners, financiers or employees;
- agreeing and documenting changes during the life of the contract; and
- ensuring compliance with the terms and conditions of contracts.

Contract risk

Western organizations have always carried on business through contracts rather than based on relationships of trust that may be more evident in some other parts of the world. The Western business culture is based on documenting agreements in contracts and seeking remedies through the courts where contracts are not fulfilled. Organizations commonly find themselves tied in to a complex array of contracts, agreed by different people, committing to a variety of service level agreements with an increasingly diverse range of customers, suppliers, partners, financiers, etc. The management and performance of these contracts is vital to profitability, retention of customers and supply chain relationships and reputation. However, the process through which contracts are agreed, and their subsequent terms, can expose organizations on both sides of the contracting relationship to significant risks.

However, at the time of contract negotiation, competitive market dynamics and economic downturns can result in a greater number of contracts being negotiated on buyers' terms which increases suppliers' exposure to a greater number of unidentified risks. Confusion in contracts can also arise because of a lack of consistency between countries or organizations and due to language and cultural barriers. However, contract risk encompasses not only the negotiation of the contract but operates through the contract's entire lifetime, until all the terms of the contract are satisfied.

Regulatory, market and resource changes may remove the whole basis underlying a contract after it has been executed. What may have previously been acceptable contractual terms may no longer be appropriate if levels of risk increase in relation to risk appetite or there are changes to the risk/return trade-off. What is initially laid out in a contract may therefore cease to be relevant 1, 2 or 5 years later when market or economic forces take an unexpected turn. This may require contract re-negotiation or if this is not possible exposes the contracting parties to an unforeseen risk.

Contract risk management

Contract risk management focuses on understanding the risks inherent in contracts; designing risk management solutions to those risks; and implementing robust contractual risk management processes. This is achieved through improving organizational understanding of the general components of contractual liability and risk management, undertaking individual contract risk reviews, and analyzing portfolios of contracts. Contract risk management can take place through standardization of contractual terms and conditions; policies covering the writing, checking and authorization of contracts; enforcement; and monitoring.

Post-contract review also needs to monitor compliance with contractual terms and also to determine the effect, if any, of market, technology, regulatory changes on the contract.

Case study: project risk in an engineering consultancy

'Alpha Engineering' (the name has been changed for anonymity) is a listed company with 3500 employees carrying out engineering consultancy for major industrial projects including dams, power stations and bridges. These projects were typically valued at several million pounds each, extended over several years and involved considerable uncertainty. A key management concern following a review of Alpha's financial performance was that the estimated cost of project over-runs, non-productive time and contractual penalties incurred averaged about 2% of annual turnover. This represented an opportunity loss of about £3 million per annum against reported profits of about £5 million.

The main driver of risk management in Alpha was to address the rapidly increasing cost of professional indemnity insurance that had increased premiums to several million pounds per annum and had seen its excess increase from £5000 to £500 000 per annum over the last few years. Alpha had recently appointed a risk manager, adopted an offshore 'captive' insurer and implemented a management development programme. The programme included a substantial content on contract law and risk management aimed at improving the skills of all its managers.

One of the ways in which Alpha was helping its managers to understand risk was to undertake risk assessments as part of every project bid and to reflect each risk in the price to be submitted in tender documents. During contract negotiations, each risk would then be discussed between the lead consultant and the client when the value of the risk could be discussed. Alternative proposals were presented in terms of the mitigation action or control devices that could be put in place by the client to reduce the risk. This would reduce the component of the project price that reflected that risk. Alpha found that this transparent approach to risk and its impact on project pricing would both reduce risk and lead to a more profitable outcome for both parties.

Chapter 18

Fraud and Theft Risk

Organizations face a considerable risk of fraud and theft by managers, employees, customers, suppliers and other parties. This ranges from shoplifting to credit card fraud to stealing large sums of money. The increase in e-commerce has also increased the risks of electronic fraud and theft via the internet. Enterprise risk management requires an emphasis on preventing, detecting and responding to fraud effectively through a risk-aware culture, appropriate controls, careful monitoring and audit.

Fraud and theft

In criminal law, fraud is the crime of deliberately deceiving another in order to obtain property or services without payment. However, fraud is also a common law tort, a civil wrong for which damages may be payable as a remedy. Fraud is distinguished from the crime of theft which is the illegal taking of another person's property without that person's consent. In this chapter we use the term fraud to include theft by employees.

There are many examples of fraud that can damage a company financially as well as destroy its reputation and undermine public trust. For example:

- Fraudulent financial reporting (e.g. improper revenue recognition, overstatement of assets, understatement of liabilities) such as occurred with Enron and World-Com and which is now the subject of US Sarbanes-Oxley legislation.
- Misappropriation of assets (e.g. embezzlement, payroll fraud, theft of goods, procurement fraud, counterfeiting) whether by employees, customers or suppliers.
- Revenue or assets gained by fraudulent or illegal acts (e.g. over-billing customers, deceptive sales practices, collusion amongst competitors, etc.).
- Expenses incurred or liabilities avoided by fraudulent or illegal acts (e.g. tax fraud, payroll 'ghosts', falsifying timesheet data, providing misleading information to regulators).
- Expenses or liabilities incurred for fraudulent or illegal acts (e.g. bribery, kick-backs).
- General misconduct (e.g. conflicts of interest, insider trading, discrimination, theft of competitor trade secrets, antitrust practices, environmental violations, etc.)

The public faces a constant onslaught by thieves to defraud them through scams and stealing their personal information. Credit card and identity fraud crimes have increased dramatically and the theft of sensitive, non-public protected information has increased through hacking into private computer systems and similar practices.

Fraud risk awareness

Fraud or the risk of fraud should never be ignored. An anti-fraud culture supports awareness amongst all employees that there is always the possibility that fraud is taking place. It is important to raise awareness through training programmes, beginning with the induction of new employees and thereafter as a continuing process. Particular attention should be given to training and awareness amongst those employees involved with receiving cash, purchasing and paying suppliers, and handling valuable and readily saleable inventory.

Publicity should also be given to fraud that has been exposed by the organization. This serves as a reminder to those who may be tempted to commit fraud and also provides a warning to those responsible for the management of controls that the effectiveness of controls needs to be continually monitored and improved.

Fraud risk management strategy

As for all other risks, a risk management strategy needs to be developed for fraud. The cornerstone of this strategy should be a fraud policy statement which emphasizes the organization's attitude to fraud; its determination to combat and prevent fraud; and a commitment to punishing those found guilty of wrongdoing.

The UK Financial Services Authority has stated[1] that:

"A robust fraud strategy is one that is sponsored at the highest level within a firm and embedded within the culture. While the larger firms have been forced to wake up to fraud, those that have so far remained outside the fraudsters' radar are not as developed. Fraud threats are dynamic and fraudsters constantly devise new techniques to exploit the easiest target. Firms need to continue to invest in systems and controls and manage their responses to fraud in order to avoid being targeted as the weakest link."

The fraud strategy should be followed by a fraud and theft risk assessment which identifies the likelihood and impact of fraud and theft. It helps management understand

---

[1] http://www.fsa.gov.uk/pages/Library/Communication/PR/2006/014.shtml.

the risks that are unique to its business, identify the gaps or weaknesses in control to mitigate those risks, and develop an action plan for introducing controls to reduce the risk of fraud and theft.

A risk management strategy should aim to achieve three main objectives:

- Prevention: to reduce the risk of fraud and theft from occurring in the first place;
- Detection: to discover fraud and theft when it occurs; and
- Response: to take corrective action and remedy the loss caused by the fraud or theft.

Fraud prevention

People commit fraud because of the perceived suitability of a target; the incapacity of potential fraud victims to look after their own interests; and the motivation of offenders. However, the likelihood that fraud will be committed will decrease if the potential fraudster believes that the rewards will be modest, that they will be detected or that the potential punishment will be unacceptably high (even criminals have their own risk/return trade-off model). Therefore, a comprehensive system of controls is needed to reduce the opportunity for fraud, increase the likelihood of detection and support appropriate remedial action.

The existence of a fraud strategy can itself be a deterrent as it leads to employee awareness that fraud is of concern to the organization. As for most property-related crimes, there are three prerequisites for fraud to occur: dishonesty on the part of the perpetrator; the opportunity for fraud to occur and a motive for the fraud. Each can be dealt with through fraud prevention techniques, such as:

- Dishonesty
    - Pre-employment checks on all new staff (especially checking educational qualifications and references from previous employment).
    - Careful observation of staff by supervisors and the identification of lifestyles that are not supported by salaries.
    - Severe discipline for offenders – (the fraud response plan – see below).
    - Effective moral leadership by senior managers (e.g. managers who inflate expense claims are unlikely to engender a culture of honesty).

- Opportunity
    - Separation of duties where possible to avoid individual employees having access to cash, inventory, or other assets and also having the authority to cover such fraud.

- Controls over inputs (especially cash receipts).
- Controls over processing (to ensure that transactions are not omitted).
- Controls over outputs (e.g. printing of cheques).
- Physical security of assets (especially laptop computers and similar readily saleable assets).

■ Motive
- Good employment conditions so that employees believe they are fairly remunerated.
- Instant dismissals where illegal or unethical conduct has occurred.
- Sympathetic complaints procedure so that employees feel valued, especially in circumstances of personal hardship.

Fraud prevention can also be promoted through an anti-fraud culture that creates and supports employee awareness. Such a culture is one where fraud and theft is not tolerated, no matter how minor it appears to be (e.g. taking office stationery for home use). If minor unethical practices are overlooked, for example through inflated expenses or inaccurate time recording, this may lead to a culture in which larger frauds occur. High ethical standards bring long-term benefits as customers, suppliers, employees, investors and the community realize they are dealing with a trustworthy organization. The guiding principles for an anti-fraud culture include:

■ Ensuring that business values are clearly stated and communicated;
■ Not acting in a way that could bring the organization into disrepute;
■ Acting with integrity towards colleagues, customers, suppliers, government, investors and the public;
■ Ensuring that benefits (whether to shareholders, customers, suppliers or employees) are distributed fairly and impartially;
■ Safeguarding the confidentiality of personal data;
■ Complying with legal requirements.

Fraud detection

In KPMG's *Profile of a Fraudster Survey of 2007*,[2] 70% of fraudsters were found to be between the ages of 36 and 55. 85% of perpetrators were male. In 89% of profiles the

---

[2]http://www.ey.com/global/content.nsf/International/AABS_-_RAS_-_FIDS_-_10th_Global_Fraud_Survey.

fraudsters were employees committing fraudulent acts against their own employer. Members of senior management (including Board members) represented 60% of all fraudsters. In 36% of profiles the perpetrator worked for their company for 2–5 years before committing fraud and in 22% of profiles the fraudulent employees registered more than 10 years of service at the victim's organization. The internal fraudster most often worked in the finance department followed by operations, sales or as the CEO. Misappropriation of money was the most common type of fraud. In 24% of profiles the timeframe for perpetrating fraudulent acts was less than 1 year. In 67% of profiles, fraudsters acted within a timeframe between 1 and 5 years until they were exposed or stopped their fraudulent activities (see the case study of Conrad Black later in this chapter).

External auditors do not generally find fraud. Their letters of engagement typically identify that it is not one of their roles to look for fraud. Most frauds are uncovered through the work of internal audit. The methods of discovering fraud include:

- Performing regular checks, for example, stock takes and cash counts;
- Warning signals: late payments, backlogs of work, holidays not being taken, extravagant lifestyles, multiple and/or complex interlocking company structures, payments to countries with different legal standards (e.g. Swiss banking law has different privacy rules), missing audit trails, large money transfers before public holidays, etc.
- Whistleblowers.

Whistle blowing or an anonymous reporting hotline allows for suspicions to be reported by those who are not personally involved. People must be encouraged to raise the alarm about possible fraud. An anti-fraud culture will be important in reinforcing the need for employees to express their concerns. However, management must realize that loyalties among workers, fear of the consequences and having unsubstantiated suspicions may prevent people from coming forward. Of course, management has to be aware of the risk of malicious accusations or of suspicions that prove unfounded, whether anonymous or otherwise. The Public Interest Disclosure Act of 1999 provides some protection for whistleblowers and guidance to management.

Fraud response

The organization's fraud response plan should describe the arrangements for dealing with suspected cases of fraud, theft or corruption. It should provide procedures for evidence gathering to support any disciplinary or legal action. The fraud response plan also has a deterrent value as it should reinforce the organization's commitment to high legal, ethical and moral standards and its approach to those who fail to meet those standards.

The organization's response to fraud may include:

- Internal disciplinary action, in accordance with personnel policies, including dismissal.
- Civil litigation for recovery of the loss from the fraudster.
- Criminal prosecution through the police.

The response to any suspicion of fraud should be the formation of an investigation team. The actions of the investigation team will be driven by the organization's policy as to whether internal disciplinary, civil or criminal proceedings are expected. This will in turn influence the method of collection, storage and documentation of physical evidence and interview statements. Individual responsibilities for fraud response should be allocated to:

- Managers, to whom employees should report their suspicions. Managers should have an agreed, standard response in relation to any reported incidence of fraud or theft.
- Chief financial officer, who should have overall responsibility for the organizational response to fraud including the investigation. However, this role may be delegated to a fraud or internal security officer.
- Human Resources staff, who will have responsibility for disciplinary procedures and issues of employment law and practice.
- Internal auditors, who will most likely have the task of investigating the fraud and who should review the adequacy of internal controls.
- Audit committee, to whom notice of any significant fraud needs to be reported. They should review the details of all frauds, in order to identify control weaknesses.
- External auditors, particularly if the fraud is material, or reflects a significant internal control weakness. Auditors will also have expertise which will help the organizational response.
- Legal advisers, in relation to internal disciplinary action, or any civil or criminal action.
- Public relations, if the fraud is sufficiently large that it will come to public attention.
- Police, where it is the organization's policy to prosecute all those suspected of fraud.
- Insurers, where there is likely to be a claim.

Fraud and IT security

IT systems provide an additional opportunity for fraud. IT systems are subject to the accidental or deliberate alteration of data and controls must exist to prevent unauthorised access to data and to secure the integrity of data. This is particularly important with the increase in e-commerce. The lack of transparency with on-line processing of data across multiple sites in a network and a reduced reliance on paperwork leaves open the ability for internal or external fraudsters to disguise their fraud.

Particular problems for computer and data security have resulted from the growth of distributed data processing. Fraud can be carried out by customers who deny orders were placed via the internet and subsequently reject payments made on credit card transactions via the internet, but the main risks are: hacking via the internet; computer virus or worm; electronic eavesdropping into confidential information; etc. Commonly used controls for improving computer security from fraud or disruption through hacking and viruses include the protection of sensitive data through firewalls, anti-virus software and data encryption.

The increased use of e-commerce by businesses has increased the potential for hacking. Hacking is the ability to obtain unauthorised access to a computer system. Hacking can take many forms:

- 'Denial of service' attacks that overload a website with a well-organized increase in traffic that can force the website offline and result in lost revenue as well as a loss of brand image and reputation.
- Access to systems by breach of password security and tampering with files; Keystroke logging software that captures the keys pressed on a keyboard (such as passwords) and sends a log of these to the hacker via the internet.
- 'Trojans', apparently harmless software that contains malicious code designed to give control of a computer system to a hacker.
- 'Phishing', the use of deliberately misleading e-mails and websites designed to trick recipients into divulging personal financial data such as credit card numbers, passwords, etc.

A virus is a computer program that is capable of self-replication, which allows it to spread between infected computers. The virus can alter or delete files or even erase the entire contents of a computer hard disk drive. A worm can randomly over-write or change pieces of data within a file. Staff awareness needs to be increased about the threats involved and they should not be permitted to use unauthorised software. Data transferred between computer systems must be checked before opening files. Attachments to e-mails from unknown sources must similarly be treated with caution.

Competitive intensity has increased so protecting customer databases from competitor access or fraudulent use (especially credit card fraud) is important. The UK Data Protection Act has made it essential to maintain the confidentiality of data.

The main controls that can be used against viruses include virus detection and protection software which scans for viruses, alerts the user and removes the virus. The control used to restrict access to an organization's computer system over the internet is a firewall. A firewall comprises a combination of hardware and software located between the company's private network (intranet) and the public network (internet). It is a set of control procedures established to allow public access to some parts of the organization's computer system (i.e., outside the firewall) while restricting access to other parts of the system (i.e., inside the firewall). Data encryption enables data to be converted into a non-readable format before transmission and then re-converted after transmission. The data can only be read by a receiver with a matching encryption key. This method is commonly used for on-line purchases using credit cards. Digital envelopes can send the encryption key in a message separately to the encrypted message.

Because experienced hackers can find ways around firewalls and avoid, at least in the short-term, virus protection software and additional security to prevent hacking has become more important. The security methods include:

- Vulnerability or penetration testing: deliberate attempts by the organization to breach its own security;
- Intrusion detection: regular monitoring to determine when the network is being attacked;
- Scanning of all e-mails received and rejection of spam e-mail;
- Network forensics: a new science that can be used after a security breach to find out how the network was compromised, from where the attack originated and what the hacker was able to do. Evidence can be used to protect against similar attempts in the future and may assist a prosecution.

Serious and committed attempts to breach a computer system are likely to be successful, while the cost of a completely secure computer system will usually be prohibitive (except for government). The real aim of information security is to increase the cost in time and money to hackers who want to gain unauthorised access to the network.

Fraud, internal control and internal audit

Anti-fraud activities are an essential element of the internal control system. The role of internal audit and the audit committee of the Board in preventing fraud is therefore critical. To minimize risk, the Board or audit committee must understand the fraud risk, and implement controls that can detect and deter these activities. The audit committee must use fraud risk assessments to ensure that adequate internal controls are in place and that fraud risk is part of the annual internal audit plan.

An organization's fraud policy should explain the role of internal audit in relation to fraud. Internal audit should be responsible for:

- Planning and evaluating the design and effectiveness of anti-fraud controls;
- Assisting in the organization's fraud risk assessment and helping draw conclusions about the appropriate mitigation strategies; and
- Reporting to the audit committee on internal control assessments, audits, investigations, and related activities.

Proper internal controls and distribution of duties should be designed to make it as difficult as possible to commit fraud. The risk of fraud is substantially reduced by segregating duties so that no one person has too much control in any one financial area. When various people handle different aspects of transactions, this provides a deterrent to fraud while increasing the chance of identifying any fraud that may have occurred.

Some of the more common internal controls that mitigate the more likely opportunities for fraud and theft include the separation of responsibilities between:

- authorising supplier invoices and signing cheques;
- signing cheques and reconciling the bank account;
- updating accounts receivable records and banking customer monies;
- updating accounts receivable records and issuing credit notes or writing off debts;
- handling physical inventory and writing off obsolete, damaged or missing inventory from inventory records;
- controlling stocks of pre-numbered invoices and cheques and using those forms.

Internal audit can also often take a key role in investigating cases of fraud or irregularity, whether arising from external or internal sources. The fraud policy may encourage employees to inform the Head of Internal Audit of any attempted, suspected or actual fraud as soon as is possible.

There have been high profile cases of fraud over recent years, many of which have involved the top management of organizations. The risk of this kind of fraud is particularly difficult because the Board and audit committee will rely extensively on management assurances and internal control, which may be compromised by top managers. The following four case studies highlight this risk.

Case study: Parmalat

In December 2003, Italian dairy-foods group Parmalat, with 36 000 employees in thirty countries, went into bankruptcy protection with US$ 8–10 billion of vanished assets. The company was 51% owned by the Tanzi family.

Parmalat defaulted on a US$ 185 million bond payment that prompted auditors and banks to scrutinise the company's financial accounting records. Thirty-eight per cent of Parmalat's assets were supposedly held in a bank account in the Cayman Islands but no such account ever existed. Letters received from the bank by auditors were forgeries. Tanzi admitted that he knew the accounts were falsified to hide losses and the falsified balance sheet was used to enable Parmalat to continue borrowing. Tanzi also confessed to misappropriating US$ 620 million, although prosecutors believe the amount could be as much as US$ 1 billion.

Parmalat has been one of the largest financial frauds in history. The company falsified its accounts over a 15-year period. This was not identified by two firms of auditors, Grant Thornton and Deloitte Touche Tohmatsu. At least 20 people have been involved in the fraud, including members of the Tanzi family, the chief financial officer, board members and the company's lawyers. Calisto Tanzi the founder and chief executive was arrested on suspicion of fraud, embezzlement, false accounting and misleading investors and is currently in prison in Italy.

Case study: Conrad Black

Conrad Black was one of the most powerful newspaper magnates in the world, controlling Hollinger International, which through its affiliates published several high profile newspapers including the UK *Daily Telegraph* and the US *Chicago Sun Times*.

In 2003, Hollinger International reported to the US Securities and Exchange Commission details of misconduct at the company, including violations of fiduciary obligations by officers, including Conrad Black. Hollinger's report accused Black and some of his senior colleagues at Hollinger of running a "corporate kleptocracy." Black subsequently resigned as the CEO of Hollinger.

Black had diverted company funds for his personal benefit from money due to Hollinger after it sold some of its publishing assets. He had also illegally taken company documents. In 2007, Black was convicted in US federal court of three counts of mail and wire fraud and one count of obstruction of justice. He was sentenced to 78 months in prison and required to repay Hollinger $6.1 million and a fine of $125 000.

Case study: Enron

In December 2001, US energy trader Enron collapsed. Enron was the largest bankruptcy in US history. Even though the United States was believed by many to be the most regulated financial market in the world, it was evident from Enron's collapse that investors were not properly informed about the significance of off-balance sheet transactions. US accounting rules may have contributed to this, in that they were more concerned with the strict legal ownership of investment vehicles rather than with their effective control. Enron may have actively lobbied against changing the treatment of special purpose entities used in off-balance sheet financing in US financial reporting with the aim of continuing its deception.

The failure of Enron also highlighted the over-dependence of an auditor on one particular client, the employment of staff by Enron who had previously worked for their auditors, the process of audit appointments and re-appointments, the rotation of audit partners and how auditors are monitored and regulated.

Former chief executive Kenneth Lay was convicted of securities fraud in 2006 but died before sentencing and his conviction was then set aside. Enron's former chief financial officer Andrew Fastow was sentenced in 2006 to 6 years in prison for stealing from Enron and devising schemes to deceive investors about the energy company's true financial condition. Lawyers have to date won settlements totalling $US 7.3 billion from banks including JPMorgan Chase, Bank of America, and Citigroup.

As a consequence of the failure of Enron and WorldCom, the United States introduced Sarbanes-Oxley legislation to address many of the criticisms of reporting and auditing practice. In their comments on the failure of Enron, the Association of Certified Chartered Accountants recommended a global set of principles-based financial reporting standards and a global code of corporate governance, arguing that legalistic, rules-based standards encourage creative, loophole-based practice. Subsequently, the United States has begun to move towards adopting International Financial Reporting Standards, already used or in process of being adopted by most other countries (see Chapter 10).

Case study: WorldCom

WorldCom filed for bankruptcy protection in June 2002. It was the biggest corporate fraud in history. The company used accounting tricks, largely by treating operating expenses as capital expenditure to conceal a deteriorating financial condition and to inflate profits. WorldCom (now renamed MCI) admitted in March 2004 that the total amount by which it had misled investors over the previous 10 years was almost $US75 billion and reduced its stated pre-tax profits for 2001 and 2002 by that amount.

WorldCom stock prices began falling in late 1999 as businesses reduced their spending on telecom services and equipment. A series of debt downgrades had raised borrowing costs for WorldCom, which was struggling with about US$ 32 billion in debt.

Former WorldCom chief executive Bernie Ebbers resigned in April 2002 amid questions about US$ 366 million in personal loans from the company and a federal probe of its accounting practices. In 2005, he was convicted of fraud and conspiracy as a result of WorldCom's false financial reporting. He is currently serving a 25-year prison term. Scott Sullivan, former chief financial officer, entered a guilty plea and was sentenced to 5 years in prison as part of a plea agreement in which he testified against Ebbers.

The US Securities and Exchange Commission said WorldCom had committed 'accounting improprieties of unprecedented magnitude' – proof, it said, of the need for reform in the regulation of corporate accounting.

Chapter 19

Risk, Regulation and the Environment

This chapter is concerned with external pressures on the organization, in particular the impact of regulation and the impact of climate change. There is considerable regulation in most countries and the United Kingdom, where much, regulation derives from its membership of the European Union. Climate change risk is one example of how external risks can emerge quite suddenly and potentially have significant impact on whole industries and supply chains. Its high profile as a risk at the time of writing has resulted in it being covered separately.

Risk and regulation

While many aspects of enterprise risk management are concerned with improving performance through a risk-based approach to achieving objectives and controlling operations, the compliance function is also important. Compliance and regulatory costs can be a significant burden on organizations. Every country and every industry has a different set of regulations governing many aspects of how individual companies or industries operate, while all companies have to comply with generic regulations such as health and safety and data protection. It is impossible to produce even a partial list of regulations because of the sheer scale of regulation. This scale highlights the risk of not being aware of or complying with regulations which can lead to penalties and reputational damage at the enterprise level. Those responsible for enterprise risk management need to ensure that affected managers and functions are all aware of the relevant legislation and regulations and ensure compliance.

The costs of meeting compliance regulations such as Basel II for financial institutions and Sarbanes-Oxley for US-listed companies have been immense. In its 2006 report *Risk, Responsibility and Regulation – Whose risk is it anyway?*,[1] the UK's Better Regulation Commission wrote:

> "The relationship between risk, responsibility and regulation is rapidly emerging as an important theme of policy development. In it lies great opportunity, not only to reduce dramatically the burdens of regulation on society but also to

---

[1] http://archive.cabinetoffice.gov.uk/brc/upload/assets/www.brc.gov.uk/risk_res_reg.pdf.

reinforce national qualities of self-reliance, resilience and a spirit of adventure. But there is also a danger that if the relationship is unbalanced, we slip into a cycle of increased regulation to meet the demands of increased risk aversion".

The report explained that the public response, often encouraged by the media, to a perceived risk (whether it emerges over time or arises from a specific incident) is usually to call for regulation – the result being a 'regulatory spiral'. The legal background of many politicians encourages them to reach first for legislative solutions to problems rather than to look for alternative solutions. Getting an important Bill through Parliament has also been seen as a good way to progress a political or public service career. The Better Regulation Commission has argued that the entanglement of risk and regulation is unsustainable and undesirable. They called for a change of culture, recognizing that this required political leadership and policy change. This would ensure that where it was appropriate for governments to intervene through regulation, that this was done on the basis that it was demonstrably the best possible option. A subsequent report, *Public Risk: The next frontier for better regulation*[2] published in 2008 has led to the establishment of a Risk and Regulation Advisory Council.

Regulatory compliance risk

Compliance risks often arise from the awareness and understanding of regulations but also from interpretation and judgement on 'grey areas' of business practices. This is particularly so as institutions such as the UK Financial Services Authority moves towards more 'principles-based' regulations, in which interpretation becomes even more important.

The process of managing compliance risk includes the following steps:

- Defining 'compliance risk' and responsibilities. Organizations should having a clear understanding of what compliance risk means, and this should be communicated to all relevant staff. Compliance risk should be seen as the responsibility of the whole organization and not viewed as something in which only the compliance function has a responsibility.
- Compliance culture. Organizations should demonstrate the positive aspects of compliance (rather than as an annoying or bureaucratic set of rules) through a compliance culture and reinforce desired behaviours as essential in successfully managing compliance risk.

---

[2]http://archive.cabinetoffice.gov.uk/brc/upload/assets/www.brc.gov.uk/public_risk_report_070108.pdf.

■ Governance. The Board and senior managers should have a clear commitment to compliance and the risk management of compliance.

■ Compliance risk assessment process. The compliance risk assessment process can determine priorities and drive compliance work plans around the areas where risk is greatest. Risk assessment methods can also help ensure that compliance is effective. Compliance risk management should also be aligned with internal control and internal audit functions.

■ Compliance monitoring. As for other risks, monitoring of compliance performance needs to be carried out on a regular basis, through desk-based audits of processes and documentation and internal audit reviews. Reviews can range from the simple testing of whether an organization adheres to a specific regulatory requirement to a more holistic assessment of the risks faced by the organization as a whole.

■ Evaluating compliance performance. Organizations should measure the effectiveness of their efforts to manage compliance risk. This can involve an assessment of whether it is achieving the desired compliance culture and behaviour, assessing the behaviour of individual staff and business units, and assessing the effectiveness of the contribution of the compliance function to managing compliance risk.

However, compliance should not only be seen as a restrictive exercise, as regulation can sometimes follow the acceptance of good practice and the need to apply a higher standard of practice more widely. It can therefore be used as a lever of improvement. As such, organizations may prefer not only to comply with legislation and regulation but also to change their business processes by simultaneous compliance and improvement action. In this way compliance becomes less a burden and more the opportunity to enhance organizational processes.

Managing regulatory compliance and review

A key function, usually of specialist departments within organizations, is to ensure compliance with regulations. Compliance enables the avoidance of sanctions such as penalties and the negative effect on reputation that flows from penalties and public exposure. It also enables reporting to the public where this is required. Risk and compliance are increasingly being seen as an integrated function, with 'Risk and Compliance' management roles being increasingly advertised.

The compliance function, whether centralized or decentralized is concerned with leading enterprise compliance efforts, designing and implementing internal controls, policies and procedures to assure compliance with applicable laws and regulations and professional codes; managing the risk of non-compliance; advising and supporting the internal audit function; undertaking any investigations into regulatory and compliance issues; and responding to requests for information from regulatory bodies.

Regulatory review involves:

- Risk management of regulatory compliance.
- Environmental scanning to determine new and proposed regulations.
- Assessment and implementation of new regulatory requirements.
- Training and awareness programmes for employees.
- Internal controls for compliance assurance.
- Compliance health checks.
- Benchmarking compliance systems against industry best practice.
- Measuring, monitoring and reporting on compliance.
- Cost effectiveness of compliance and reporting systems.
- Reducing the risk of regulatory intervention.

One example of the likely increase in regulatory burden over time, which also provides opportunities, is climate change and the impact of greenhouse gas emissions. There are also proposals by various governments, notably Australia, for emissions trading schemes, supplementing or replacing direct government intervention with market forces. Climate change risk is used here, not as an example of regulation, but as an example of environmental (in the broadest sense of that word's usage) change increasingly affecting all organizations.

Climate change risk

Climate change has been called the most important issue facing the world in the twenty-first century. Scientists generally agree that the rate of global warming is increasing and it is predicted that future warming this century will be $3\,°C$ above twentieth century levels. This is likely to lead to significant rises in sea levels, increasing drought in many parts of the world and could lead to severe political, social and economic consequences.

Organizations need to consider the economic instability likely to occur during climate change, which may manifest itself through changes in supply networks, employment, interest rates and currency values. The severity of future climate change will force governments to impose additional regulatory costs on all businesses which are deemed to be contributing to the problem. There are also legal risks for companies if they fail to take climate change seriously and the risks of litigation will be increased if companies act irresponsibly. A company's reputation could also be damaged by not taking climate change seriously and failing to disclose relevant information to investors and other interested parties.

Organizations need to seek reliable scientific evidence about how climate change may affect their business models. This involves assessing climate risks over different timescales and through developing alternative scenarios; quantifying the possible risks using an appropriate method for the regions in which the organization operates; and evaluating the likely success of business strategies in the light of this information.

In their 2008 report *Climate changes your business*[3] KPMG identified the aviation, healthcare, oil and gas, tourism, transport, and financial services sectors as those most at risk of climate change. The oil and gas sector faces the greatest risk with recent attempts by energy firms to diversify into the renewable energy sector being offset by the upheaval the industry faces as countries shift towards having a low carbon economy. Financial institutions were also found to be particularly exposed to climate risks as a result of their investment portfolios and the increasing environmental awareness amongst their customer bases. The tourism sector was deemed to be underestimating the physical effects climate change will have on many of the most popular holiday resorts. The telecommunications, chemicals and food and beverages sectors faced comparatively less risk.

Lloyd's insurance report *Climate Change: Adapt or Bust*[4] urges the insurance industry to act now or face the risks associated with climate change. The report showed that in the last year, natural catastrophes killed 97 000 people and cost the insurance industry $83 billion – more than ever before. Lloyd's argued that with new weather patterns, exposures are changing and the insurance industry needs to take a new approach to underwriting, recommending that pricing and capital allocation models needed to be regularly updated to reflect the latest scientific evidence.

Perhaps the key issue raised by climate change is that of sustainability – how will organizations sustain and improve their performance as environmental resources are depleted and climate changes.

Climate change risk management

The enterprise risk management approach is as applicable to climate change as to other risks facing the organization. Sustainability is the concept that links climate change with enterprise risk management. Serious consideration should be given to:

■   The long-term nature of climate change and its variable effects in different regions, and

---

[3] http://www.kpmg.nl/Docs/Corporate_Site/Publicaties/Climate_Changes_Your_Business.pdf.
[4] http://www.lloyds.com/NR/rdonlyres/38782611-5ED3-4FDC-85A4-5DEAA88A2DA0/0/FINAL360climatechangereport.pdf.

▓ The indirect effects. While direct effects may be relatively easier to identify and assess, indirect effects are much more difficult.

A comprehensive guide to climate change risk management which applies the AS/NZS4360 Risk Management Standard was produced by the Australian Government in 2006 as *Climate Change Impacts & Risk Management*[5]. The risks associated with climate change will have to be assessed by businesses as part of their strategic planning process and especially where long-term capital investments are being considered. The risks of climate change are that it could lead to:

▓ Loss of markets.
▓ Loss of resources.
▓ Loss of infrastructure.
▓ Increased operating costs.
▓ Increased regulatory costs through additional reporting and proposed carbon trading measures.
▓ Changes in the political, social and economic context in which commercial decisions are made.

The risks of climate change to an organization may range from its reputation as a reliable provider of products or services to its ability to provide public services. This may arise directly from changes to climate but also from a chain of consequences which may affect the organization's ability to serve its customers. However, neither likelihood nor consequence can be estimated with any certainty. In the context of climate change risk assessment, uncertainty arises because, although evidence supports a changing climate, there is insufficient knowledge about the speed and magnitude of the changes or what impact the changes will actually have.

To manage the risks of climate change it is necessary to define how climate is assumed to change in the future. This is achieved by using climate change scenarios which provide alternative but plausible summaries of the changes to climate that could apply in particular geographical regions and in particular timescales. Scenarios can provide a consistent and efficient basis for assessing climate-related risks for different industries and organizations.

Because of the long time scales involved, the risk treatment of climate change involves substantial strategic planning and resource allocation decisions that are quite different from short-term, reactive adjustments. Climate change risk treatment can include technological and capital investment change. These are significant decisions when the likelihood and impact of climate change is so uncertain in terms of timing

---

[5]http://www.climatechange.gov.au/impacts/publications/pubs/risk-management.pdf.

and effect. One means of avoiding under- or over-adaptation is for organizations to take a balanced approach to managing climate and non-climate risks. This is best achieved by integrating climate change risk management with the broader enterprise risk management process.

Adaptive management is an important strategy for dealing with climate change uncertainties. It is the process of putting in place flexible and incremental changes based on regular monitoring and the revision of plans using information available at the time, rather than relying on one-off, large-scale treatments. Adaptive management leaves scope for decisions about treatments to be reviewed in the future as improved information becomes available about the nature and effect of climate change risks. An advantage of this approach is that it reduces the potential for over-adaptation, while providing scope for an organization to strengthen its risk treatment should it become apparent in the future that the organization is under-adapting to one or more climate change risks.

The Global Reporting Initiative (GRI)[6] is a not-for-profit entity which promotes the disclosure by organizations of their sustainability performance. The GRI vision is that reporting on economic, environmental, and social performance by all organizations should be as routine and comparable as financial reporting. The GRI has produced a Sustainability Reporting Framework and Sustainability Reporting Guidelines which provide guidance for organizations for disclosure about their sustainability performance. The Reporting Framework facilitates transparency and accountability by organizations across the world.

Research published by GRI and KPMG Sustainability in 2007 *Reporting the Business Implications of Climate Change in Sustainability Reports*[7] critiques current practices on reporting and climate change, and questions how organizations are currently responding to this issue. The research found that although most businesses report on climate change, the majority avoid reporting the risks posed by this environmental threat. Instead they extensively report on new business opportunities arising from it, such as establishing carbon funds.

Regulatory compliance and climate change are but two examples of external risks which face all organizations to some extent, and which need to be considered as part of the organization's enterprise risk management.

---

[6]http://www.globalreporting.org/Home.

[7]http://www.globalreporting.org/NR/rdonlyres/C451A32E-A046-493B-9C62-7020325F1E54/0/ClimateChange_GRI_KPMG07.pdf.

Chapter 20

Risk and Business Continuity Management

A crisis can be caused by any number of factors, some of which have already been introduced in earlier chapters: a stock market disruption such as that caused by Enron/WorldCom or more recently in the US sub-prime mortgage market; by the failure of a key computer system or key supplier or the loss of a key employee; by human action such as the September 11 terrorist attacks; or by a natural disaster such as floods or hurricanes. Enterprise risk management uses business continuity as the key mechanism by which a response to crisis can take place, effects mitigated, and a return to normal operations as quickly as possible, including the restoration of any reputational damage.

Risk of crisis

There are a number of differences between enterprise risk management (ERM) and its specific application to business continuity management (BCM). ERM focuses on undertaking a thorough enterprise-wide identification and assessment of risk, and evaluating risk in relation to its likelihood and impact before identifying an appropriate risk response. BCM is concerned only with events that cause a significant business disruption, it is not concerned with probability (which will usually be low) but with the impact of an event and the time required for an organization to return to normal business operations.

For example in the United Kingdom the Civil Contingencies Act, 2004 requires all emergency services and local authorities to actively prepare and plan for emergencies. Local authorities also have an obligation under the Act to actively lead the promotion of business continuity practices in their geographical areas.

Business continuity management

As for other risks, risk identification and assessment is needed so that the organization is able to catalogue the crises which may impact its business. However, by its very nature, a crisis has a low likelihood but a very significant impact so risk management needs to take this into consideration. Risk reduction should already have taken place and this chapter is concerned with the actions necessary should the risk eventuate. In the event of a crisis event, mitigation will take place through enacting the business continuity plan (or disaster recovery plan). Business continuity management involves the development of strategies, plans and actions which provide protection and alternative modes of operation for those activities which, if interrupted, might bring a seriously damaging impact or critical loss to an organization.

Business continuity management is defined by the Business Continuity Institute[1] as a process that identifies potential impacts that threaten an organization and provides a framework for building resilience and the capability for an effective response that safeguards the interests of its key stakeholders, reputation, brand and value creating activities. Business continuity (or disaster recovery) planning takes place in order to recover from business-critical events after a disaster or extended disruption has taken place.

Although specifically related to IT systems, the Business Continuity Institute has established a business continuity life cycle with six stages:

1. Understanding the business through business impact analysis and risk assessment and control.
2. Establishing business continuity management (BCM) strategies.
3. Developing and implementing BCM response including detailed plans; relationships with other organizations; crisis management; sourcing and outsourcing; emergency response; communications and public relations.
4. Building and embedding a BCM culture through employee education, training and awareness.
5. Exercising, maintenance and audit through rehearsals and testing, and audit processes.
6. Implementing a BCM programme with Board commitment and participation, strategy, policies, accountabilities, resources, information systems, etc.

British Standard BS 25999[2] contains some key elements for business continuity management (BCM):

■   BCM Policy: a clear, unambiguous and appropriately resourced policy.
■   Understanding the organization. In order to apply appropriate business continuity

---

[1] http://www.thebci.org/.

[2] http://www.bsi-global.com/en/Assessment-and-certification-services/management-systems/Standards-and-Schemes/BS-25999/.

strategies and tactics the organization has to be fully understood, including its critical activities, resources, duties, obligations, threats, risks and overall risk appetite.

■ Developing and implementing a BCM response. The tactical means by which business continuity is delivered. These include incident management structures, incident management and business continuity plans.

■ Exercising, maintenance, audit and self-assessment of the BCM culture. Without testing the BCM response an organization cannot be certain that they will meet their requirements. Exercise, maintenance and review processes will enable the business continuity capability to continue to meet the organization's goals.

■ Embedding BCM into the organizational culture. Business continuity should become part of the way that the organization is managed.

Business impact analysis

A business impact analysis helps to define critical business processes. This is important because once a crisis occurs, all efforts must be taken to return to effective business operations within a realistic timescale. A distinction needs to be made here between the primary business processes which need priority and the secondary ones which can take a little longer. As every organization will have limited resources it is critical to understand where it needs to focus its recovery efforts.

Risk assessment of the impact may include consideration of any of the following risks:

■ Loss of IT systems and data.

■ Loss of key employees (e.g. the Twin Towers terrorist incident caused the loss of many staff in some organizations) or of key skills.

■ Fire or extreme weather (hurricane, floods, high winds, etc.) leading to loss of, or substantial damage preventing access to site.

■ Loss of telecommunications (including computer network).

■ Loss of utilities (electricity, gas, water, sewerage).

■ Damage to image, brand or reputation, negative press publicity, etc.

■ Employee loss of life or serious injury.

■ Threat to customer health or product safety leading to product recall or liability claim.

■ Disruption to supply chain.

■ Pressure group protest (e.g. animal rights activists).

■ Protracted industrial action.

■ Environmental accident (e.g. Bhopal, Chernobyl).

■ Terrorist damage.

Emergency response

A key element of business continuity management is an emergency plan, in effect the first response to a crisis at the time it is happening. Of primary concern is the evacuation of affected people (employees, customers, visitors, etc.), the alerting of emergency services, and only if it can be done safely, the removal of critical business documents and files (although good business continuity planning will have arranged for secure storage and/or off-site backup data).

Media management is important in the immediate response to a crisis because a company which does not communicate with its employees, customers, suppliers, investors, or affected public can lose the trust of these groups. This will have an adverse impact on the company's reputation which can lead to the loss of staff and customers.

The case study of Marks & Spencer at the end of this chapter provides an example of emergency response and the learning that can lead to improvements in business continuity.

Business continuity planning

The Business Continuity Plan should be simple enough so that it can be executed without any problems during a crisis. The purpose of the plan is to:

■ manage the risks which could result in disastrous events and thus minimize the likelihood of a disaster occurring;

■ reduce the time taken to recover if an incident does occur; and

■ minimize the risks involved in the recovery process by making the critical decisions in advance in stress-free conditions. This is because critical decisions made during the stress of a crisis have a high risk of being wrong, ineffective, and costly.

Business continuity planning involves making a risk assessment and developing a contingency plan to address those risks. The business continuity plan should identify:

■ The roles and responsibilities of key individuals.

■ Back-up facilities for all data.

■ Alternative sites to continue operations.

■ Replacement equipment providers.

■ Staffing requirements and the work necessary to restore business-critical information to enable the organization to continue operating.

■ The time involved to restore business operations and business-critical information.

■ Media communication.

■ Ongoing communication to affected employees, customers, suppliers, financiers, etc.

■ Close liaison with insurers.

Testing and monitoring

Once the business continuity plan has been designed and approved it needs to be tested under realistic conditions as untested plans can easily fail. It is also important to educate everyone in the company about the business continuity plan. Employees will be the first ones to react to (or in some cases prevent) an incident, so the success or failure of the plan depends largely on the way it is implemented by employees. If people are not properly trained regarding emergency response and the business continuity plan, its likelihood of success is seriously diminished.

After testing, it is important to re-evaluate the plan on a regular basis and retest it as sites, equipment and business processes can change on a regular basis. For example if a company buys new equipment on which it is heavily dependent, the business continuity plan needs to be revised to take this into account. The Business Continuity Plan should be a living document, which needs to adapt to changing business conditions and as business requirements change.

If a crisis does occur, it is important to evaluate the effectiveness of the business continuity plan while the event is fresh in everyone's minds. While a crisis has serious effects, it also provides a valuable learning experience that can be used to help in preventing or responding to future crises.

Case study: Marks & Spencer

In June 1996, the police were alerted by a coded message from the Irish Republican Army, a terrorist group that a bomb was placed in the Manchester city centre. A total of 173 Marks & Spencer staff were working in the store that morning and were evacuated by police. However, the evacuation point was unusable as it was within the police cordon. Once the bomb, which had been placed close to the store, detonated, staff who were injured, many by flying glass, were taken to hospital and others were sent home. Those staff did not have their personal possessions and the transport system was disrupted so this presented difficulties that had not been foreseen. Employees were told to report to the store closest to their home the next day. The company attempted to contact those not on duty that day to give them advice about reporting to work, however the regional telephone network no longer operated. Telephone services to the Manchester store were re-routed following co-operation with the telecommunications provider.

Staff required a great deal of emotional support in the aftermath, exacerbated by the loss of their personal possessions. There were also a great many press queries that called for a company response. Subsequently, stock was removed from the store and computer equipment was sent for cleaning and data recovery. Staff were allocated to different stores during the rebuilding process and Marks & Spencer announced the opening of new stores in Manchester to replace the damaged one.

Marks & Spencer improved their business continuity plan as a result of their learning from the crisis, which they summarized as '4 Ps':

■   People issues which will be with the organization for an extended period of time.
■   Press handling.
■   Product availability for customers, and ensuring the organization's reputation remains intact throughout the response.
■   Premises – understanding what is in each location in terms of possessions, equipment and stock is essential to subsequent salvage efforts.[3]

---

[3]The full case study is available at http://www.londonprepared.gov.uk/businesscontinuity/casestudies/mands.pdf.

Chapter 21

Risk and Insurance

Insurance is a form of risk management primarily used to hedge against the risk of a loss which is unlikely but has a high impact. Insurance, once thought of as an early line of defence against risk, is increasingly seen as a last resort. The increased cost of insurance and the recognition that prevention is superior to indemnity, has led to insurance now being seen more as a risk mitigation device of last resort, that is when all other controls and actions have failed, or as a result of events (e.g. natural disasters) over which the organization has no control.

Insurance involves the payment of a premium to an insurer, who will pay the sum assured to recompense a loss suffered by the insured. An insurer is able to offer this cover on the basis of probabilities assigned to the occurrence of particular events and the pooling of risks by many insured parties. The premium cost will be influenced by the type of risk, the experience of the insured with prior claims and the extent of risk management carried out by the insured in order to prevent or mitigate risk. Purchasing insurance is one method of controlling the financial effect of uncertain future events that carry the risk of significant loss.

Nature of insurance

Insurance is defined as the equitable transfer of the risk of a loss, from one entity to another, in exchange for a premium. An insurer is a company selling the insurance. The insurance rating that applies to a risk is a judgment made by the insurer about the likelihood and extent of loss which is used to determine the premium, to be charged for a specified amount of insurance coverage. This rating is based on the prior experience of the insurer with similar risks.

Contracts of insurance spread the risk over as large a body of organizations as is possible. In this way, the premium paid by any one insured or policyholder is relatively small compared to the financial loss which that party might suffer in the event of the risk eventuating.

The purpose of insurance is to compensate the insured organization which suffered the loss or damage covered by the insurance policy. The insurance principle of indemnity is to place the insured organization in the same position financially as it was in immediately before the loss or damage took place. Therefore, the insured should be no better and no worse off than it was before the loss or damage occurred. Indemnity can include:

■ A payment of money equal to the value of the loss or damage.
■ The replacement of the lost or damaged item.
■ The repair of a damaged item.
■ Restoration, for example rebuilding a property destroyed by fire.

Insurers

Insurance companies may be classified into two main groups:

■ Life insurance companies, which insure the lives of individual people.
■ General insurance companies, which sell other types of mainly property-related insurance.

In addition, there are some specialty insurers:
■ Reinsurance companies are insurance companies that sell policies to other insurance companies, allowing insurers themselves to spread their risks and protect themselves from very large losses. The reinsurance market is dominated by a few very large companies with large reserves.
■ Captive insurers are limited-purpose insurance companies established for the specific purpose of financing risks faced by their parent organization. A 'captive' is an in-house self-insurance vehicle. Captives may be a subsidiary of the self-insured parent company or a 'mutual' captive which insures the collective risks of members of an industrial, professional, commercial or trade association. Captives represent commercial, economic and tax advantages to their sponsors because of the reductions in costs they help create and for the ease of insurance risk management and the flexibility for cash flows they generate.

Insurance contracts and the law

A contract of insurance is legally binding on the insurer and the insured and can be enforced by the courts. However, to be a valid contract, certain conditions must be satisfied:

■ Insurable interest: the insured must suffer a loss if the item insured is lost or damaged.

■ Utmost good faith: the insured must disclose all material facts about the risk to the insurer, and the insurer must disclose to the insured the full details and terms of the insurance policy and cover provided.

■ Indemnity: insurance cover compensates the insured for loss or damage sustained, but does not permit the insured to make a profit.

■ Likelihood of the event occurring: insurance contracts (excluding life assurance) are designed to protect against events that may or may not occur; that is, the events are possibilities rather than certainties.

Types of risk for insurance purposes

There are two broad categories of risk:

■ Fundamental risks
■ Particular risks.

Fundamental risks tend to affect large numbers of people or organizations or a whole geographic region. These risks are often termed 'acts of God' or 'forces of nature' and cannot be controlled. Examples include the effects of weather, for example flooding, hurricanes, earthquake, etc. Although the effect of these events can be devastating, most of these risks are not insurable and governments will often play a role in providing compensation and assistance to affected persons (such as the aftermath of Hurricane Katrina in New Orleans).

Particular risks are those which cannot be predicted but where the effects can be controlled, at least to some extent. These risks arise from business decisions such as the need to store chemicals for use in a production system. Although various actions can be taken to reduce the risk of these events occurring and to mitigate their effects, particular risks are insurable.

Fundamental and particular risks offer only the chance of loss, not of gain. By contrast, speculative risks offer the possibility of gain as well as loss. Trading risks are speculative risks and are therefore not insurable through a contract of insurance, although as we saw in Chapter 12, hedging contracts are similar in their effect to an insurance policy.

Types of insurance

Any risk that can be quantified in terms of a financial loss can potentially be insured. A single insurance policy may cover multiple risks. The main types of insurance for organizations are listed below.

Property damage insurance provides protection against risks to buildings, plant and equipment, such as through fire or weather damage. This class of insurance includes specialised forms of insurance such as fire insurance, flood insurance, earthquake insurance, etc.

Burglary insures the organization's assets against theft.

Business interruption or consequential loss of profits insurance supplements property damage insurance by compensating the organization for the profits it has lost while recovering from a loss that was covered by a property damage insurance policy.

Public liability insurance protects the business against the financial risk of being found liable to a third party for death or injury, loss or damage to property or a loss resulting from the insured's negligence.

Product liability insurance covers damage or injury caused to another business or person by the failure of the organization's product.

Employers' liability, workers' compensation or sickness and accident insurance covers employee medical costs and loss of earnings following a work-related accident or illness.

Fidelity guarantee covers losses resulting from misappropriation by employees who embezzle or steal from the organization or its clients.

Directors' and officers' (or D&O) liability insurance protects an organization from costs associated with litigation and the personal liability of directors and officers resulting from mistakes for which they are liable.

Professional indemnity insurance protects organizations from legal action for losses incurred as a result of poor advice if a client suffers a material, financial or physical loss directly attributed to negligent acts or advice. Professional indemnity insurance is primarily relevant to professional service firms such as accountants, lawyers, architects and consultants, etc.

Motor vehicle (or automotive) insurance covers either replacement or repair of damage to the vehicle caused by an accident and legal liability claims against the driver for personal injury or damage to another vehicle or property.

Builders' insurance covers the risk of physical loss or damage to property during construction. This is commonly an 'all risks' insurance which covers a variety of risks of loss or damage including fire, theft, accidental damage, etc.

Machinery breakdown provides protection when mechanical or electrical plant and machinery in a factory breaks down. A similar policy exists for computers.

Marine insurance and marine cargo insurance cover the loss or damage to ships at sea or on inland waterways, and of the cargo that may be on those ships.

Travel insurance provides cover for those who travel and indemnifies medical expenses, loss of personal belongings, travel delay, personal liability, etc.

Crop insurance for agricultural businesses covers loss or damage to growing or stored products caused by weather, hail, drought, frost damage, insects, or disease.

Credit insurance (see Chapter 15) indemnifies some or all of a debt to a lender in the event of default by a borrower.

Life insurance (often called life assurance or key person insurance) usually over a key employee or manager, provides a monetary benefit to an organization in compensation for the loss suffered by the organization while a suitable replacement is being found. This will typically reflect the key manager's knowledge, skills, business relationships, etc. However, unlike general insurance, no financial loss needs to be proven, as the sum insured is paid on the event of death.

This list is not exhaustive. Other kinds of specialist insurance include kidnap and ransom insurance, terrorism insurance, environmental pollution, etc.

Organizations will typically use the services of an insurance broker, whose role is to advise on the types of insurance needs, sums assured, etc. The broker will then identify the most cost-effective insurers and policies and act on behalf of the organization to buy insurance policies, taking a commission as a fee. The broker will frequently also provide advice to the organization on ways of mitigating risk through loss prevention and thereby reducing claims experience and so reducing the cost of insurance premiums. A broker will also provide advice in relation to making claims on the insurer for losses sustained. Enterprise risk management would be incomplete without an organization buying adequate insurance as a method of risk transfer for those risks where mitigation action and controls have failed to prevent a loss from occurring.

Chapter 22

Risk in Banking and Operational Risk

Financial services products have become more complex as the business environment has become more uncertain. Regulation is also increasing as the public, press and politicians demand greater accountability. Banks and financial institutions, by virtue of their role in carrying out transactions on behalf of third parties, their focus on borrowing and lending from others, their often speculative trading in their own right (e.g. in foreign currencies and derivatives), and their high degree of regulation, face a number of risks specific to the nature of their business.

Banking risk arises largely from a mismatch between assets and liabilities. If their assets and liabilities were matched, borrowing and lending would have the same maturity dates, the same interest rates and would be in the same currencies. The only remaining risk, as for non-financial institutions, would then be credit risk, that is the risk of a defaulting borrower (see Chapter 15). Matching in practice is of course virtually impossible as banks need to take advantage of available opportunities in their borrowing and lending decisions as those opportunities arise.

Risk categorization

Although we considered risk categorization in general in Chapter 5, the nature of banking is that a sector-specific categorization has arisen. Categories of risk for banks and other financial institutions are:

- Credit risk or the risk of default, that is that a borrower will fail to repay the principal borrowed and/or the interest on the amount borrowed. Using securitization, credit risk can be transferred to third parties, so the impact of default is wider than that faced by a particular financial institution (the global impact of the US sub-prime crisis is an example of this).
- Liquidity risk is the risk that a bank is unable to meet its commitments when required to do so, that is a default by the bank itself (this happened in the United Kingdom with Northern Rock). Liquidity risk is a result of losses which need to be covered by capital. A bank's capital requirement is based on a standardized definition of assets and capital so that it can be risk-weighted. The capital ratio is the percentage of a bank's capital to its risk-weighted assets.

■ Interest rate risk is the risk of changing interest rates and the effect this has on the bank's margin between the borrowing and lending rate, especially where there is interest rate volatility or an unbalanced mix of fixed and floating interest rates.

■ Market risk is the loss in the value of a portfolio of trading assets (currencies, commodities, bonds, derivatives, etc). Increases in the size of the trading portfolio increases bank's financial exposure. Market risk is also known as systematic risk.

■ Country risk is the ability and willingness of borrowers in a foreign country to meet their obligations. The assessment of country risk relies on analysis of the country's economy and often subjective judgments about social and political factors (Zimbabwe is a case where country risk is extremely high).

■ Operational risk. This is defined by the Basel Committee on Banking Supervision as the risk of direct or indirect loss resulting from inadequate or failed internal processes, people and systems or from external events which include poor information systems or risk management procedures (see later in this chapter).

Risk regulation and value at risk (VaR)

The most popular and traditional measure of risk is volatility, but for investors, risk is about the odds of losing rather than gaining money. This involves assessing the 'worst case' scenario. Regulators require banks to measure their market risk using a risk measurement model which is used to calculate the value at risk (VaR). VaR is based on the assumption that investors care mainly about the probability of a large loss. The VaR of a portfolio is the maximum loss on a portfolio occurring within a given length of time with a given small probability. Banks can measure their value at risk through models developed internally or by a standardized approach using a risk-weighting process developed by the Basel Committee on Banking Supervision.

VaR calculates the maximum loss expected (or worst case scenario) on an investment, over a given time period and given a specified degree of confidence. Calculating VaR involves using three components: a time period, a confidence level and a loss amount or percentage loss. There are three methods of calculating VaR: historical, variance–covariance, and Monte Carlo simulation. Actual daily trading gains or losses are then compared to the estimated VaR over a period of time. If actual results are frequently worse than the estimated VaR then corrective action needs to be taken.

Basel II

For banks and regulated financial institutions, the Basel Committee on Banking Supervision has had an important impact, particularly as it affects risk and internal control.

Part of the Bank for International Settlements, the objectives of the Basel Committee are to enhance the understanding of key supervisory issues and improve the quality of banking supervision globally. Guidelines and standards are developed, but the most important guidelines introduced by the Basel Committee[1] include:

- Basel Committee on Banking Supervision. 1994. *Risk Management Guidelines for Derivatives.*
- Basel Committee on Banking Supervision. 1998. *Framework for the Evaluation of Internal Control.*
- Basel Committee on Banking Supervision. 2001. *Sound Practices for the Management and Supervision of Operational Risk.*

A particular focus of attention is the latest version of Basel II. These are international standards for banking laws and regulations aimed at helping to protect the international financial system from the results of the collapse of a major bank or series of banks. Basel II has established rigorous risk and capital management requirements to ensure that each bank holds reserves sufficient to guard against its risk exposure given its lending and investment practices.

Banks also have to comply with the operational risk management guidance of the Basel Committee. Basel II has raised operational risk management to the top of the agenda of financial institutions around the world. Operational risk includes systems risks, such as hardware or software failure, issues over availability and integrity of data, and utility failures, and external events (e.g. computer hacking, terrorist attack, vandalism or supplier failure.)

Sound practices for the management and supervision of operational risk

In 2003, the Risk Management Group of the Basel Committee on Banking Supervision established a framework for the effective management and supervision of operational risk, for use by banks and supervisory authorities when evaluating operational risk management policies and practices.

The Committee recognized that the approach for operational risk management chosen by an individual bank depended on its size and sophistication and the nature and complexity of its activities. However, clear strategies and oversight by the Board of Directors and senior management, a strong operational risk culture and internal control culture (including, among other things, clear lines of responsibility and segregation

---

[1] Further information is available from the bank's website www.bis.org/bcbs/.

of duties), effective internal reporting, and contingency planning were all identified as crucial elements of an effective operational risk management framework for banks of any size and scope.

Operational risk was defined as 'the risk of loss resulting from inadequate or failed internal processes, people and systems or from external events'. This definition includes legal risk but excludes strategic and reputational risk. A clear understanding by banks of what is meant by operational risk is critical to the effective management and control of this risk category which should include the full range of material operational risks facing the bank and the most significant causes of severe operational losses.

Operational risk is particularly important as banks are skilled at using quantitative techniques to assess credit, liquidity, interest rate and market risk. They are not however, equally skilled at making subjective judgments about the risk of processes, people and systems, where little or no objective information is available. However, it is this kind of risk that caused the failure of Barings Bank (see the case study later in this chapter).

Operational risk identified by the Basel Committee as having the potential to result in substantial losses for banks include:

- Internal fraud, for example misreporting of positions, employee theft, and insider trading by an employee.

- External fraud, for example through robbery, forgery, cheque kiting (the practice of exploiting the time period during which cheques clear through the banking system and the different days upon which the payee's account is credited and the payer's account is debited with the amount of any cheque which can inflate the balance in both bank accounts), and damage from computer hacking.

- Employment practices and workplace safety including workers compensation claims, violation of employee health and safety rules, organized labour activities, discrimination claims, and general liability.

- Clients, products and business practices such as fiduciary breaches, misuse of confidential customer information, improper trading activities on the bank's account, money laundering, and sale of unauthorized products.

- Damage to physical assets through terrorism, vandalism, earthquakes, fires and floods.

- Business disruption and system failures following IT hardware and software failures, telecommunication problems, and utility outages.

- Execution, delivery and process management. This includes data entry errors, collateral management failures, incomplete legal documentation, unapproved access to client accounts, counterparty mis-performance, and vendor disputes.

The Basel Committee's Sound Practices for the Management and Supervision of Operational Risk[2] identified 10 principles for risk management of operational risk:

1. The board of directors should be aware of the major aspects of the bank's operational risks and should approve and periodically review the bank's operational risk management framework.

2. The board of directors should ensure that the bank's operational risk management framework is subject to effective and comprehensive internal audit by trained and competent staff. The internal audit function should not be directly responsible for operational risk management.

3. Senior management should have responsibility for implementing the operational risk management framework approved by the board of directors and implementing policies, processes and procedures for managing operational risk in all of the bank's material products, activities, processes and systems. All levels of staff should understand their responsibilities with respect to operational risk management.

4. Banks should identify and assess the operational risk inherent in all material products, activities, processes and systems. Banks should also ensure that before new products, activities, processes and systems are introduced, the operational risk inherent in them is subject to adequate assessment procedures.

5. Banks should implement a process to regularly monitor operational risks and material exposure to losses. There should be regular reporting of relevant information to senior management and the board of directors that supports the management of operational risk.

6. Banks should have policies, processes and procedures to control and/or mitigate material operational risks. Banks should periodically review their risk limitation and control strategies and should adjust their operational risks using appropriate strategies, in light of their overall risk appetite.

7. Banks should have in place contingency and business continuity plans to ensure their ability to operate on an ongoing basis and limit losses in the event of severe business disruption.

8. Banking supervisors should require that all banks, regardless of size, have an effective framework in place to identify, assess, monitor and control/mitigate material operational risks as part of an overall approach to risk management.

9. Supervisors should conduct, directly or indirectly, regular independent evaluation of a bank's policies, procedures and practices related to operational risks.

---

[2] Available to download from http://www.bis.org/publ/bcbs96.pdf.

Supervisors should ensure that there are appropriate mechanisms in place which allow them to remain apprised of developments at banks.

10. Banks should make sufficient public disclosure to allow market participants to assess their approach to operational risk management.

Enterprise risk management in the banking sector presents challenges to banks that have readily accepted the quantitative techniques of value at risk but that have found it more difficult to understand and address the more qualitative judgments involved in assessing operational risk. For non-bank institutions, what banks call operational risk is at the core of the enterprise risk management process. Two cases, one many years ago and one more recent, highlight the risk to banks where judgments about operational risk and internal controls are inadequate.

Case study: Barings Bank

Barings Bank was Britain's oldest bank, having existed for 200 years before it collapsed in 1995 as a result of uncontrolled derivatives trading by Nick Leeson in the bank's Singapore office. Nick Leeson was a 26-year-old dealer who lost £800 million in unauthorised dealings in derivatives trading from his base in Singapore. Leeson suppressed information on account '88888' which he used for trading between 1992 and 1995, which management was unaware of. The losses wiped out the Bank's capital.

There are many risk management and control lessons to be learned from the failure of Barings. As only a small amount of money (a margin) is needed to establish a derivatives position, it is possible to commit to financial obligations beyond an organization's ability to pay. Barings had placed Nick Leeson in charge of both the dealing desk and the back office. The back office records, confirms and settles trades made by the front office and provides the necessary checks to prevent unauthorised trading and minimize the potential for fraud and embezzlement. In this dual position, Leeson was able to relay false information back to the London head office.

An internal audit report in August 1994 concluded that Leeson's dual responsibility for both the front and back office was an excessive concentration of powers and warned of the risk that Leeson could override controls. There was also a lack of supervision of Leeson by Barings' managers, either in Singapore or London. The internal auditors' responsibility was to make sure the directors were aware of the risk they were facing by not implementing the separation of duties. However, directors did not implement the internal audit recommendations. Their response was that there was insufficient work for a full-time treasury and risk manager.

Senior managers of Barings had only a superficial knowledge of derivatives, did not understand the risks of the business, did not articulate the bank's risk appetite or implement strategies and control procedures appropriate to those risks. When the Singapore exchange made margin demands on Barings, large amounts of cash had to be paid out but still no steps were taken by the London head office to investigate the matter. Eventually, the amounts required were so great that Barings was forced to call in receivers. The trading positions taken out by Leeson were unhedged and the cost of closing out the open contracts was US$ 1.4 billion. Leeson was charged with fraud for deceiving his superiors about the riskiness of his activities and the scale of his losses and was sentenced to six and a half years in prison in Singapore.

The information in this case study comes from the *Report of the Board of Banking Supervision (BoBS) Inquiry into the Circumstances of the Collapse of Barings.*

Case study: Société Générale

In 2008, Société Générale, one of the largest European banks reported a £4.9 billion loss caused by a trader making fraudulent wrong-way bets on stock index futures. This was three times the loss caused by Nick Leeson at Barings Bank in 1995. Société Générale was a leader in derivatives and considered one of the best risk managers in the world. Before the discovery of the fraud, Société Générale had been preparing to announce pretax profit for 2007 of €5.5 billion. The case followed similar frauds by employees who understood their bank's risk management systems and found ways to circumvent those systems, for example at Amaranth Advisers in 2006, Allied Irish Banks in 2002, and Kidder Peabody in 1994.

Part D. Evaluating Risk Management

In this final part, we take a step back and look at the processes that provide assurance that enterprise risk management is effective. Chapter 23 explains the role of the audit committee and internal control in relation to ERM. Chapter 24 looks at the inter-relationship between risk management and audit. Chapter 25 highlights some of the key ideas from this book and considers the future of enterprise risk management.

Chapter 23

The Audit Committee, Enterprise Risk Management and Internal Control

In Chapter 2 we described the role of the Board and of the audit committee from a corporate governance perspective. In this chapter, we are concerned with the role of governance and the audit committee in relation to risk management and internal control.

In Chapter 2, we also presented a simple model of governance, risk and control that reflected an integrated approach to enterprise risk management (ERM). In this model repeated here as Figure 23.1, the Board of Directors, often working through the audit committee, set the organizational risk appetite and ensure that enterprise risk management is put in place. ERM results in a set of internal controls that provides assurance about both conformance and performance aspects of the role of the Board. This whole process is subject to audit and the audit committee carries out a monitoring process throughout.

Role of the audit committee in the risk management of financial statements

Financial statements are one of the main ways in which organizations communicate with the outside world and to investors and lenders in particular. Financial reports therefore need to fairly present the financial performance and position of an organization. This was dealt with in detail in Chapter 10.

The role of the audit committee as the delegate of the Board of Directors is critical to the risk management of financial statement preparation and presentation. However, it is not the duty of the audit committee to carry out functions that belong to others, such as management's responsibility for the preparation of financial statements, or auditors for the planning and conduct of audits. However, audit committees need to satisfy themselves that there is a proper system and allocation of responsibilities for the day-to-day monitoring of financial controls although they should not do that monitoring themselves.

The audit committee should review the significant financial reporting issues and judgments made in connection with the preparation of the company's financial

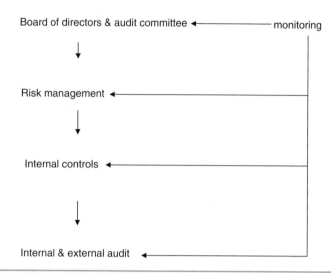

Figure 23.1   A model of governance, risk and control.

statements, interim reports, preliminary announcements and other related statements. Although it is management's responsibility to prepare financial statements, the audit committee should consider the significant accounting policies, any changes to those policies and any significant estimates and judgments. Management should inform the audit committee of the methods used to account for significant or unusual transactions where the accounting treatment is open to different approaches. Taking the advice of the external auditors, the audit committee should consider whether the company has adopted appropriate accounting policies and made appropriate estimates and judgments. The audit committee should review the clarity and completeness of disclosures made in the financial statements.

Under Sarbanes Oxley legislation, the audit committee's primary role is to exercise oversight over the financial statements and the internal and external audit functions. While this is an important role in all countries, it does not adequately address the role of the audit committee in enterprise-wide risk management – the whole area of risk that includes, but is far from limited to, risk of mis-statements in financial reports.

Role of the audit committee in enterprise risk management and internal control

The audit committee should review the company's internal financial controls and, unless expressly addressed by a separate Board risk committee composed of independent directors, the company's internal control and risk management systems.

The Smith Guidance for audit committees (Financial Reporting Council, 2005) explains:

The company's management is responsible for the identification, assessment, management and monitoring of risk, for developing, operating and monitoring the system of internal control and for providing assurance to the Board that it has done so ... the audit committee should receive reports from management on the effectiveness of the systems they have established and the conclusions of any testing carried out by internal and external auditors (para. 4.6).

In the United States, the New York Stock Exchange requires the audit committees of its listed companies to "discuss policies with respect to risk assessment and risk management." The related commentary continues:

"While it is the job of the CEO and senior management to assess and manage the company's exposure to risk, the audit committee must discuss guidelines and policies to govern the process by which this is handled. The audit committee should discuss the company's major financial risk exposures and the steps management has taken to monitor and control such exposures. The audit committee is not required to be the sole body responsible for risk assessment and management, but, as stated above, the committee must discuss guidelines and policies to govern the process by which risk assessment and management is undertaken. Many companies, particularly financial companies, manage and assess their risk through mechanisms other than the audit committee. The processes these companies have in place should be reviewed in a general manner by the audit committee, but they need not be replaced by the audit committee." [1]

Reviewing the effectiveness of internal control

Reviewing the effectiveness of internal control is one of the Board's responsibilities and needs to be carried out on a continuous basis. Directors are expected to apply the same standard of care when reviewing the effectiveness of internal control as when exercising their general duties. The Board should regularly review reports on internal control in order to carry out an annual assessment for the purpose of making its public statement on internal control to ensure that it has considered all significant aspects of internal control. It is important that any review of internal controls is not limited to financial controls.

Reports from management to the Board should provide a balanced assessment of the significant risks and the effectiveness of the system of internal control in

---

[1] http://www.nyse.com/pdfs/finalcorpgovrules.pdf.

managing those risks. Any significant control failings or weaknesses identified should be discussed in the reports, including the impact that they have had, could have had, or may have, on the company and the actions being taken to rectify them (Turnbull Guidance, para. 30, Institute of Chartered Accountants in England & Wales, 1999). When reviewing management reports on internal control, the Board should:

- Consider the significant risks and assess how they have been identified, evaluated and managed.
- Assess the effectiveness of internal controls in managing the significant risks, having regard to any significant weaknesses in internal control.
- Consider whether actions are being taken promptly to remedy any weaknesses.
- Consider whether the findings indicate a need for more exhaustive monitoring of the system of internal control.

One practical approach used by a professional services firm that specializes in risk-based internal control is the five questions it suggests any audit (or risk) committee should ask management on a regular basis:

1. What new risks have arisen since the risk register was last reviewed which should now be considered?
2. Are there any risks that are no longer applicable that can now be removed from the risk register?
3. What assurance can the Board take from management that key controls already in place to manage risks are operating effectively?
4. What events are on the horizon which may impact on the organization's ability to manage its risks?
5. Have any risk events actually occurred? If so, what lessons have been learned in relation to the control environment or control procedures?

(adapted from RSM Robson Rhodes, now part of Grant Thornton)

Assessment of control

The Board's annual assessment should consider[2]:

- Any changes since the last annual assessment in the nature and extent of significant risks, and the company's ability to respond to changes in its business and the external environment.

---

[2]Institute of Chartered Accountants in England & Wales. 1999. Internal Control: Guidance for Directors on the Combined Code (Turnbull Report), para. 33.

- The scope and quality of management's ongoing monitoring of risks and of the system of internal control and the work of the internal audit function and other providers of assurance.
- The extent and frequency of the communication of the results of the monitoring to the Board which enables it to build up a cumulative assessment of the state of control in the company and the effectiveness with which risk is being managed.
- The incidence of significant control weaknesses that have been identified during the period and the extent to which they have resulted in unforeseen outcomes that have had, or could have, a material impact on the company's financial performance.
- The effectiveness of the company's public reporting processes.

The Board's statement on internal control should disclose that there is an ongoing process for identifying, evaluating and managing the significant risks faced by the company, that it has been in place for the year and up to the date of approval of the annual report and accounts, and that it has been regularly reviewed by the Board and conforms to the Turnbull Guidance. Boards should look on their internal control statement as an opportunity to communicate to their shareholders how they manage risk and internal control. Boards are required to confirm in their annual report that necessary action has been or is being taken to remedy any significant failings or weaknesses identified from their review of the effectiveness of the internal control system, and to include in the annual report such information as is considered necessary to assist shareholders' understanding of the main features of the company's risk management processes and system of internal control.

The Board must acknowledge that it is responsible for the company's system of internal control and for reviewing its effectiveness. It should also explain that the system is designed to manage rather than eliminate the risk of failure to achieve business objectives, and can only provide reasonable but not absolute assurance against material mis-statement or loss. The Board should also disclose the process it has applied to deal with material internal control aspects of any significant problems disclosed in the annual report and accounts.

Integrating the audit committee, ERM and internal control

As shown in Figure 23.1, the role of the audit committee as the key governance body responsible for risk management is an important one. The audit committee needs to be fully committed to enterprise risk management, making clear the organizational risk appetite, implementing a risk management strategy (including the components described in Part B of this book), and covering all the risks faced by the organization (including but not limited to those in Part C). The audit committee then needs to ensure that controls are risk-based following risk assessments compared with the organizational risk appetite, rather than enforcing controls that are historically or politically derived rather than being linked to risks (this was argued in Chapter 9). Risk management and risk-based controls should then be followed by risk-based audit (see also Chapter 24) with the audit committee continually monitoring the effectiveness of each of the risk management, internal control and audit processes as well as the integration between those processes.

Two case studies follow. The first example is that of Old Mutual plc, a financial services company which appears to have adopted an integrated approach to the role of governance, enterprise risk management and internal control. The second example is that of Northern Rock, an apparent failure of governance, risk management and control.

Case study: Old Mutual[3] plc

Old Mutual had funds under management in 2007 of £279 billion (22% in Europe, 15% in South Africa, 61% in the United States and 2% in the rest of world). It operates in Europe mainly through Skandia, the Swedish insurance company acquired in 2006. Its South African financial services business, comprising life and asset management business, has at its core one of the largest distribution capabilities in the South African industry. Old Mutual has also built significant asset management and life assurance businesses in the USA through a number of acquisitions during the past 6 years. Operations in India, China and Australia are part of a strategy to take the company's business skills into other developing markets.

The following information about Old Mutual's approach to enterprise risk management and control is taken from the company's 2006 annual report:

Risk management

The Board acknowledges its overall responsibility for the Group's system of internal control and for reviewing its effectiveness, while the role of executive management is to implement Board policies on risk and control.

Executive management has implemented an internal control system designed to facilitate the effective and efficient operation of the Group and its business units and aimed at enabling management to respond appropriately to significant risks to

---

[3]http://www.oldmutual.com/vpage.jsp?page_id=2073.

achieving the Group's business objectives. It should be noted that the system is designed to manage, rather than eliminate, the risk of failure to achieve the Group's business objectives, and can only provide reasonable, and not absolute, assurance against material mis-statement or loss.

This system of internal control helps to ensure the quality of internal and external reporting, compliance with applicable laws and regulations, and internal policies with respect to the conduct of business. The Board has reviewed the effectiveness of the system of internal control during and at the end of the year. This review covered all material controls, including financial, operational and compliance controls and risk management systems.

The Board is of the view that there is a sufficient ongoing process for identifying, evaluating and managing the significant risks faced by the Group, and that this process has been in place for the year ended December 31, 2006 and up to the date of approval of this Report. The process accords with the Turnbull Guidance set out in 'Internal Control Guidance for Directors on the Combined Code' and is regularly reviewed by the Board.

Approach to risk management

Creating shareholder value is the Group's overriding business objective, and the Group therefore derives its approach to risk management and control from a shareholder value perspective. As a result, the risk process is based on an enterprise risk management concept, which takes a holistic approach to managing risks on an enterprise-wide basis. This involves focusing on the identification of the key risks that affect the achievement of Group's objectives. Such risks are firstly understood on an inherent basis, which involves understanding the main drivers to such risks in the absence of any controls. Thereafter there is an assessment of the residual level of risks, taking into account the controls that are in place to manage such risks. Where the residual level is outside the risk appetite, further controls and action are defined to bring the risks within the risk appetite. An important aspect of this approach is the recognition that risk management is not limited solely to the downside or risk avoidance, but is about taking risk knowingly.

In order to meet its ERM objectives, the Group applies the ERM framework issued in September 2004 by COSO (Committee of Sponsoring Organisations of the Treadway Commission). This risk framework contains the following components: (i) a robust risk governance structure; (ii) risk appetites established at Group and subsidiary level; (iii) Group-wide risk policies; and (iv) methodologies that focus on risk identification, risk measurement, risk assessment, action plans, monitoring and reporting. Each component is explained in more detail below.

Risk governance

The Group's risk governance model is based on three lines of defence. This model distinguishes between functions owning and managing risks, functions overseeing risks, and functions providing independent assurance.

Under the first line of defence, the Board sets the Group's risk appetite, approves the strategy for managing risk and is responsible for the Group's system of internal control. The Group Chief Executive, supported by the Management Board, has overall responsibility for the management of risks facing the Group and is supported in the management of these risks by management at the operating subsidiaries. Management and staff within each business have the primary responsibility for managing risk. They are required to take responsibility for the identification, assessment, management, monitoring and reporting of enterprise risks arising within their respective areas.

The second line of defence comprises, firstly, the Group Chief Executive supported by the Old Mutual Executive and the principal subsidiary and business unit management performing risk monitoring and oversight, and, secondly, the Group Finance Director, Group Head of Risk & Compliance, subsidiary Chief Risk Officers, supported by their respective Finance and Risk functions, and other specialist inhouse functions at company and subsidiary levels, who provide technical support and advice to operating management to assist them with the identification, assessment, management, monitoring and reporting of financial and non-financial risks. The Group risk function recommends Group risk principles to the Board for approval, provides objective oversight and co-ordinates ERM activities in conjunction with other specialist risk-related functions. Group risk is not, however, accountable for the day-to-day management of financial and non-financial risks.

The third line of defence is designed to provide independent objective assurance on the effectiveness of the management of enterprise risks across the Group. This is provided to the Board through the Group internal audit function, the external auditors and the Group Audit and Risk Committee, supported by audit committees at subsidiaries.

Internal audit

The Group internal audit function operates on a decentralized basis, with teams established at all major businesses. Reports are submitted directly to the Group Internal Audit Director, who in turn reports to the Chairman of the Group Audit and Risk Committee and the Group Chief Executive. Internal audit carries out regular risk-focused reviews of the control environment and reports on these to local executive management. It also enjoys unrestricted access to the audit committees of the Group's principal subsidiaries.

The internal audit function has recently moved to a single audit methodology, updated and aligned to current international standards by a Professional Practice Unit, which is a centralized function responsible for ensuring quality and consistency of internal audit working practices and staff competency around the Group. The roll-out of this methodology has coincided with the change to the TeamMate™ software, which is now used by all internal auditors across the Group.

The next major review of internal audit by external experts is planned for 2008, in keeping with the IIA Inc. standards of professional practice.

Risk appetite

The fundamental purpose of the Group's risk appetite is to define how much risk the Group is willing to take. Risks or events falling outside the agreed risk appetite are identified for immediate remedial action and subjected to executive management and the Group Audit Committee oversight. The Group's risk appetite encompasses: (i) volatility and quantum of returns to shareholders: (ii) value for money for customers; (iii) financial strength ratings; (iv) regulatory solvency; and (v) how risks are monitored and controlled. Compliance with the risk appetite is monitored through the quarterly business review process.

Group risk principles

Group risk principles have been established for each major risk category to which the Group is exposed. These are designed to provide management teams across the Group with guiding principles and requirements within which to manage risks. Business unit risk policies expand on these principles and contain detailed requirements for the specific business concerned.

Adherence to these principles provides the Board and the company's stakeholders with assurance that high-level common standards are consistently applied throughout the Group and also contributes to how the Group governs itself.

Risk methodologies

Risk identification

Strategic objectives reflect management's choice as to how the Group will seek to create value for its stakeholders. Strategic objectives are translated into business unit objectives. Risks (and risk events) are then identified that would prevent the achievement of both the strategic and business objectives, that is objective-setting is a pre-condition to the risk management process as well as an ongoing process. For this reason, risk identification is part of the annual business planning process as well as an ongoing process. The resultant risks are recorded in a risk log, with details of risk owners, existing controls or actions to mitigate the risks and any associated time frame, and a measure of the residual risk. Where the residual risk is deemed to be outside the risk appetite, it is transferred to a control log for remedial action.

Risk assessment and measurement

Various means of assessing and measuring enterprise risks and risk events are used throughout the Group. These include estimating the financial impact and the likelihood of risk occurrence, trend and traffic light assessments and high/medium/low assessments.

Action plans

Action plans to implement the risk management strategy in respect of key risks or to remedy a material breakdown in control are recorded on risk and control logs maintained by each business grouping.

Monitoring and control

The Board regularly receives and reviews on risks and controls across the Group. These reviews cover all material controls, including financial, operational and compliance controls and risk management systems.

Management teams in each subsidiary and business unit have performed annual reviews of the control environment in their business and have produced reports reflecting appropriate assurances.

Risk monitoring is undertaken at Group, principal subsidiary and business unit level by management, ERM functions, specialized risk management functions, internal audit and subsidiary audit committees.

The following are some of the other key processes of risk monitoring used around the Group:

■ The Group Finance Director provides the Board with monthly performance information, which includes key performance and risk indicators. These are complementary to the monthly management reports, which include a status report on key risks to the achievability of business objectives.

■ Items on risk logs and control logs (which contain details of any control failures) are reported pursuant to an escalation protocol to the appropriate level of Management Board or committee, where rectification procedures and progress are closely monitored. Planned corrective actions are independently monitored for timely completion by internal audit and, as appropriate, by the Group Audit and Risk Committee and Board.

■ Exposure reporting, risk concentrations and solvency and capital adequacy reports are submitted to the relevant credit and capital management committees in the normal course of business. Where exposures are in excess of limits, they are treated in the same way as control breakdowns and reported on the relevant control log for audit committee review.

Reporting

As part of the Board's annual review process, the Chief Executive of each of the Group's major businesses completes a Letter of Representation. This letter confirms that there has been no indication of any significant business risk occurring, nor any material malfunction in controls, procedures or systems during the reporting period, resulting in loss or reputational damage, which impacts negatively on the attainment of the business's objectives during the year and up to the date of approval of the annual report. Exceptions are noted and reported. In addition the letter confirms that the business unit will continue as a going concern for the year ahead. The collated results of these letters are reported to the Group Audit and Risk Committee via a Letter of Representation from the Group Chief Executive.

Monthly management reports, reports by the Group Finance Director, risk logs, control logs and exposure reports described under "Monitoring and control" above also form part of the reporting process.

Case study: Northern Rock – a failure of risk management?

In September 2007 Northern Rock plc was a top five UK mortgage lender, on the FTSE 100 index with over £100 billion in assets. Northern Rock raised over 70% of the money it used in its growing mortgage lending business from banks and other financial institutions. Following the global credit crunch that resulted from the crisis in the US sub-prime (high risk) mortgage sector, banks stopped lending to each other and Northern Rock could not raise sufficient cash to cover its liabilities.

A bank run on Northern Rock by its customers (the first on a UK bank for 150 years) led to the government providing 'lender of last resort' facilities and guarantees for the bank's depositors totalling about £20 billion. The result was a 90% fall in the bank's share price, a deteriorating credit rating and a loss of reputation. The CEO subsequently resigned and several directors also left the Board. Following the failure to find a buyer, the UK Government nationalized Northern Rock in early 2008.

Northern Rock had a formal approach to risk management, including liquidity, credit, operational and market risk, fully described in its Securities and Exchange Commission filings. The company's 2006 annual report, the last before its crisis, described its approach to risk management. Excerpts from that annual report include[4]:

The Risk Committee met four times during 2006. The main role of the Risk Committee is to review, on behalf of the Board, the key risks inherent in the business, the system of control necessary to manage such risks, and to present its findings to the Board. This responsibility requires the Risk Committee to keep under review the effectiveness of the Group's system of internal controls, which includes financial, operational, compliance and risk management controls and to foster a culture that emphasizes and demonstrates the benefits of a risk-based approach to internal control and management of the Group. The Risk Committee fulfils this remit by reinforcing management's control consciousness and making appropriate recommendations to the Board on all significant matters relating to the Group's risk strategy and policies. Other responsibilities of the Risk Committee include keeping under review the effectiveness of the Group's risk management infrastructure. This involves an assessment of risk management procedures (for the identification, measurement and control of key risk exposures) in accordance with changes in the operating environment. It is also primarily responsible for considering any major findings of the Financial Services Authority and management's response to any risk management review undertaken by internal audit or the external auditors. To assist the Board in discharging its responsibilities for the setting of Risk Policy, the Risk Committee periodically reviews the Group's credit risk, interest rate risk, liquidity risk and operational risk exposures in relation to the Board's risk appetite and the Group's capital adequacy. As part of the implementation of the International Convergence of Capital Measurement and Capital Standards: Revised Framework (commonly known as Basel II) the Committee has responsibility for monitoring the performance of the company's Basel credit rating systems and reviewing reports prepared by the company's Basel designated committees. The Risk Committee also ensures that the public disclosure of information regarding the Group's risk management policies and key risk exposures is in accordance with statutory requirements and financial reporting standards.

Internal control

The Board of Directors is responsible for the Group's system of internal control and for annually reviewing its effectiveness. The system of internal control is designed to manage risk rather than eliminate it and in this regard, the Board considers that

---

[4]The full annual report is available from http://companyinfo.northernrock.co.uk/downloads/results/res2006PR_AnnualReportAndAccounts.pdf.

Northern Rock is a well-controlled, risk-averse business that continues to adopt a prudent stance in the management of risk. The Board has reviewed the effectiveness of the system of internal control and is satisfied that there is a sound system of internal control that safeguards shareholders' investments and the company's assets. Where necessary, the Board confirms that action has been taken or is being taken to remedy any significant failings or weaknesses identified from its review of the effectiveness of the internal control system. In accordance with the guidance set out in the Turnbull Guidance, the company has an ongoing process for identifying, evaluating and managing the significant risks faced by it.

In Northern Rock's operating and business review in the 2006 annual report, it described its risks as follows:

The principal risks the Group manages are as follows[5]:

- Credit risk: the risk arising from the possibility that the Group will incur losses from the failure of customers and counterparties to meet their obligations.
- Liquidity risk: the risk that the Group is unable to meet its obligations as they fall due.
- Operational risk: Operational risk is defined as the risk arising from the Group's people, processes, systems and assets.
- Market risk: the risk that changes in the level of interest rates, the rate of exchange between currencies or the price of securities or other financial contracts, including derivatives, will have an adverse impact on the results of operations or financial condition of the Group.

The Group's approach to managing each of these is set out below.

Credit risk

The objective of credit risk management is to enable the Group to achieve sustainable and superior risk versus reward performance while maintaining credit risk exposure in line with approved risk appetite. Credit risk is the risk of loss if another party fails to meet its financial obligations to the Group, including failing to perform them in a timely manner. Credit risk occurs mainly in the Group's loans and investment assets, and in derivative contracts. Good credit risk management is

---

[5] http://companyinfo.northernrock.co.uk/downloads/results/res2006PR_AnnualReportAndAccounts.pdf.

essential to ensure that the Group's cost advantage is not undermined by poor quality loans.

Liquidity risk

Liquidity risk arises from the mismatch in the cashflows generated from current and expected assets, liabilities and derivatives. The Group's liquidity policy is to ensure that it is able to meet retail withdrawals, repay wholesale funds as they fall due, and meet current lending requirements. It also ensures that it meets FSA liquidity rules, which require the Group to be able to meet its sterling obligations without recourse to the wholesale money markets for a period of at least five business days. To ensure that it meets these requirements, the Group has approved a Liquidity and Treasury Assets Policy Statement, compliance with which enables it to meet both the requirements of the FSA and internal policy requirements. This is achieved by managing a diversified portfolio of high quality liquid assets, and a balanced maturity portfolio of wholesale and retail funds. Longer term funds are raised through the Group's Medium-Term Note programmes. The Board reviews the Policy Statement annually, and on a more frequent basis if any significant changes are proposed or required. As well as approving the types of liquid asset that may be bought, the Liquidity and Treasury Assets Policy Statement sets out approved operational limits and establishes operational guidelines for managing the Group's liquidity risk. The Treasury Director monitors liquidity on a daily basis, using daily cashflow liquidity and sterling stock liquidity reports, together with daily movement reports, portfolio analyses and maturity profiles. The Board receives monthly liquidity reports analysing the liquid assets and showing the percentages of assets held in each asset type.

Operational risk

Operational risk is the risk of opportunities foregone, reputational damage or financial losses, resulting from inadequacies or failures in internal processes, people or systems, or from external events. The three main categories of operational risk losses are direct financial losses, indirect losses due to impairment of the Group's reputation, and potential earnings foregone because of the lack of operational ability to process business.

The key components of operational risk are systems and processes, technology, customers, external events and relationships, people, reconciliation and accounting, new activities and legal and compliance. To minimize operational risk, the Group has implemented a Risk Policy and an Operational Risk Policy. Management Board directors and senior line managers are primarily responsible for ensuring effective operational risk management exists within their areas – in particular, the setting of tolerances, monitoring and reporting of operational risks. Where appropriate, Northern Rock establishes suitable cost-effective processes to mitigate or transfer operational risk exposures. Operational risks are controlled and managed on a decentralized basis, with responsibility and authority to mitigate these risks delegated to the relevant line management. Northern Rock's support functions provide corporate policies, processes and reporting mechanisms as appropriate to the 'front line' functions for the range of operational risks faced.

Market risk

Market risk is the risk that changes in the level of interest rates, the rate of exchange between currencies or the price of securities or other financial contracts, including derivatives, will have an adverse impact on the results of operations or financial condition of the Group. The principal market risks to which we are exposed are interest rate risk and foreign exchange (currency) risk. The principal financial instruments that expose us to such risks are loans, deposits, securities and derivatives, none of which are used for trading purposes. To manage our exposure to market risk, the Board has adopted a Balance Sheet Structural Risk Management and Hedging Policy Statement. This sets out our policy for managing balance sheet market risk, and the use of derivatives in achieving this. It enables the Board to assess, monitor and manage the current and expected interest rate risk, credit risk and currency risk in the balance sheet in line with the Group's overall risk policies.

Northern Rock's assets were sound so there was no significant credit risk. Market risk was also well managed in terms of interest rate and foreign exchange exposure. However, despite formal procedures and a demonstrated compliance with regulations, there was an assumption by managers that access to funds would continue unimpeded. The US sub-prime crisis led to liquidity risk materializing, far greater than had been foreseen by Northern Rock and causing its demise. The consequence was also the loss of reputation that followed press reports which blamed the bank's management for not having a contingency plan to cover the possibility of disruption to its funding.

References

Financial Reporting Council. 2005. Guidance on Audit Committees (The Smith Guidance), Financial Reporting Council, London.
Institute of Chartered Accountants in England & Wales. 1999. Internal Control: Guidance for Directors on the Combined Code, (Turnbull Report).

Chapter 24

Enterprise Risk Management and the Audit Function

As we saw in Chapter 23, the role of the audit committee is to drive and monitor enterprise risk management (ERM) and a risk-based approach to both internal control and audit. The role of internal audit and the risk-based approach to audit was described in Chapter 9 while the role of external audit was covered in Chapter 2. In summary, we saw in Chapter 9 that internal audit is an independent, objective assurance and consulting activity. Its core role with regard to ERM is to provide objective assurance to the Board on the effectiveness of risk management. By contrast, we saw in Chapter 2 that external auditors are independent firms of accountants who conduct audits on behalf of their client organization and report to the Board and shareholders. In their report, external auditors express an opinion on whether financial statements present a true and fair view (or in the United States are presented fairly) and comply with applicable accounting standards.

▌ External audit

Audit is a periodic examination of the accounting records of a company carried out by an independent auditor to ensure that those records have been properly maintained and to express an opinion on the financial statements which are prepared on the basis of those records. An audit includes examination, on a test basis, of evidence relevant to the amounts and disclosures in financial statements. It also includes an assessment of significant estimates and judgments made by directors in the preparation of financial statements, and whether accounting policies are appropriate, consistent and adequately disclosed. Each year the auditors present their report to shareholders, giving their opinion (in the United Kingdom) as to whether the financial statements give a true and fair view and are properly prepared in accordance with the Companies Act and applicable accounting standards.

The auditor's opinion to shareholders clearly expresses the basis of their opinion. Two particular elements of a standard audit report are:

■ The auditors' report whether the organization has kept proper accounting records, or if they have not received all the information and explanations they required for the audit, or if information specified by law is not disclosed.

■ The auditors are not required to consider whether the Board's statements on internal control cover all risks and controls, or form an opinion on the effectiveness of the Group's corporate governance procedures or its risk and control procedures.

This second point is particularly important as it shows that the external auditors have no duty or responsibility to consider risk management or internal control, although they may identify weaknesses and bring these to the attention of management and the Board through an annual management letter. Most of the internal control weaknesses are likely to be limited to those affecting financial reporting, consistent with the requirements of Sarbanes Oxley. Consequently, the assurance of effective risk management and internal control must come from management and the organizations' internal audit function, each monitored by the audit committee.

Internal audit

In 2004, the Institute of Internal Auditors (IIA) issued a position paper on *The Role of Internal Auditing in Enterprise-wide Risk Management.*[1] The purpose was aimed at assisting chief internal auditors to respond to enterprise risk management issues in their organizations.

The Institute emphasized that management remains responsible for risk management. Internal auditors should provide advice, and challenge or support management's decisions on risk, as opposed to making risk management decisions themselves. Internal auditing's core role with regard to ERM is to provide objective assurance to the board on the effectiveness of an organization's ERM activities to help ensure key business risks are being managed appropriately and that the system of internal control is operating effectively.

The IIA position paper listed the roles internal auditing should play throughout the ERM process. The core internal auditing roles that relate to ERM are:

■ Giving assurance on risk management processes.
■ Giving assurance that risks are correctly evaluated.
■ Evaluating risk management processes.

---

[1] Available to download from http://www.theiia.org/guidance/standards-and-practices/position-papers/current-position-papers/.

- Evaluating the reporting of key risks.
- Reviewing the management of key risks.

Other legitimate internal auditing roles relating to ERM are:

- Facilitating the identification and evaluation of risks.
- Coaching management in responding to risks.
- Coordinating ERM activities.
- Consolidating risk reporting.
- Maintaining and developing the ERM framework.
- Championing the establishment of ERM.
- Developing a risk management strategy for Board approval.

However, the IIA also listed the roles internal auditing should not play in ERM:

- Setting the risk appetite.
- Imposing risk management processes.
- Providing management assurance on risks.
- Taking decisions on risk responses.
- Implementing risk responses on management's behalf.
- Being accountable for risk management.

The relationship between risk management and internal audit

Internal auditors and risk managers share some knowledge, skills and values. Both, for example, understand corporate governance requirements, have project management, analytical and facilitation skills and value having a healthy balance of risk rather than extreme risk-taking or avoidance behaviours. However, risk managers provide services only to the management of the organization and do not provide independent and objective assurance to the audit committee. Internal auditors who seek to extend their role to ERM underestimate risk managers' specialist areas of knowledge (such as risk transfer and risk quantification and modelling techniques) which are outside the body of knowledge for most internal auditors. Any internal auditor who cannot demonstrate the appropriate skills and knowledge should not undertake work in the area of risk management. Furthermore, the head of internal audit should not provide consulting services in this area if adequate skills and knowledge are not available within the internal audit function and cannot be obtained from elsewhere.

Internal auditors will not just focus on financial control (although this is the focus of Sarbanes-Oxley) but also on enterprise-wide risk management and internal control systems that go beyond financial controls (see Chapter 9 for a description of different types of control). Internal auditors should focus on matters of high risk and where significant control deficiencies have been found, they should identify the actions necessary to remedy those deficiencies. This is the risk-based approach to control described in Chapter 9. The role of the head of internal audit is to develop an audit plan based on an assessment of significant risks, submit this to the audit committee for approval, implement the agreed plan and maintain a professional audit team to carry out the plan. Part of the internal audit role is to provide assurance to the Board and audit committee that the risk management system and the controls to mitigate risk are effective.

Risk managers are responsible for identifying, assessing, estimating, evaluating treating and reporting risk within the structure of an enterprise risk management system. This process will consider the work of internal audit and may well identify risks and controls that receive inadequate internal audit attention.

Therefore, while the roles of internal audit and risk management are independent, they each influence the other significantly. In an organization with a risk culture, both roles will be seen as mutually reinforcing.

Risk in auditing

In the auditing process, it is important to understand risk as it affects the process of auditing itself, and to understand why neither internal nor external audit is risk-free.

Some risks are *inherent risks*, that is, they follow from the nature of the business and its environment, such as market demand, competitive conditions, natural disasters, human error, fraud and theft and strategic mismanagement, for example the failure to respond to market change or expansion into unprofitable markets. Controls are put in place to mitigate against these risks.

However there are also risks that relate to the *failure of controls* and control systems, such as failure to control password access to computer systems, failure to comply with documented procedures, having inadequate insurance cover, or not properly evaluating the credit worthiness of a customer.

But even when controls are effective, they cannot guarantee the elimination of risk. Changing circumstances lead to control systems becoming out of date, the actions of people are often unpredictable and the cost of control may outweigh the benefits. *Residual risk* is that risk which remains after controls have been implemented and it is for management and the Board to decide whether or not the level of residual risk is acceptable in terms of the organizational risk appetite. The auditor's responsibility is to ensure that managers understand the consequences of the level of residual risk that they implicitly or explicitly accept.

Even auditing cannot provide complete assurance that systems and processes are all operating effectively. Therefore *audit risk* relates to the inability of the audit process to detect control failures.

When the head of internal audit believes that management has accepted a level of residual risk that may be unacceptable to the organization, she/he should discuss this with management. If the issue is not resolved, the head of internal audit and senior management should report the matter to the audit committee for resolution.

Effectiveness of internal audit

The Institute of Internal Auditors has produced guidelines[2] for the audit committee's oversight of internal auditing. This involves:

- Reviewing and approving the internal audit activity's charter.
- Ensuring communication and reporting lines between the head of internal auditing and the audit committee.
- Reviewing internal audit staffing and ensuring that the function has the necessary resources.
- Reviewing and assessing the annual internal audit plan.
- Overseeing the coordination of the internal auditor with the external auditor to ensure proper coverage and minimize duplication of efforts.
- Reviewing periodic reports on the results of the internal auditors' work which should include significant risk exposure and control issues, corporate governance issues, and other matters needed or requested by the audit committee and senior management.
- Reviewing management's responsiveness to internal audit findings and recommendations.
- Monitoring and assessing internal audit effectiveness through a quality assurance and improvement program that covers all aspects of the internal audit activity and continuously monitors its effectiveness. External assessments, such as quality assurance reviews, should be conducted at least once every five years by a qualified, independent reviewer from outside the organization.
- The internal audit activity should evaluate and contribute to the improvement of risk management, control, and governance processes using a systematic and disciplined approach.

---

[2]http://www.iia.org.au/pdf/StandardsMatterAUwebreadycopyAugust2006.pdf.

A study by Beasley et al. (2008) found that ERM had the greatest impact on internal audit's activities when five factors were present:

■ the organization's ERM process was more completely in place,

■ the CFO and audit committee had called for greater internal audit activity related to ERM,

■ the chief internal auditor's tenure was longer,

■ the organization was in the banking industry or was an educational institution, and

■ the internal audit function had provided more ERM leadership.

External audit cannot be relied on beyond its scope to provide an opinion on financial statements. Internal audit has a crucial role in reviewing the effectiveness of enterprise risk management and risk-based controls. Consequently, the relationship between the chief risk officer and the head of internal audit is an important one and the oversight of the audit committee is crucial to ensure the effectiveness of the integrated process. The following case study of ABC is an example of the need for integration between risk management and internal audit.

A case study of ABC: Risk, control and internal audit

ABC (the name has been changed to preserve anonymity) is a small listed services company which, through the adoption of enterprise risk management, changed its focus from a concern with financial statements to a broader appreciation of risk but was forced to change its internal audit function to one that supported this approach.

ABC's Board of Directors took its responsibilities to shareholders seriously. Over recent years it had tried to improve its corporate governance processes in the light of the Combined Code. Management prepared monthly accounts for the Board and annual accounts for investors. The annual accounts were audited. Although ABC's Board took overall responsibility for the company's accounts, it delegated the detail of supervising the quality of the information and liaising with the external auditors to its audit committee. A few years previously, the Board had established its first audit committee. In its first year, the audit committee focused on improving confidence in the company's financial statements and subsequently formed a view that ABC's internal financial controls were effective. This view was supported by the external auditors, who considered the company's financial management and reporting to be sound.

ABC had an approach to internal control that allowed delegated decision-making within a framework of policies and financial regulations. It had put a lot of effort into recruiting and training the best people, but the complexity of service provision and high staff turnover owing to industry competition for experienced staff led to a significant staff turnover. To overcome this risk, key work practices had been documented as standard procedures and a quality management system had been introduced. Budgetary control was also quite strict.

The audit committee relied on a wide range of evidence in considering the effectiveness of ABC's internal controls. These included reports by external and internal auditors; management assurances about risk management and controls; the results of inspections by taxation authorities; the performance measurement system; the quality assurance system; the business planning and budgeting process; and business continuity planning to cover the possible loss of its building and information system.

The audit committee recognized that it had always relied heavily on financial controls and was unsure whether the non-financial controls gave the Board sufficient assurance that risk was being managed effectively. A major form of internal control for ABC was its internal audit function. The company had thought for many years that it was more likely to achieve objective and cost-effective judgments about its internal controls by outsourcing this to a professional accounting firm. Although the internal audit provided a lot of assurance about financial controls and the quality of financial statements, ABC's audit committee became increasingly concerned with broader issues of control over the business operations. This was partly a reflection of the importance placed by the Combined Code on risk management. As a result, the Board agreed that the remit of the audit committee should be extended to encompass risk management.

In the audit committee's second year of existence, ABC appointed a risk manager who implemented a comprehensive system of identifying and assessing risks, and of developing a risk register, the contents of which were reported regularly to the Board. Although the board was satisfied with the risk management processes that were in place, the audit committee felt that it didn't have sufficient independent and objective assurance that the risk management system and internal controls were effective. The audit committee asked the internal audit provider to spend less time auditing financial systems and more time auditing the broader risk management system and internal controls, that is to take a more risk-based internal audit approach.

Over the next year, ABC's audit committee became disillusioned with the internal audit provider, which had continued to take a traditional financial systems approach, rather than focusing on broader risk management issues. The audit committee considered that the major risk facing the company was a failure to achieve its business objectives, which could cause ABC to lose its market position in a competitive environment. The internal audit provider had failed to respond to these concerns, so the committee decided to put the work out to tender as a risk-based internal audit.

ABC soon appointed a new internal firm, which reviewed ABC's risk management system and recommended a new internal audit plan based on an assessment of the major risks. The risk register was improved and the audit committee received a higher level of assurance that controls were effective and that risks were being managed in accordance with ABC's appetite for risk. Financial controls remained important, but they no longer dominated internal audit, while many non-financial controls came to be seen as just as important as the financial ones.

Financial reports and systems are crucial for all organizations. But in ABC's case there were far more important risks facing the organization and a need for controls beyond the traditional financial ones. Once an organization has sound financial controls and can rely on its systems for timely and accurate financial reports, all risks need to be assessed – particularly those relating to the achievement of organizational objectives. Internal controls need to be put in place to manage those risks and a risk-based internal audit approach should support enterprise risk management and internal controls by providing assurance to the audit committee about their effectiveness. Only through a combination of effective risk management, internal control, and internal and external audit can a Board of Directors fulfil its governance responsibilities.

Reference

Beasley MS, Clune R, Hermanson DR. 2008. The Impact of Enterprise Risk Management on the Internal Audit Function. *Journal of Forensic Accounting* IX:1–20.

Chapter 25

The Future of Enterprise Risk Management

This chapter is at the same time a summary of key concepts but also a look to the future and an optimistic view of enterprise risk management (ERM). In looking forward, we need to consider whether ERM is just another management fad, doomed to be replaced by some new concept in the years to come.

We sincerely hope this is not the case, because the integration of governance, risk and control in ERM is a far more holistic approach to understanding and improving organizational functioning than any piecemeal approach can be. As an integrated approach, ERM encompasses strategy, goal setting and performance measurement, and balances the need for conformance with the need for performance. ERM also provides a means by which the plethora of management controls that exist in most organizations can be replaced by a risk-based approach to control.

In reviewing the book and presenting an optimistic picture of the future for risk management, we summarize some key points in the form of questions.

What is risk management?

Every organization faces a number of risks of varying levels of seriousness. Risk can be seen both in terms of threat (something going wrong) and opportunity (achieving, or not achieving, business objectives). It can be financial (e.g. incurring bad debts) or non-financial (e.g. pollution), although most risks will eventually be reflected in deteriorating financial performance. Risk management is concerned with identifying risks, assessing their likelihood and impact, and developing appropriate responses in the context of the organization's appetite for risk. This may involve accepting some risks, while transferring others through hedging or insurance; treating them to reduce their potential impact; or exercising mitigation through risk-based control. Risk management is also concerned with reporting and monitoring risks before and after they are treated and with improving the effectiveness of the risk management process.

However, at the level of the enterprise, there is a portfolio of many risks which result from the aggregation of each individual risk, from different sources and across all business activities. Top management and the Board needs aggregated information about the high-level, strategic risks faced by the organization, and assurance that lower level more operational risks are being managed effectively throughout the organization. Hence, not only must top management and the Board focus on the management of the key strategic risks facing the organization, but it must also rely on the organization's risk management and control system.

What is ERM?

ERM encompasses[1]:

■ Aligning risk appetite with strategy so that management considers the entity's risk appetite in evaluating strategic alternatives, setting objectives and developing mechanisms to manage related risks.

■ Enhancing risk response decisions by providing the rigour to identify and select among alternative risk responses – avoidance, reduction, sharing and acceptance.

■ Reducing operational surprises and losses through an enhanced capability to identify potential events and responses to those events.

■ Identifying and managing multiple and cross-enterprise risks – the myriad of risks affecting different parts of the organization. ERM facilitates effective response to the interrelated impacts, and enables an integrated response to multiple risks.

■ Seizing opportunities by considering a full range of potential events, management is positioned to identify and proactively realize opportunities.

■ Improving deployment of capital. Obtaining robust risk information allows management to effectively assess overall capital needs and enhance capital allocation.

■ The capabilities inherent in ERM help management achieve the entity's performance and profitability targets and help prevent loss of resources. ERM helps ensure effective reporting and compliance with laws and regulations, and helps avoid damage to the entity's reputation and associated consequences. In sum, ERM helps an entity get to where it wants to go and avoid pitfalls and surprises along the way.

As Part C of this book has shown, there are many aspects to risk management and control at the enterprise level: financial reporting; financial decision making; the use

---

[1] http://www.coso.org/documents/COSO_ERM_ExecutiveSummary.pdf.

of derivatives for hedging; information systems; employee health and safety; credit risk; strategic and business risk relevant to different businesses according to their circumstances; project and contract risk; the risk of fraud; risks associated with the environment and regulation; business continuity management; insurance; and risks specific to banks and financial institutions. What all these risks have in common is their linkage to the corporate governance agenda, and the applicability of the ERM structure described in Part B that encapsulates these and other risks facing the whole enterprise.

What are the benefits of ERM?

ERM can make a significant contribution towards helping an organization manage the risks to achieving its objectives. The benefits of ERM include:[2]

- greater likelihood of achieving corporate objectives;
- consolidated reporting of disparate risks at Board level;
- improved understanding of the key risks and their wider implications;
- identification and sharing of cross business risks;
- greater management focus on the issues that really matter;
- fewer surprises or crises;
- more focus internally on doing the right things in the right way;
- increased likelihood of change initiatives being achieved;
- capability to take on greater risk for greater reward; and
- more informed risk-taking and decision-making.

What does an ERM system look like?

ERM as a system is led by a chief risk officer (CRO, by whatever title that role is called). The CRO is responsible for establishing the system by which risks are:

- identified and described so that they can be understood and communicated;
- assessed;
- estimated in terms of their likelihood and consequence;

---

[2] http://www.theiia.org/guidance/standards-and-practices/position-papers/current-position-papers/.

- evaluated in terms of significance;
- treated through avoidance, reduction, sharing and acceptance strategies;
- reported in terms of gross (before controls) and net (or residual, after controls) terms.

The CRO will work with the Board, through its audit or risk committee to:

- develop a strategy and policy for risk management,
- incorporate risk into the strategic planning process,
- establish the organization's risk appetite,
- embed an appropriate attitude towards risk into the organization's culture,
- operate a risk management group with supporting processes (e.g. risk registers) to monitor risk,
- develop (with other managers) an internal control system that is consistent with the organization's risk appetite and mitigation strategies.

Risk and control go hand in hand. Whilst it is fairly easy to conceive of a control system that excludes risk management, the exclusion of control from ERM does not make sense.

What is internal control?

Internal controls are the policies and procedures used by directors and managers to help ensure the effective and efficient conduct of the business; the safeguarding of assets; regulatory compliance; the prevention and detection of fraud and error; the accuracy and completeness of accounting records; and the timely preparation of reliable financial information. These controls, along with the control environment (the attitudes of managers and directors on the significance of control; the organization's values, style, structure, responsibilities and competence) make up the internal control system.

Internal controls may be financial, such as variance analysis, stock recording systems and fixed asset registers, but a control system must look much further than that. Non-financial controls include numeric targets and performance indicators such as customer satisfaction, employee turnover and product wastage. These are quantitative controls because they involve numeric (although non-financial) measurement. But many controls are qualitative. They include policies and procedures; physical access controls; the structure of authority and reporting relationships; and a whole host of human resource controls, such as employment contracts, job descriptions, training programmes and performance appraisals.

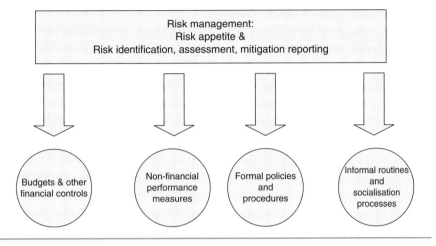

Figure 25.1   Risk management as the driver of management control.

Towards an ERM paradigm of control

Risk management has been adopted by corporate governance, a consequence of high profile corporate failures and the myriad public enquiries and reports that have followed such failures. It sits, sometimes uncomfortably, alongside a management control paradigm in which financial, quantitative and qualitative controls have emerged over time for internal political purposes or to guard against weaknesses (which may no longer exist), all of which become historically institutionalized as part of the organizational *modus operandi*.

Governance, at least in the post-Sarbanes-Oxley world of US financial reporting, is concerned with conformance and compliance. However, in the post-Cadbury world of most non-US regulation, governance is equally and perhaps more importantly concerned with performance (International Federation of Accountants, 2006). The conformance/performance dichotomy has been recognized by Chartered Institute of Management Accountants (2003).

We propose the replacement of the historical–political management control paradigm with an ERM paradigm where all management controls, whether accounting-based, non-financial targets and measures, policies and procedures, informal and social controls are not historically or politically derived but exist only in relation to the assessment, mitigation and control of risks. The risk-based approach to control is shown in Figure 25.1. In the ERM paradigm of control, new controls should emerge and be discarded through a lifecycle as the likelihood and consequence of new risks are identified and as old risks fade away. In this risk-based approach to control, controls are only relevant if they mitigate risks and those controls can be discarded where they are merely legacies of historical and political decisions. However, new controls must emerge whenever necessary to mitigate identified risks where no controls previously existed.

In this paradigm, risk-based internal auditing is just another form of control, although an essential one that provides assurance to the Board that risk management processes are operating as they should be; that management responses to risks are adequate; and that the whole set of risk-based controls are effective in mitigating risks.

In this ERM paradigm of control, the audit committee plays a fundamental role in coordinating ERM, control, internal and external audit.

What does the audit committee do?

The audit committee helps the Board of Directors to fulfil its stewardship duty by monitoring and reviewing the system of internal controls and risk management; internal and external audit; and the financial information provided to shareholders. It monitors and directs the internal audit function and oversees the relationship between the external auditors and the company, assessing the effectiveness of the auditors every year and making recommendations to the Board concerning their appointment or removal.

The audit committee reviews the effectiveness of internal controls by assessing the significant risks facing the company and the effectiveness of controls in managing those risks. This review covers financial, operational and compliance controls as well as risk management systems.

ERM as an emerging area of practice

ERM is undergoing almost continual change, partly as a result of the continual development and refinement of processes by organizations like COSO, the Institute of Risk Management and the Institute of Internal Auditors, and partly by academic insights that help to develop our understanding of risk management and its role in society (e.g. Collier et al., 2007; Power, 2007). Development is also continuing through the professional service firms who engage in continual improvement of their products, to try to stay one step ahead of their competitors and aim to provide superior advice to their clients.

Practice of course also develops by individual risk managers developing new tools and techniques, proving the value of those tools and techniques and communicating those improvements through industry publications and conferences.

We should have great optimism for the future development of ERM and for the risk-based approach to control and audit. Managers with functional interests in risk are being coordinated by chief risk officers. Internal and external auditors are increasingly taking a risk-based approach. And Boards of Directors and audit committees are increasingly seeing ERM as providing an overarching framework through which their governance responsibilities can be fulfilled.

References

Chartered Institute of Management Accountants. 2003. *Enterprise Governance: Getting the Balance Right*. CIMA & IFAC.

Collier PM, Berry AJ, Burke GT. 2007. *Risk and Management Accounting: Best Practice Guidelines for Enterprise-wide Internal Control Procedures*. Oxford: Elsevier.

International Federation of Accountants. 2006. *Internal Controls – A Review of Current Developments*. New York: Professional Accountants in Business Committee.

Power M. 2007. *Organized Uncertainty: Designing a World of Risk Management*. Oxford: Oxford University Press.

Index